Composers of the **Twentieth** *Century*

The Music of

YALE UNIVERSITY PRESS   New Haven and London

Charles Ives

PHILIP LAMBERT

Set in Monotype Garamond type by The Marathon Group, Inc., Durham, North Carolina.
Printed in the United States of America by Edwards Brothers, Ann Arbor, Michigan.

Library of Congress Cataloging-in-Publication Data
Lambert, Philip, 1958–

  The music of Charles Ives / Philip Lambert.

    p. cm. — (Composers of the twentieth century)

  Includes bibliographical references (p.) and index.

  ISBN 0-300-06522-1

  1. Ives, Charles, 1874–1954—Criticism and interpretation.
I. Title. II. Series.
ML410.I94L36   1997
780'.92—dc20
[B]   96-38979
                                    CIP
                                    MN

A catalogue record for this book is available from the British Library.

The paper in this book meets the guidelines for permanence and durability of the Committee on Production Guidelines for Book Longevity of the Council on Library Resources.

10 9 8 7 6 5 4 3 2 1

Contents

For my mother
and
in memory of my father

Preface

We have come to know Charles Ives as a kind of split personality. The side we know best is Ives the artist, the composer of expressive, colorful music that captures the essence of nineteenth-century America and speaks in tongues comprehensible only to the human spirit. The other side is Ives the experimenter, the creator of complex, difficult, often humorous short pieces filled with innovative compositional ideas and constructed upon elaborate musical edifices. The compositions by Ives the artist are well known and well loved by the concert-going public; they include *Three Places in New England,* the Third Symphony, and the *Concord* Sonata. The works of Ives the experimenter often mystify the average music lover and are familiar only to a handful of serious enthusiasts; they include pieces with such unusual titles as *Tone Roads, In Re Con Moto Et Al,* and *Chromâtimelôdtune.* Ives the artist is impulsive, given to free flights of fancy; Ives the experimenter is deliberate, absorbed in careful compositional calculations. Ives the artist is the author of *Essays Before a Sonata;* Ives the experimenter wrote *Memos.* Ives the artist is a genius; Ives the experimenter is an eccentric. Ives the artist speaks from the soul; Ives the experimenter speaks from the intellect.

Yet the musicians and scholars who have created these images have not always looked at both sides with the same eyes. They have held Ives the artist to the highest musical and artistic standards, but they have tended to take Ives the experimenter less seriously. They have not ignored this Ives—indeed, they have been eager to champion his musical innovations as prophecies of important twentieth-century trends. But they have not always approached his compositional efforts with the same level of expectation. They have regarded this Ives more with amusement and condescension than with serious critical scrutiny. Ives the experimenter has become that strange uncle whose odd behavior the family accepts and allows as long as nobody gets hurt.

What the dual imagery overlooks is the common artistic and aesthetic basis for all of Ives's work. To see it, we need only apply to Ives the experimenter the values and standards that have traditionally been reserved for the other Ives. That was my goal in writing this book. In giving Ives the experimenter more serious and unpatronizing attention, I aim to bring this Ives into the mainstream, to elevate and promote the status of his contribution to a diverse catalogue of expressive resources. I regard the works of Ives the experimenter as serious and necessary compositional efforts whose worth is at least proportionate to the countless hours he spent on them. I treat Ives the experimenter as a composer rather than as a crank. Ultimately my aim is to merge these and other personalities into a single Ives: artist, experimenter, philosopher, humanitarian, wit, patriot, guide to the human spirit.

To accomplish these objectives, we will follow several paths through the music that has traditionally been associated with Ives the experimenter. One path will feature the musical structures of his pieces, revealing particular compositional trends and interrelationships within Ives's oeuvre. Another will lead us through chronologies that illuminate the evolution of Ives's compositional technique from early musical tinkerings through the confident workmanship of his mature writing. The portrait that emerges will be richly informative about Ives's compositional values and the musical language of one sizable segment of his work. It will represent one piece in the diverse, complex puzzle we must ultimately assemble to reach a full understanding of the composer and his music.

Part of the process of merging the personalities is to recognize compositional techniques usually deemed experimental occurring in music that has customarily been associated with the "nonexperimental" category. Such cross-pollinations are especially evident in the Second String Quartet, the *Robert Browning Overture, The Fourth of July,* and the Fourth Symphony. Though relationships between different types of pieces will suggest to some readers that certain efforts have served as "experiments" for others, our purposes here will discourage such judgments. Rather, we will retain our focus on the compositional techniques themselves, as they appear in music written for any purpose, on any scale, and with any result. We will simply consider any connections between works of disparate scope within the broader context of the compositional trends and artistic developments we are following.

The book is organized into two parts, preceded by an introduction. In the introductory chapter, "The Composer and His Language," I identify the central issues connected with this area of Ives's work and examine the composer's writings about technical composition. I also explore the origins of these views and techniques, as outlined in some of the composer's earliest sketches and compositional ideas. In Part One, "Tools and Materials," I offer an initial examination of how Ives's attitudes and approaches are manifested in fundamental elements of his compositional language. I give an overview of his basic technical apparatus. In Part Two, "Cyclic Substance," I build on Part One to illuminate the most sophisticated aspect of Ives's work, his deployment of musical structures based on cyclic principles. Chapters Two, Four, Five, Seven and Nine are expository. They describe compositional techniques and evolutionary trends as they appear in numerous different works. Chapters Three, Six, and Eight, the "Analysis" chapters, are illustrative. Each explores a single work in full detail to place techniques and trends from surrounding chapters into complete musical contexts. The last chapter, Chapter Ten, is a study of Ives's sketches for what would have been his ultimate artistic statement: the *Universe Symphony*. In surveying the symphony's philosophical and musical ideas, we will touch upon the principal themes of the entire study and gain a concluding perspective on this aspect of Ives's creative life.

I have adopted a few methodological and notational practices throughout. The first mention of a composition in the text is usually accompanied by a date, as given and explained in the alphabetical list of works in Appendix A. A question mark beside a date indicates that some speculation was involved in the dating. Appendix B lists all works discussed, in general chronological order. The music in the examples is taken directly from the most reliable original source—usually original sketches and related materials—and may include corrections of errors in published scores, made without comment.

Pitch references are based on the Acoustical Society of America standard: middle $C = C_4$, and so on. Such designations are used only when analytically relevant or useful for clarity.

Unless indicated otherwise, all music in examples sounds as written.

References to specific measures in musical examples will often take the form of a measure number followed by a colon and then the beat number. For example, "m. 3:2" refers to measure 3, beat 2; and "m. 3:2−4" refers to a span of beats, measure 3, beats 2 through 4. A measure number without a beat designation refers to that measure in its entirety.

I assume in the analyses that the reader has a thorough background in the concepts and language of current post-tonal theory. Some additional explanatory or theoretical matters are taken up in footnotes. In the analytic commentary I employ standard pitch-class (pc) labels, where C = 0 and 10 = T and 11 = E. Order positions (op) are *italicized*. Unless otherwise specified, the term *interval* is used to mean "ordered pitch-class interval" (Babbitt's "directed interval")— the result of subtracting the first pc from the second (mod 12). Notation of pitch-class sets is as follows: (prime form) or [normal form] or {some other specifically defined form}; an ordering of pitch classes or intervals is notated as an <ordered string>.

Acknowledgments

The *Music of Charles Ives* is the culmination of some ten years of work and stands as evidence of a number of valuable influences and associations. Robert Gauldin contributed unsurpassed musical expertise and copious general wisdom to my first serious study of Ives's music when I was a graduate student at the Eastman School of Music in the mid 1980s. In more recent times I have reaped many rewards from my association with H. Wiley Hitchcock, J. Peter Burkholder, and other members of the Ives Society board and scholarly community. My research during nine years on the faculty of Baruch College of the City University of New York (CUNY) has been supported by released-time grants from the School of Liberal Arts and Sciences, and by two grants from the PSC-CUNY Research Award Program. I am also grateful to the staff and librarians at the Sibley Music Library of the Eastman School of Music, the John Herrick Jackson Music Library of Yale University, the New York Public Library, and various CUNY libraries, especially those at Baruch College and the Graduate Center. For their steadfast support over the sometimes rough and rocky roads that ultimately led to this publication, I thank Allen Forte, the general editor of the series, and Harry Haskell of Yale University Press. Susan Abel edited the manuscript with considerable care and precision. I am indebted to Sally Goldfarb and Joseph N. Straus for their legal counsel, and to Paul Carter for his care and dedication in producing the musical examples.

The final years of this book's long gestation period were marked by two happy events: my marriage to Diane Taublieb in 1993, and the birth of our daughter, Alice Jeanette Lambert, in 1995. It gives me great pleasure to associate Diane and Alice with the conclusion of a project that I have always primarily associated with my parents, whose support and encouragement was vital in the early stages. It is with a renewed appreciation of my parents' influence and my debt to them, revealed more and more vividly with each passing day of my own parenthood, that I respectfully and gratefully dedicate this book to my mother, and to my father's memory.

1 The Composer and His Language

The story of Ives's musical upbringing is a familiar one. As a youth he showed prodigious talent and was tutored and coached by his father. He felt a spiritual affinity with the elder Ives, and absorbed from him a liberal perspective on music and artistic expression that he would carry with him throughout his life. George Ives was fabled as a musical experimenter and seeker of new sounds, and these activities certainly fostered progressive tendencies in his son. As Burkholder emphasizes, however, the progressivism went hand in hand with an "assured, disciplined technique";[1] Charles Ives's early development as a musical innovator is no more important than his training in traditional music fundamentals. His early growth was also enriched by his exposure to sundry musical experiences as a young participant in the musical life of his hometown of Danbury, Connecticut.[2] As a drummer in his father's bands, a vocalist in church, a piano student and recitalist, and a church organist, he began to cultivate a keen awareness of music's expressive and artistic power.

The details of Ives's adulthood and musical maturity are also familiar, and they are studies in contrasts. While expending the effort necessary to succeed in the insurance industry, he was also producing musical works of disparate sizes and types. He wrote delicate songs and enormous symphonies. He wrote music of extraordinary complexity and sublime beauty, usually without hearing it performed. He wrote in styles that mocked music indigenous to American culture and in styles that followed and paid reverence to the traditions out of which such music evolved. The central ideas in his music include thoughtful metaphysical questions and jovial evocations of programmatic images. His musical language includes frankly tonal, marginally tonal, tonally centric, and densely atonal idioms, incorporating compositional techniques that range from the freely formed to the rigidly schematized. He had no patrons to please or publishers to satisfy, and his music reflects all the idiosyncrasies and paradoxes of a composer who answers only to his own whims and agendas.

Technique and "Experimentation"

To make sense of this vast diversity, recent students of Ives's music have identified a basic duality in his work and compositional attitudes. Burkholder explains the duality as a "strict dichotomy between private inquiry and public performance" in the approaches of both Ives and his father. The results of private inquiry, according to Burkholder, are "experiments," intended not for public performance but as elaborate sketches trying out progressive ideas, while the pieces suitable for public presentation are "concert" works that are less technically oriented and more freely inspired.[3] To put it another way, the experiments are part of a trend of "research" into new possibilities for musical organization, while the concert pieces aspire to be works of art in the conventional sense.[4] Ives himself supports separate consideration for his private and experimental compositions by referring to them as "studies" (for example, *Memos,* 56), "memos in notes" (*Memos,* 64), and "not . . . definitely completed works of art" (*Memos,* 111).

Let us examine this widely accepted dualism. A judgment placing a work in one category or the other is a reflection on the *beginning* of the compositional process. To call certain works experimental is to say that Ives evinced a desire to try new ideas when he wrote those works, and had no expectation of public presentation. To use the label *concert* implies that the composer was initially less concerned with experimentation and was anticipating public exposure. But suppose we turn the tables to emphasize not initial motivations but ultimate compositional goals. Ives's goals are a part of his basic views of music, which, as Burkholder has demonstrated, are firmly rooted in Western art-music traditions.[5] They are apparent throughout Ives's life, from his boyhood exposure to conventional and progressive sounds to his mature creations in various idioms. Ives's ideas about what music is and what it should do are those shared by anyone who contemplates such things: that great music is both profoundly expressive and skillfully organized. His most basic goal is to produce music that exhibits both these characteristics.[6] When he writes music designed to try out new, progressive ideas—and which manifests an attitude that might be termed experimental—he is particularly concerned with organization. Expressive content is also important, but if he ultimately feels that a piece has not succeeded on both counts he is inclined to criticize it and highlight what he sees as an inability to meet high artistic expectations. Similarly, when he is not concerned with new compositional techniques, the expressive content in his music may seem to take the lead. But of course its success will also be dependent on its organization, whether exemplified by traditional formal structures, familiar developmental devices, treatment of borrowed material, or any number of other factors.

The two facets are inevitably interdependent. From the point of view of organization, expression is an outcome, a result of the constructive decisions made in the compositional process. A work's language may be wildly unorthodox or stubbornly conventional, but the way it is organized will determine its expressive success. From the point of view of expression, organization is a means to an end. The composer begins with an idea to be expressed and then searches for the right tools to communicate it. The compositional process is a continual interaction between the two perspectives, as expressive desires inspire organizational tools and new techniques of organization suggest further expressive possibilities.[7]

Our shift of perspective away from initial motivations and toward ultimate goals can bring about important revisions in our understanding of Ives's attitudes and development. For example, it has been common to see an experimental work as a kind of proving ground for ideas that might be used later in concert music. Ives supports this notion when he says that the "memos in notes . . . opened up things naturally that later were used naturally and spontaneously" (*Memos*, 64). In Burkholder's words, "Ives later incorporated many of the ideas he had first developed in his 'memos in notes' into his music for public performance."[8] And Charles Ward constructs a paradigm for Ives's compositional process in which "experiments" are a "necessary prerequisite" for large-scale compositions.[9] The suggestion is that Ives's early works fall into either the experimental or the nonexperimental category, while his later music effects a kind of synthesis of the earlier categories by employing earlier experimental techniques alongside "nonexperimental" ideas.[10]

Although it is true that Ives reuses ideas, it is a mistake to suggest that experimental pieces exist solely for the purpose of supplying material for other music. His goals are more ambitious than that. We owe him the assumption that he approaches one of these works with the same ideals that he has for any other compositional effort. Each experiment deserves to be considered on its own terms, to be evaluated for its own organization and expressivity, independent of any other music it may have influenced. Once we have taken this view, it is easy to see Ives's compositional evolution not as a continuum from experiment to concert piece but as a typical progression of compositional trends toward greater sophistication and maturity. If Ives seems in his early experimental works to be excessively concerned with organization, this is surely a mark of immaturity— evidence of a composer struggling to find a voice. Surely there are also early works that suffer from a lack of attention to organization. In neither case can the goal of expressivity be achieved. In later works, on the other hand, we may find many ways in which Ives moves closer to his goals. He may do this by employing techniques from earlier "experiments" within a piece that is not essentially "experimental" in conception, or by writing freely inspired music that does not incorporate such techniques, or by employing "experimental" techniques almost exclusively. It becomes very difficult to use the word *experimental* to describe the efforts of a composer who has by then become very experienced with his resources and confident in his technique.

How, then, can we characterize that area of Ives's work that has been known as experimental, using language that forsakes initial motivations for the actual ideas and methods he uses to pursue his artistic goals? The common thread in these works is a reliance on pattern and logic in the formation and development of musical ideas. The structures typically display distinctive compositional designs based on schemes involving pitches, chords, rhythms, metrical structures, formal units, expressive markings, instrumentations, and the like. It is music that can be rigidly organized, exactingly contrived, formulaic. It is not experimental but *systematic;* we will refer to this area of Ives's work as systematic composition. In applying this concept we do not, of course, mean that Ives pursued a uniform "system of composition," but that he developed tools that are systematic in nature and applied them to satisfy particular expressive needs.

Previous studies of Ives's music have focused more on other aspects of its organization. His treatment of borrowed material has been extensively explored, most notably and comprehensively in a recent work by Burkholder.[11] Other aspects of Ives's technique that are becoming better understood include his use of stylistic diversity and his strategies for motivic development.[12] But the attention given to the systematic aspect of his work has too often taken the form of superficial observations about techniques that anticipate later twentieth-century trends. It is the goal of this study to give systematic methods a more exalted status, to recognize them as some of the many tools Ives has at his disposal to pursue his compositional objectives, and to consider the place of these methods within the full chronology of the composer's work and compositional evolution.

One way of understanding how systematic composition fits in with Ives's overall artistic goals and evolution is to consider what the composer himself says about this aspect of his work. Doing so, however, can be a difficult enterprise, as readers of the Ives literature well know, for his major writings about music easily suggest incompatible views on matters of technique and artistry. We have come to know his *Essays Before a Sonata* as a tribute to the ineffable in art—spirit, soul, abstract philosophical messages[13]—whereas the *Memos* seem to favor exactly the opposite qualities—structure, organization, technique. But just as a broader consideration of experimental and concert music yields a common basis in certain fundamental artistic beliefs, so does a new reading of the *Essays* and *Memos* reveal a more consistent articulation of these beliefs than initial impressions may suggest. Though these two works have been amply studied over the years, we owe them yet another visit.

One issue attending any discussion of *Essays* and *Memos* is the contrasting purposes for which they were written. Ives wrote the *Essays* in the years before 1920 as a philosophical backdrop for the *Concord* Sonata, while he wrote the *Memos* in the 1930s as a remembrance of virtually all of his earlier compositional activities. The distinction of purpose is crucial, according to Burkholder, but was overlooked when the first historical and biographical perspectives on Ives were formed.[14] While the *Memos* were regarded as the valuable source of musical commentary that they are, the *Essays* were ascribed a significance broader than that indicated by their stated purpose. They were seen not as philosophical ruminations relating to a specific work and specific period in Ives's creative life but as a kind of artistic manifesto for his entire oeuvre. In reality, as Burkholder observes, the *Essays* express views Ives fully developed only at the end of his composing years. They are his "final, hard-won synthesis of the many conflicting views of music he had either held or encountered during his lifetime."[15] Burkholder asserts that we cannot weigh all of Ives's musical values against those of the *Essays,* because in so doing we will deprive Ives of his "history and diversity," we will judge music written at earlier stages of Ives's development on the basis of artistic ideals he formulated only in later years.[16]

And indeed Ives has been unfairly pigeonholed, owing to misperceptions of the *Essays.* But we should not be too quick to dismiss absolutely any possible relevance of the *Essays* to Ives's earlier work. If the *Essays* accomplish a synthesis of earlier views, then the seeds and roots of their main ideas lie within the views being synthesized. They articulate artistic values whose individual components may appear in less refined manifestations throughout his earlier music. When Ives wrote the *Essays,* he had some twenty-five years of composing behind him—during which he had produced music in a diversity of styles and idioms, using a variety of systematic and nonsystematic methods—and he did not ignore this legacy as he formulated his "hard-won synthesis." Without misrepresenting the position of the *Essays* in Ives's intellectual development, we can gain valuable insights into his earlier music—even his systematic music—by exploring their principal themes.

One of the main ideas is a fundamental artistic duality for which the *Essays* are renowned. Ives defines the most profound qualities of art as *substance,* consisting of a "body of conviction," a strong artistic "spirit," a moral and artistic high ground. It is, as Kavanaugh points out, an "Ivesian equivalent of the Kantian noumenal reality, known to the moral consciousness, or the Platonic good, true and beautiful essence of the universe."[17] He contrasts this with the *manner* of art, its form or external reality.[18] Ives discusses manner and substance at great length in the *Essays.* Though he says that substance is "practically indescribable" (p. 75), he offers a reasonably clear definition by listing its attributes and drawing comparisons with nonsubstantial art, artists, and ideas. He says substance is composed of "reality, quality, spirit" (p. 75). He contrasts the substance and nonsubstance, respectively, of Emerson and Poe (p. 76), Thoreau and Debussy (p. 82), Beethoven and Richard Strauss (pp. 82–86), introspection and observation (p. 86), genius and talent (p. 88), and truth and repose (p. 88). From these and other descriptions, one aspect of the fundamental duality is clear; we know what substance is and what it is not. And yet the concept of manner is not so clear. If manner is a work's external reality, it would have to be necessary for the communication of substance; as Ives says, manner is the means by which substance is "translated into expression" (p. 75). Yet at other times he also refers to manner in a very different way, implying not that manner is a necessary conduit but that it is the opposite of substance, the trivial and shallow counterpart of substance's profundity. For example: "Substance has something to do with character. Manner has nothing to do with it" (p. 77); "The substance of a tune comes from somewhere near the soul, and the manner comes from—God knows where" (p. 77); "Substance tends to create affection; manner prejudice" (p. 78); "We would be inclined to say that Thoreau leaned toward substance and Debussy towards manner" (p. 82). But Ives cannot really mean that manner is bad, since he also acknowledges that it is omnipresent and necessary. What he must mean is that manner that does not reflect substance is bad, and that in such cases the manner itself receives undue attention. In his explicatory comparisons the word *manner* actually means "nonsubstance," or "manner without substance." We might rephrase his statements with more precision: "Substance has something to do with character; manner-without-substance has nothing to do with it"; "Substance tends to create affection, nonsubstance prejudice"; and so forth. It is only in the final pages of the *Essays* that Ives seems to recognize the importance of both sides of the duality, when he speaks of "using in their true relation, as much as one can, these higher and lower dual values" (p. 100). As Burkholder notes, "manner is necessary for art—one could argue that it *is* art, although Ives does not say as much—but must assume its true relation to substance, proceeding from and depending upon the spirit."[19]

Thus manner can be good or bad, depending on its source, which might or might not be substance. Music may have manner without substance, but it cannot have substance without manner. Let us recast Ives's terms into a more general conceptual framework. We start where the artist begins: with a certain set of *values* that will be projected into the work. These values represent the guiding spirit of his creation, the source of his inspiration. If these values are of the highest spiritual strength and moral character, they are values of substance. Otherwise, they can exhibit any number of undesirable qualities—superficiality, materialism, unoriginality, intellectual simplicity, to name a few. Ives criticizes Wagner, for example, for an "undercurrent of make-believe" in his music, for his overemphasis on "the repose of pride" rather than the "truth of humility," and for choosing "the representative rather than the spirit itself" (pp. 72, 74). In other words, Ives rejects Wagner's original values because of their spiritual weakness. Ives's criticisms of Debussy single out a "sentimentality deadening something within" and a "sensual sensuousness" in Debussy's attitude toward nature (pp. 73, 82). That is, he also finds that Debussy prefers spiritually vacuous qualities over values of substance. The works of Bach and Beethoven, by contrast, are held up as exemplars of great art (pp. 73–74); the original values of these composers are values of substance.

After the initial inspiration, the model of Ives's beliefs would continue with the three additional stages shown below. The second stage is the intellectual process of translating original values into terms that are capable of artistic realization—the conception of concrete *ideas* that will reflect the initiating values. Ives describes the progression from values to ideas using a biological metaphor: "Substance in a human-art-quality suggests the body of a conviction which has its birth in the spiritual consciousness, whose youth is nourished in the moral consciousness, and whose maturity as a result of all this growth is then represented in a mental image" (p. 75). And at this point it is just an image. These ideas are not specific musical constructs but general visions of the scope and character of the artwork. They both reflect the quality and profundity (or lack thereof) of the original values and look ahead to the specific materials that will give them musical life.

Values ⟶ Ideas ⟶ Manner ⟶ Realization

The third stage translates the mental image from stage two into concrete musical structures—Ives's *manner*. This move from ideas to manner is the progression from conception to composition, from the ideas that formulate a work to the details of the way these ideas are communicated. And once again, the manner will be deficient only if it reflects nonsubstantial original values. Finally, stage four is the *realization* of the finished work—for music, the performance. This is included here as the natural and essential conclusion of the process, although Ives devotes little attention to it in the *Essays* (perhaps because he had all too little experience with it).[20]

A related concept in the *Essays* is Ives's notion of beauty. One statement on this subject may be the work's most quoted passage: "Beauty in music is too often confused with something that lets the ears lie back in an easy chair. Many sounds that we are used to do not bother us, and for that reason we are inclined to call them beautiful" (p. 97). But in general Ives is as inconsistent in his discussion of beauty as he is in his definition of manner. On the one hand, there is the "easy-chair" beauty, consisting of the "sounds that we are used to," the clichéd and unchallenging musical conventions that result from "a kind of a first necessary physical impression" (p. 76). Ives says, "when a new or unfamiliar work is accepted as beautiful on its first hearing, its fundamental quality is one that tends to put the mind to sleep" (p. 97). This definition of beauty also underlies statements such as: "We like the beautiful and don't like the ugly; therefore, what we like is beautiful and what we don't like is ugly . . ." (p. 77). On the other hand, Ives also adopts a definition of beauty that is more vague and abstract, that is a reflection of the spiritual essence of a work. This artistic beauty is roughly equivalent to substance. It brings to mind Emerson's thoughts on beauty in *Nature,* when he speaks of a "high and divine beauty . . . found in combination with the human will."[21] And it is this definition that Ives has in mind when he speaks of "moral beauty" (p. 77, quoting François Roussel-Despierres), and when he claims that "Probably nobody knows what actual beauty is" (p. 76). He invokes this definition of beauty when he admits "that manner has a great deal to do with the beauty of substance, and that to make a too arbitrary division or distinction between [manner and substance] is to interfere, to some extent, with an art's beauty and unity" (p. 97).

Thus Ives's concept of beauty embodies both sides of the duality. Easy-chair beauty is a variety of manner-without-substance—a conventionally structured manner that reflects a musically unoriginal and intellectually shallow substance. Artistic beauty is manifested in manner that does reflect substance, revealing moral strength and spiritual depth. Ives acknowledges the dual definition, even while doubting that a distinction can easily be made: "Beauty, in its common conception, has nothing to do with . . . substance, unless it be granted that its outward aspect, or the expression between sensuous beauty and spiritual beauty, can be always and distinctly known, which it cannot, as the art of music is still in its infancy" (p. 76).

Now we can take these main ideas of the *Essays*—manner, substance, and beauty—and see how they might be applied to the *Memos* and to systematic writing in general. Since manner is necessary to art, we now know better than to condemn the discussion of technical details in *Memos* or the focus on method and design in systematic music simply because they place value on a highly organized manner. The issue is whether the initial compositional values reflected by a systematic manner are values of substance.

It is a thorny question, because Ives sometimes avoids addressing it or seems to deny that "systematic substance" is possible. In his discussion of Emerson in chapter two of the *Essays* (pp. 11–36), for example, he praises qualities such as vagueness and eschewal of order and logic in Emerson's writings.[22] Elsewhere in *Essays* (p. 77), Ives criticizes "the sculptors' over-insistence on the 'mold'; the outer rather than the inner subject or content of his statue," and "overinterest in the multiplicity of techniques, in the idiomatic." In *Memos* (p. 78) he describes modern music as "too intellectual—the brain has [been] working a little more than that bigger muscle underneath (what you may call it, spirit, inner blast, soul?)." And an inscription in the margin of sketches for his song "Majority" avers that music constructed in a "calculated, diagram, design way . . . is a weak substitute for inspiration."[23]

But Ives is not utterly denouncing regularity and organization, nor is he denying the possibility that systematic methods are potential communicators of substance. He does indeed praise Emerson's spontaneity and freedom of inspiration, but he does so only to explain particular aspects of Emerson's work, not to deny other ways of achieving the same spiritual transcendence. He says, for example, "Vagueness is at times an indication of nearness to a perfect truth" (*Essays*, 22). It is *at times* an indication; the implication is that in other circumstances other qualities may serve as indicators. David Michael Hertz observes that Ives derived from Emerson not only a sense of spontaneity and freedom but also an appreciation of "a kind of Emersonian organicism" that would lead to more precise compositional strategies.[24] And when Ives denigrates the sculptor and modern music, he is simply illustrating the undesirability of manner-without-substance, without offering any suggestions for how manner in these examples could reflect substance. When he criticizes organizing principles in "Majority," he indicates only that such procedures cannot be the sole inspirational source, not that they have no role to play in good music; they may indeed have one, for example, as technical means of communicating more substantive inspirations.

Elsewhere, Ives does suggest ways that a systematic manner can reflect values of substance. One way is implicit in his criticisms of music that relies too heavily on convention, when he rails against "mellifluous sounds, perfect cadences, perfect ladies, perfect programs," and "one-syllable gossip for the soft-ears-and-stomachs, easy for their bodies, . . . art prostituted for commercialism" (*Memos*, 73, 134). He often makes such statements as a means of emphasizing his own innovations—he uses himself to demonstrate the value of progressive thinking of the kind that goes into systematic composition. Sometimes his condemnations of tradition take the form of criticisms of technique. In *Essays* (98), for example, he says that "unity is, too generally conceived of, or too easily accepted as analogous to form; and form as analogous to custom; and custom to habit." In *Memos* (86), he criticizes those who value "workmanship" in music. When they use this word, he says, they "mean just one and the same thing, 'groove made technique,' reflecting almost literally some sofa-cushion formulism which they've slept on for generations—the little, usual, tried-out, played-out expediences in harmony, melody, time—(rhythm is beyond them)—every right sound (sound or unsound) in just the nice way they've always seen it done, etc. etc." But once again, the technique he criticizes is that of a composer who is unoriginal and uninspired, who falls back on tradition without attempting to break new ground. Pathbreaking technique, such as we see in the systematic writing, is desirable and therefore can be a reflection of substance.

In fact, when Ives uses the term *workmanship* to describe music that is both organized and original, the word takes on positive connotations. In *Memos* (91), he describes *Hallowe'en,* a meticulously crafted systematic work, as "one of the most carefully worked out (technically speaking), and one of the best pieces (from the standpoint of workmanship) that I've ever done." Then he surveys some of the work's systematic characteristics, as if to confirm that these well-reasoned and novel procedures are part of what makes *Hallowe'en* one of his "best pieces." Later he adds, "I happened to get exactly the effect I had in mind, which is the only ([or] at least an important) function of good workmanship." Ives added the phrase in parentheses sometime after writing the rest of the sentence.[25] Clearly, good, progressive workmanship is a component of good music. It is not the only thing of value, but it is important.

At one point in *Memos* (31 – 32) Ives even uses the phrase *technical substance* to refer to well-organized and innovative structural details. Referring to the music critic who ignores this aspect of music, he says,

> If he should sometime be compelled to listen, or try to hear, and then try to tell others what is going on in this music, first from a technical standpoint (enough to know that he has sensed what the technical substance

implies), not in too much or every detail . . . but in the fundamental problems that have to do with all music in general, . . . what would he say? Of course here we are referring to a kind of music that he is not much accustomed to, and which he has not trained himself to listen to and hear. What would he tell the public about what is taking place, as to its form, as to its tone-associations, as to its rhythms, as to its tonalities (poly-, a-, or others), its division of tones, as to the recurrence or sequences of the musical thought, its sound-centers, the relation of the different groups of tones and intensities, etc. etc.?

Ives leaves no doubt that all these things that the critic misses are things of value, aspects of music that can form part of "technical substance."

Another way that technique can reflect substance has to do with the role of the intellect. Ives explains that there is a part of substance that is associated with intellectual depth and strength. Early in the *Essays,* for example, he says that music should have meaning "perhaps of a spiritual nature, in the expression of which the intellect has some part" (p. 4). Shortly thereafter, he singles out "mental, moral, or spiritual" qualities as among the highest artistic values (pp. 7–8). And in the Emerson chapter, while recognizing that "the intellect is never a whole," he explains that the intellect "is where the soul finds things" (p. 24). These comments bring to mind Ives's references, elsewhere than in his discussions of substance, to intellectual values in music. In *Memos* (p. 63), for example, he describes pieces that "were in part made to strengthen the ear muscles, the mind muscles, and perhaps the Soul muscles too." And he says the intensely systematic work *In Re Con Moto Et Al* is "if not good music (though today I think it is), at least good exercise for strengthening the muscles in the mind— and I'm not sure that it doesn't help some in the muscles of the heart and soul (wherever they are!)" (*Memos,* 101). Music can embody intellectual depth through profound philosophical messages, or references to literary figures and trends, or displays of the complexity and expressive power of music, among others. But surely systematic writing is one of the most effective ways. The systematic compositional process is *ipso facto* an intellectual act, more so than any other approach.

Further, when Ives discusses beauty in the *Essays,* he assumes that there is an intellectual component of perception. He implies that the beauty of substance is something that can be appreciated only by those who are sufficiently open to a concept of music expanded to encompass the forces of intellect. A listener who knows only easy-chair beauty is a listener who is intellectually confined and lazy, who is unwilling to acknowledge a kind of artistic beauty that may include sounds that would not be "beautiful" in a conventional way. This is what Ives means when he says "My God! What has sound got to do with music!" (*Essays,* 84)—the "music" is the substance that narrow-minded listeners miss by limiting their understanding of beauty to certain sounds only.[26] But a listener who recognizes the beauty inherent in true substance is intellectually open to unconventional sounds and intellectually capable of seeing beauty in systematic complexity and compositional sophistication. Again Ives's views echo Emerson's in *Nature:* "There is still another aspect under which the beauty of the world may be viewed, namely, as it becomes an object of the intellect. . . . The intellect searches out the absolute order of things as they stand in the mind of God, and without the color of affection."[27]

Ives has still more to say about the issues of intellectual sophistication and technical complexity in his essay on insurance.[28] After a deep, complicated exposé of guidelines for insurance agents in determining amounts of coverage, he writes,

> For what are technical complexities, anyway? Whence do they come if not from the natural evolution of the business? Why make believe they don't exist? Why not see if they have their lessons for us—and, if so, learn to use them or not use them, so that, in any event, our work may be made more valuable and comprehensive.
>
> The method outlined in this paper, or any similar one, becomes less and less complicated the more thoroughly it is learned and the longer it is practiced. Whoever takes the trouble to know whatever he has to know, whether it be a problem of "transmitting the molecular force," or of "selling a book," in as perfect a way as he is capable [of], and then keeps *at it and at it* until all sides of his problem may become as clear to him as the sun was to Galileo, *will* find a way of making his message clear to the dullest listener. Truth always finds a natural way of telling her story, and a natural way is an effective way, simple or not.
>
> All fundamental aspects of anything—moral values or an organized business activity—have their complex side; all are part of the natural laws coming up from the roots. Any man, in any valuable work—no matter how limited his capabilities and power of expression seem to him at the start—who sincerely seeks to find the truths and essentials so often confused with or covered up by the immediate and superficial, and who constantly tries, as well as he knows how, to present them in preference to the easier, the more expedient, or the less substantial, will find a way to the *kind* of success he wants. And the way will be simple enough to be understood by the many, and complex enough to be of some value to all![29]

He could essentially be talking about his systematic music. He urges us to take the time to understand technical complexity and find out how we can learn from it. What we will find are basic "truths and essentials" that are often obscured by the "immediate and superficial" and that should be preferred to the "easier, the more expedient, or the less substantial." In other words, the complex inner core is where we find substance. And substance is complex because it reflects the complexity of the world itself. In the process of understanding it we learn more about ourselves and our environment.

Contemporary analysts have occasionally addressed the issue of associating substance with technique. Perhaps the first was Dennis Marshall, who showed that Ives's borrowed material is "at the very core of his compositional thought."[30] Ives selects and uses borrowed materials, according to Marshall, so that their "musical characteristics and interrelationships" will "form a part of the real *substance* of [Ives's] musical art."[31] Larry Starr also confronts the issue, asserting that "Ives's often peculiar manner is . . . in fact *necessary* to the appropriate expression of his substance."[32] Starr, in his analysis of Ives's song "Ann Street," finds that a pattern of stylistic change, which might seem simply an aspect of manner, actually "helps illuminate the inner musical 'substance'" of the song.[33] To put it in the language we are using here, the song's manner reflects values of substance both because it has artistic beauty and because it appeals to the scrutinizing intellect.[34]

The value of technique was clear in Ives's mind when he wrote the *Essays*. If it tends to linger in the background of the work, that is only because his main purpose in the *Essays* is to define and describe substance, the higher artistic value that technique serves to communicate. But just because *Memos* conversely places primary focus on technique, we should not assume that its main purpose is to investigate manner. In the end both the *Essays* and the *Memos* help us to understand the nature and qualities of artistic substance. While the *Essays* do this abstractly, with philosophical ruminations about art and aesthetics, the *Memos* do it pragmatically, by illuminating the necessary technical roots of substance.

Aspects of Systematic Composition

On our journey through Ives's musical language, we will be guided by a few basic questions. Why did Ives write systematic music? What was it about systematic methods that he found appealing and worthy of precious hours of his time? And what are the values of substance that particular systematic methods help to communicate? But before we can start to answer these questions, we must ask a simpler one: What are the basic characteristics of systematic composition?

Calculation. The compositional process of creating and implementing systematic methods is cerebral and abstract. And yet this is not its most distinctive feature—the same could also be said of other approaches. We could, for example, speak of intellectualism in music written without calculation to express a philosophical idea, or in music that is simply organized according to some general principle of thematic or motivic unity. What distinguishes systematic writing from other intellectually centered approaches is the role of calculation—of compositional strategies involving precise measurements and exactingly formulated relationships among musical entities. The process may resemble a mathematical activity, and the result may often be modeled with mathematical operations.

Structural Models. The goal of a calculation process is often to create or realize a specific plan, a structural model, for musical relationships. The model may be a registral shape, a prescription for pitch or rhythmic relationships, or a formal design. It can be an important source of musical unity and structure, and as such can be an effective means of supplanting tonal forces. One type of model, for example, is essentially a visual image that might be given any number of musical representations; a "wedge" model, for example, might be realized by a mirroring of melodies or a succession of incrementally structured chords, or by some combination of both. Other types of models are formed from pure musical relationships, such as orderings of pitch classes or intervals. Still other types are distortions or elaborations of customary or familiar models, such as those of a fugue or march. The act of modeling, in its broadest definition, is central to Ives's compositional technique, encompassing not only the formation and execution of contrived plans but also that most characteristic feature of his non-systematic music, the treatment of borrowed material. Burkholder demonstrates this convincingly in his discussion of the various ways existing music can serve as a model. He finds that "modeling is the seminal technique, appearing in Ives's earliest compositions, continuing until his last works, and underlying many of the later procedures."[35]

Patterns. Virtually all of Ives's systematic methods, and many of his structural models, are based on some sort of pattern of musical entities—involving intervals, durations, transformations, and the like, and often some combination thereof. Once a pattern is established and set in motion, the musical progression becomes automated or self-generating. Ives refers to this aspect of his systematic music when he says some of his work is "based on deductions from quite simple premises, suggesting other logical premises from similar processes, but almost too self-evident to need explanation" (*Memos,* 140). This aspect gives his systematic music a predictability and regularity that stands in stark and ironic contrast to the freedom and seeming randomness that is not only pervasive but indeed flaunted in much of his other music.

Transformational Orientation. Ives's systematic structural models or self-generating patterns are often structured to place primary focus on the transformations between musical entities, not on the entities themselves. This is the case, for example, in a model based on an intervallic pattern, one of Ives's favored tools. The transformational orientation invites comparisons with other music of the period, as explored in a number of recent studies. These include Richard Cohn's studies of Bartók, in which equivalent musical entities are related by processes of "transpositional combination," and David Lewin's writings emphacizing trans- formational relationships in studies of various tonal and post-tonal musics.[36]

Pitch-Class Variety. Finally, a principle underlying many of Ives's structural models, self-generating patterns, and transformational relationships is that a variety of pitch classes should be involved. In many cases, this concern trans- lates to some method of completing the aggregate, inviting provocative but usu- ally unproductive comparisons with twelve-tone music. The comparisons are more apt with pre-twelve-tone music, where pitch-class saturation and equaliza- tion are common methods of denying tonal incursions. Webern, for example, claims to have followed a simple guiding principle in writing atonal music: "until all twelve notes have occurred, none of them may occur again."[37] Similarly, Ives's close associate Carl Ruggles was said to have felt that a melody should not repeat a pitch class until the note has left the "consciousness of a listener," usu- ally requiring at least seven intervening tones.[38]

Musical "Sense": The Origins of Ives's Systematic Music

The five aspects are present in music from throughout Ives's composing years, roughly the late 1880s through the mid 1920s. The earliest evidence survives in sketches and exercises composed when Ives was a teen and just beginning to blossom as a musician and composer. In his *Memos* Ives recalls that his father endorsed and encouraged unorthodox ideas during this period, alongside con- ventional musical studies (*Memos,* 46–48, 114–115).

In speaking about his father in *Memos,* Ives makes some revealing comments about his early perspective on systematic composition and the nature of his father's influence on progressive ideas. The early experiments, he says—and at this point they are indeed experiments—were simply "boy's fooling" (*Memos,* 46). He thereby suggests that the application of unconventional musical ideas is different from "real" composition—that it is more like playing musical games, stepping outside the bounds of conventional music student decorum. But then in the same sentence he recalls what his father told him about this type of com- positional activity: "it must be done with some sense behind it (maybe not very much or too good a sense, but something more than just thoughtless fooling)." In other words, a musical game is permissible if it has a sound intellectual basis, if it is an exercise not only for the playful imagination but also for the rational one. It must make "sense." As Ives said of his later systematic work, "shorter pieces like these . . . were in part made to strengthen the ear muscles, the mind muscles, and perhaps the Soul muscles too" (*Memos*, 63). Ultimately, his goal is to elevate the writing beyond the level of boy's fooling: "But doing things like this (half horsing) would suggest and get one used to technical processes that could be developed in something more serious later, and quite naturally" (*Memos*, 61).

Much of the boy's fooling (or in some cases, "father's fooling") that Ives specifically mentions in *Memos* has to do with combinations of two keys:

> [Father encouraged] playing left-hand accompaniment in one key and tune in right hand in another. (*Memos*, 46)

> If you can play a tune in one key, why can't a feller, if he feels like [it], play one in two keys? (*Memos*, 47)

> I couldn't have been over ten years old when [Father] would occasionally have us sing, for instance, a tune like *The Swanee River* in the key of E♭, but play the accompaniment in the key of C. (*Memos*, 115)

Ives also recalls (*Memos*, 46) writing down music with these sorts of key juxtapositions, no doubt referring at least to the three bitonal arrangements of "London Bridge" that survive among his early manuscripts.[39]

A simple tonal juxtaposition hardly approaches the sophistication of true systematic composition. And yet the exercises Ives describes already display, to some degree, the "sense" behind a boy's fooling and the salient features of his systematic methods. First of all, a bitonal juxtaposition is an intellectual exercise—"good for our minds and our ears" (*Memos*, 47). The act of maintaining separate but parallel thought processes, unfolding melodic structure and rhythms in one key against harmonic functions in another, requires a type of intellectual facility and discipline that prefigure the systematic calculations in later works, where such processes are more conscious and overt. Second, such an exercise is thoroughly controlled by structural models. One model is the structure of the existing tune, prescribing the melodic line, rhythm, and harmonic progression. Another is the model of "bitonality," prescribing a constant opposition between the keys of two rhythmically aligned continuities.[40] A third way that the bitonal exercises reflect systematic values is that the melodic-harmonic and bitonal models exhibit a kind of self-generating pattern—not the type based on some contrived formula but the type in which a particular structural relationship, in this case a bitonal opposition, is established and then allowed to perpetuate itself without impediment. Fourth, the bitonal model also reflects a transformational orientation in the relationships between its two keys, if the scale of one key is viewed as essentially a transposition of the other. Finally, we could even say that a bitonal exercise exhibits a concern for pitch-class variety, since the opposing keys are typically quite different in pitch-class content.

Still, the systematic elements in a bitonal model are shadows of their later selves. Let us now look at an early experiment in which the components of systematic composition are more strongly anticipated. Another early musical activity Ives mentions in his *Memos* is a technique of "playing the chromatic scale in different octaves, and seeing how fast you could do it." This, he says, produces "wide jumps in the counterpoint and lines."[41] In Example 1.1 two excerpts are transcribed from a copybook belonging to George Ives that includes sketches and exercises by both father and son.[42] Example 1.1A is a sketch of a "wide-jumps" chromatic scale, and 1.1B is a short organ piece that implements the wide-jumps treatment as it appears in the sketch. Below the organ score Ives inscribes: "played as Postlude after Organ Concert Bap[tist] Ch[urch] Danbury Friday May 8 1891."

Ives recalls that "gradually, as the ears got used to the intervals, I found that I was beginning to use them more and more seriously, that these wide-interval lines could make musical sense" (*Memos,* 44). Now we can see precisely what Ives means by that phrase. Measure 1 of the sketch (Ex. 1.1A) states the first five notes of the scale in a rhythm and contour that is duplicated for the next five notes in m. 2; m. 2 is $T+5$ of m. 1.[43] In the postlude (Ex. 1.1B) this material appears in mm. 3–6 of the right hand, answered canonically in mm. 4–7 of the left hand. Chromatic ideas also begin the postlude: in mm. 1–2, the right hand falls chromatically from E to G while the left hand rises from C to G. Then in m. 3, as the right hand begins the wide jumps, the left hand continues its chromatic ascent, completing the scale with the C that begins its canonic answer in m. 4.

The most obvious evidence of the aspects of systematic composition in both the sketch and the postlude is the pitch-class succession itself—a chromatic scale is aggregate completion of the most elemental kind. But the scalar ordering influences not only the parts of the postlude that are literally derived from the sketch. Indeed, the chromatic scale saturates the texture, making this particular ordering of the aggregate a pervasive structural model that prescribes the relative positioning of virtually every note. In addition, the model of the scale ordering supplies the realization of another model in the first two measures: this is the "wedge," portrayed by the two converging chromatic lines. And this is followed by the canonic treatment of the wide-jumps material in mm. 3–7, thus realizing a model handed down from contrapuntal traditions. Fundamental to all the models are patterns and transformations: the transformational relationship

A.

B.

Example 1.1. George Ives's copybook, pp. 68, 71

between the first two measures in the wide-jumps scale, the self-generating logic of the scale itself, the inevitable progress of two lines related as wedge voices or by canonic answer. The postlude is an amalgam of the products of calculation processes that are prevalent throughout Ives's systematic music.

George Ives's copybook contains other systematic sketches by the young Charles Ives. One is simply a chord, shown in Example 1.2, formed from a self-generating pattern of decreasing interval sizes.[44] Beginning with the lowest note, the intervals between adjacent notes become gradually smaller by increments of one, from interval 11 between the lowest two notes to interval 3 between the highest two. ("Oct" presumably means 8va.) Ives uses a chord such as this in some later music, but this may be his first lesson in the pitch-class variety inherent in a decreasing interval sequence. Only eight different pitch classes (pc's) will be generated before a repetition occurs; starting on C, as shown here,

Example 1.2. Chord notated in George Ives's copybook, p. 165

the eighth pc is the G♯, and the two highest notes (C and D♯) repeat pc's that appear elsewhere in the chord. Although at first glance it may seem curious that Ives did not continue the sequence to its logical conclusion with intervals 2 and 1 at the top of the chord, perhaps it was just this concern for pc variety that motivated him to stop at interval 3, even though the next pc generated would be new (F). Perhaps he saw no need to continue since he had already ended with two duplications, and his objective, finding out how many different pc's the pattern would generate prior to repetition, was achieved.

A concern for pitch-class variety is still more obvious in the exercise from the copybook shown in Example 1.3.[45] An introductory measure outlines a converging wedge, and then measure 2, repeated as measure 5, arpeggiates black keys in the left hand against white keys in the right hand. These complementations are subsequently answered by wedges of converging half-step-related major triads. In mm. 3–4 the hands move in contrary motion to the distance of a tritone, from FM to BM, thus again exploring complete pitch-class variety by stating every possible major triad between the hands. A similar procedure is thwarted in mm. 6 and 7 when the right hand moves a tritone downward but the left hand moves upward through only five chords before discontinuing the established pattern and joining the right hand on a G-major triad at the beginning of m. 7. The chords in m. 7 could represent the beginning of another wedge that Ives, for whatever reason, never notated, but it seems more likely that this is the ending he preferred: two G-major chords together at the beginning of the measure, followed by a clash of A♭M and F♯M, as if extracted from a wedge in progress.

In several places in the copybook the younger Ives tries different methods of realizing the wedge model. Example 1.4A shows another instance of triad wedges, this one with entire octave spans in both hands.[46] Example 1.4B shows a wedge realization from the copybook that places converging chro-

Example 1.3. Wedge exercise notated in George Ives's copybook, p. 100

matic lines in a tonal-harmonic context.[47] Judging from the *Amen* repeated in the text, this short piece is apparently a four-voice choral response for a church service. Its outer voices contain converging chromatic lines, stating twelve pitch classes in moving from octave G's to a unison on middle C. But the inner voices fill out harmonies that are actually not particularly unusual— they twist and shove the potentially radical wedge into a kind of harmonic orthodoxy. As suggested in the analytic notations added in the example, the opening G-major sonority is followed by a diminished-seventh chord that acts as an applied chord preparing the A-minor chord at m. 2:1. After a moment of dissonant disorientation at m. 2:3, the final measure implies a V_3^6–I cadence in C major. Thus the initial triad connects with the final cadence to imply an

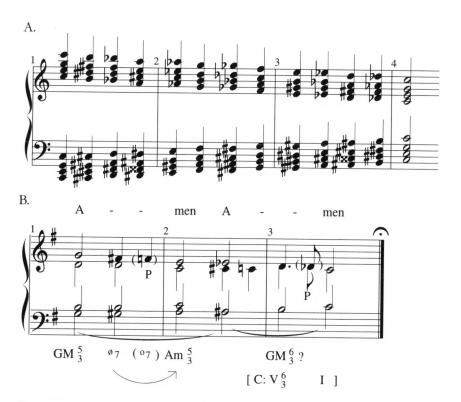

Example 1.4. George Ives's copybook, pp. 165, 68

overall V–I progression in C major. The progression is at first diverted by the move to the submediant in m. 2.

The "Amen" reveals two sides of its young composer. On the one hand, it is a simple application of principles of systematic composition, with the outer-voice chromatic lines using all twelve pitch classes to form a converging wedge. On the other hand, it is an exercise in chromatic harmony, applying principles that are not in the same sense systematic and that aspire to define structure through different means. The way the "Amen" combines the two is skillful, perhaps ingenious for a teenager, but there are also aspects that are unmistakably elementary. Compare, for example, the "Amen" with the triad wedge of Example 1.4A. The structure of the triad wedge is defined by the wedge model; we know the exercise is over when the converging lines have completed their octaves. The structure of the "Amen" is also defined by a wedge, but it is further defined by the implied harmonic progression; the sense of completion is provided both by the convergence on middle C and by the harmonic arrival. In terms of Ives's long-range objectives, we cannot criticize the pieces for lack of organization, but we can question their expressive capacities: the triad wedge is sterile and artless, while the *Amen* is limited expressively to the language of tonality that Ives will eventually want to abandon. These early efforts draw attention to the quest that Ives would pursue tirelessly in the years to follow— a quest for a musical language that would be organized and expressive, and that would also be his own.

PART I

Tools and Materials

2 Contrapuntal Foundations

ounterpoint opens a revealing window into the evolution of Ives's compositional language because it is such a distinguishing feature of his style. We have come to expect the distinctive presence of contrapuntal activity in any Ives piece, regardless of its size, instrumentation, or chronological position. In his music based on quotations and generally without systematic bases, contrapuntal textures can range from simple, transparent combinations of individual lines to juxtapositions of dense sound masses, or, in Rudolph Reti's terminology, a "polyphony of groups."[1] In Ives's systematic writing, specific contrapuntal devices often serve as vehicles for highly organized pitch and rhythmic relationships. As we sharpen our focus on one area of Ives's musical thinking and development, it is only natural to start with this most basic feature of his music.

In systematic music it is not only the contrapuntal techniques themselves that influence Ives's language; there are also strong parallels between the underlying compositional processes of contrapuntal and systematic methods. We might say that systematic writing is a kind of "strict composition," by analogy with the strict counterpoint one first encounters in contrapuntal studies. This would be distinguished from the "free composition" of Ives's concert music. The analogy carries through to many details of process and product. First of all, the act of writing counterpoint is an act of calculation—a constant process of formulating optimal materials and combinations, juggling the independence and cooperation of concurrent lines. Equally important, a fugue or canon is a structural model, prescribing a general format and structure for the presentation and development of ideas. The model's inherent patterns reflect a self-generating process that is particularly systematic in a canon, which can generate a range of possibilities depending on its length and voicing. Finally, contrapuntal writing is fundamentally dependent on a transformational orientation, relating pitch levels of subject entries in a fugue or pitch distances between voices in a canon. Contrapuntal techniques are ideally suited to carry out Ives's systematic compositional objectives, and he never stops exploiting their capabilities.

The Right Way and the Wrong Way

Ives's recollections of his early contrapuntal studies are similar to those of his early explorations of bitonality. He recalls from his father both encouragement to try something different and the admonition to use good sense and ingenuity—again, to engage in more than just "boy's fooling." Ives writes, "Father used to say, 'If you know how to write a fugue the right way *well*, then I'm willing to have you try the wrong way—*well*. But you've got to know what [you're doing] and why you're doing it.' . . . I had to practise right and know my lesson first, then he was willing to let us roam a little for fun. He somehow kept us in a good balance."[2] So in addition to writing traditional fugues—the "right way"—Ives was beginning at an early age to explore expansions of fugal conventions, writing in the "wrong way" to achieve a different kind of logic and coherence.[3]

To Ives the wrong way meant a change in the conventional key relationships. Devoted readers of the Ives literature must know his thoughts on this subject by heart: "Look at a fugue. It is, to a great extent, a rule-made thing. So, if the first statement of the theme is in a certain key, and the second statement is in a key a 5th higher, why can't (musically speaking) the third entrance sometimes go another 5th higher, and the fourth statement another 5th higher?" (*Memos*, 49). As Burkholder points out, Ives is challenging the traditional rules, but he is not challenging the idea of having rules; he simply makes up his own rules to replace the old ones.[4] The early applications of his rules include a fugal exposition and a short fugal piece, both notated in his father's copybook, with each subject entry exactly transposed (as a "real answer") a fifth higher than the previous one.[5] Ives applied these same ideas in two longer pieces from this period: the "Song for Harvest Season" (1893) for voice and organ or instruments and the *Fugue on "The Shining Shore"* (1896).[6] These are among the compositions Ives describes as his "first serious pieces quite away from the German rule book" (*Memos,* 38).

And yet it is incorrect to assume that the fugues written in the "wrong way" are simply layerings of opposing tonalities among the voices in a fugal texture, analogous to the juxtaposition of keys in a bitonal family sing-along. In fact, the objectives of a wrong-way fugue and the objectives of a bitonal layering are quite different. To recognize this difference is to learn much about George Ives's admonitions that his son should put "some sense behind" his nontraditional writing and "know what [you're doing] and why you're doing it."

We can observe the distinction in two examples of canonic writing from Ives's early years. Example 2.1 shows the canonic interlude between variations II and III of Ives's *Variations on "America"* (?1891). We will be comparing it with Example 2.2, a canonic exercise in Charles Ives's hand surviving in his father's copybook.[7]

The interlude, simply a canon based on the beginning of the tune "America," was composed to heighten the opposition between two distantly related keys. The two keys are F major in the *dux* (right hand), and, one bar later, D♭ major in the *comes* (left hand). Except for the last sonority, where all the sounds tend to coalesce, everything about the writing encourages a separation between the contrapuntal strands. Certainly, the canonic model itself contributes to this separation, as the consistent echoing invites the listener to shift attention from one voice to the other but not to merge them. And in this case the separation might be even stronger in a canon based on an unfamiliar melody, thanks to the recognizability and predictability of the tune's structure and harmony. The two strands are also distinguished by register and dynamics. In short, Ives has composed a canonic analogue to the bitonal renditions of "Swanee River" he recalls in his family sing-alongs.

The exercise (Ex. 2.2) is also a combination of two distantly related keys: *dux* in C major in the middle staff, and *comes,* an exact transposition to E♭ major (as a "real answer"), two beats later in the top staff. The bottom staff adds an accompaniment that suggests C major. Thus we have not just another hint of the bitonal family performance, but exactly the same keys Ives recalls in the case of "Swanee River" (*Memos,* 115). And yet the result is not the same as that of the sing-along or the *Variations on "America"* interlude. Rather than creating an opposition between C and E♭, Ives composes the exercise to produce a cooperation between the two lines. His objective in the exercise is actually not so different from that of a conventional contrapuntal exercise—to create lines that work alone as independent melodies but that achieve concordant results when performed together.

Of course, this is not to say that the counterpoint is harmonically conven-

Interlude (ad lib. until *)

Example 2.1. *Variations on "America,"* interlude between variations II and III. © 1949 Mercury Music Corporation. Used by Permission.

tional. It is not a canon at the minor third, with the melodic intervals adjusted to remain in the same key, as in tonal counterpoint. But it is remarkably tame for "real" counterpoint at this pitch distance, especially when compared with the bitonality of the previous example. Part of the reason for the harmonic cooperation is the conventional harmonic foundation established by the accompaniment. This implies a harmonic progression that prolongs the C-major tonic in the first three measures, moves to the dominant in m. 4, and returns to tonic in m. 6. The final four measures display a conventionally conceived increase in harmonic activity: there is a move to the subdominant at m. 6:3, a move to the submediant at m. 7:3, preceded by the hint of an applied chord, and then a concluding authentic cadence in mm. 8 and 9.

The overall effect of the canonic lines plus the accompaniment is to distort this progression mildly without straying far from its basic harmonic implications. For example, the voices together form C-minor triads in m. 1, at m. 2:1,

Example 2.2. Canon in Charles Ives's hand in George Ives's copybook, p. 101

and in the last measure. The mode shifts to C major in m. 3 due to the frequency of E♮ in the *dux,* while the *comes* adds a seventh (B♭). Similarly, dominant implications are supported in the canonic voices in m. 4, although with a B♭ instead of a B♮ as the third of the chord, and in the first half of m. 8. In general, the vertical formations throughout the exercise are either consonant intervals, especially thirds, or dissonant intervals placed in contexts where conflicts are minimized. Of the actual dissonances between the voices, only the minor second at m. 5:3 and the major second at m. 6:3 cannot be explained as some type of melodic figuration, such as a neighboring tone (as is the last eighth note of m. 2) or passing tone (last eighth note of m. 6).

Ives employs similar procedures in a canonic central section of *Psalm 67* (1898–1902), as well as in the fugal exposition, the short fugal piece, and the "Song for Harvest Season" mentioned above.[8] Viewed alongside a true tonal opposition such as that of the *Variations on "America"* interlude, the title "four-key fugue" for some of these sketches is somewhat of a misnomer.[9] The contrast shows Ives's differing responses to his father's admonitions to put some "sense" into his experimental efforts. On the one hand, the sense behind the interlude is the care Ives takes to sustain the separation—the choice of keys and temporal distance, the use of registral and dynamic separation, and the like. On the other hand, the sense behind the exercise is the care Ives takes to produce cooperation—the decisions made in the process of constructing the canonic line with an eye to the resulting simultaneities. Yet neither result seems very artistically satisfying; the interlude is a bit simplistic and crude, very much like "boy's fooling," while the exercise is excessively reliant on conventional contrapuntal principles, as if it had started out going the wrong way but had somehow become rerouted toward the right way. Again we see, as with the wedge "Amen" discussed in the previous chapter, Ives's search for methods of giving substance and a unique identity to progressive ideas.

Canonic Sense

As we move forward in the evolution of Ives's systematic writing, canon plays an increasingly prominent role. The line of development extends from his earliest uses of calculation processes in his youthful contrapuntal studies to later music in which canonic relationships simply represent one of several calculations to be made. Ives never stops searching for a more substantive and distinctive canonic "sense" that would meet the specifications articulated so many years earlier by his father.

Charles Ives's ultimate goal is a contrapuntal technique that maximizes the separation of the canonic lines. As Burkholder points out, canonic techniques are one of Ives's methods of producing layered textures.[10] Of course, the challenge is to achieve a coherent overall effect from the separate layers—to produce discrete layers that make some kind of sense when they are combined. In one respect, this is an easier task than tonal contrapuntal writing, since it puts no restrictions on melodic structure and harmonic progression.[11] But in another respect it represents a new type of challenge, because the composer must provide a new set of restrictions and sources of coherence.

The evolution of this type of writing begins with several pieces Ives composed just before and just after the turn of the century, when he was fresh out of college and obviously inspired by the contrapuntal studies he had just completed with Horatio Parker at Yale.[12] His first efforts do not achieve complete separation of canonic lines but rather push the limits of cooperation. The first *Harvest Home Chorale* (around 1902), for example, begins with a canonic passage that places the customary high value on vertical consonance but adds a new wrinkle: the voices are related by mirror inversion. The music of the passage is shown in Example 2.3. As the notations below the score indicate, only two vertical dissonances (circled) are created, and these can easily be attributed to melodic figuration. This sole surviving example of inversional canon in Ives's

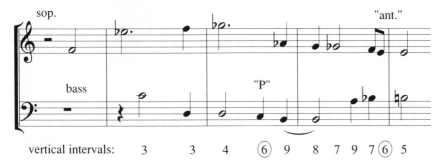

Example 2.3. *Harvest Home Chorale* No. 1, voice parts in mm. 6–10. © 1949 Mercury Music Corporation. Used by Permission.

early work draws attention to the role of inversional transformation in contrapuntal technique, and its status, along with the transpositional operations of other canonic writing, as the composer's first use of operations and calculations that will figure prominently elsewhere, in both contrapuntal and noncontrapuntal contexts.[13]

Another extension of the ideal of cooperation occurs in the center of the choral *Psalm 54* (around 1902). Example 2.4 gives the beginning of this section, which is written in double canon at T0. The vertical combinations are quite dissonant. There are dissonant clashes, for example, at mm. 16:1 (intervals <21>, bottom to top), 16:2–4 (interval E), 17:2 (interval E), and 20:2 (intervals <8TE>). But the dissonance does not result from independence of the voices, as it does in the *Variations on "America"* interlude (Ex. 2.1). Rather, the dissonances here are specifically formed in order to express the fear and tension described in the text at this point. That is, Ives constructs the canonic lines with the intent of creating particular dissonances, just as he would write the canonic line in the Example 2.2 exercise (or the canonic line in an orthodox tonal canon) so as to produce specific consonances.

The first canonic writing in which Ives achieves both greater separation and greater sense is in *From the Steeples and the Mountains* (1901–1902). This work is scored for four bell parts, written largely in four-voice canon, and trumpet and trombone, written partly in two-voice canon.[14] As regards Ives's development as a contrapuntist, the canonic writing in the brass is slightly advanced, allowing more dissonance than in earlier writing and changing the transformational relationship between voices from T9 to T8 in midstream.[15] A more significant advancement is apparent in the bells. As shown in Example 2.5, which is the beginning of a canonic passage that continues for some twenty measures thereafter, the four-voice canon in the bells combines distinct tonal layers: parts I and IV

Example 2.4. *Psalm 54*, mm. 14:2–20:4. © 1973 Merion Music, Inc. Used by Permission.

Example 2.5. *From the Steeples and the Mountains,* bell parts in mm. 15–22

state descending C-major scales in different registers, part II states a descending Db-major scale, and part III a descending B-major scale. The voices are spaced at distances of two beats (between I and II) or four beats (between II and III and between IV and III). The keys and distances are maintained throughout.

So Ives begins *Steeples* with the same kind of progressive conception of tonal juxtaposition he used in the *Variations on "America"* interlude (Ex. 2.1). But now he takes several steps to transcend anything that would resemble simple "boy's fooling." First, and most obvious, is the connection with the work's putative "program," wherein the bell parts imitate church bells.[16] With the tonal contrasts and canonic relationships Ives offers a new perspective on an old tradition that he knows well from his everyday life. Further, at the midpoint of the piece (mm. 28–30) he changes the pitch sequence to present alternate notes in the scales— in place of the original scale-degree sequence 8–7–6–5–4–3–2–1 he begins writing 8–6–4–2–7–5–3–1. He thus adds to the programmatic imagery by evoking the tradition of change bell ringing, in which this type of change could be one of several successive, methodical permutations of a scale.[17] Finally, he also adds sophistication to his canonic design by devising an overall rhythmic scheme. The beginning of the scheme is apparent in Example 2.5, with the second statement of the scale in each voice switching to dotted-quarter values. Subsequently, gradual reductions continue so that the third statements of the scales are in quarter notes, the fourth statements are in dotted eighths, and so on until the scales are being presented in sixteenth-note values in the center of the design. Then, in the second half of the piece, along with the new pitch pattern, the values begin to get larger, reversing the order of the previous diminutions. The resulting palindromic arrangement of rhythmic values, supported by the change in the pitch sequence, precisely regulates the overall rhythmic structure and gives the entire work a newfound depth of clarity and organization.

The canonic structure of *Steeples* illustrates three practices that figure prominently in Ives's later contrapuntal writing. One is the projection of a contrapuntal design over an extended passage; in Ives's later work, canon becomes a frequent means of generating a large amount of music from a limited number of ideas. The most expansive examples are a two-voice canon at To in mm. 87–125 of the third movement of the Piano Trio (1904–1911), and a four-voice, later reduced to three-voice, canon in mm. 42–73 of the second movement of the Second String Quartet (1907–1911). In the latter the pitch levels are related by perfect fifth, recalling the relations among subject entries in the early wrong-way fugal writing. Among other more compact but nonetheless pervasively canonic passages is *Hallowe'en* (1906), whose string parts juxtapose C-major, B-major, Db-major, and D-major scales in a manner similar to the *Steeples* bell parts but including inversional relationships among the voices (ascending versus descending scales) and frequent changes in the temporal canonic relationships.

The second important contrapuntal practice first seen in *Steeples* is the use of canon to support an extramusical idea. A similar approach, for example, is demonstrated in a section of *Central Park in the Dark* (1906) where Ives is depicting various "night sounds" made by "street singers," as he describes them in his program notes.[18] Example 2.6 shows a portion of the woodwind lines in this work, presenting a canon at the semitone and eighth-note temporal distance

Example 2.6. *Central Park in the Dark*, flute and oboe, mm. 65:1–71:1

to suggest an out-of-tune, out-of-phase performance by the street singers. He uses canon in a similar way to evoke images of a parade in *The Gong on the Hook and Ladder* (?1911).[19]

The third practice has to do with rhythm. Ives's use of a rhythmic scheme to add structural interest and variety in *Steeples* anticipates many strategies of this sort in later works. The next stage in the development toward greater separation of voices is a canonic rhythmic scheme that is not echoed among all the voices but that serves to distinguish one voice from another, to enhance the perception of textural stratification. Again borrowing from older practices, Ives achieves this result by applying principles of mensuration canon in the two pieces entitled *Largo Risoluto* (No. 1 and No. 2; 1906). A comment in the margin of the first work makes reference to the law of diminishing returns, pointing out that the durations of the canonic answers are subject to various proportional diminutions.[20] With several discrepancies in rhythmic values, the second voice (viola) answers the initial piano voice at T_{11} and in a 4:3 ratio, and the third voice (cello) follows in a 2:1 diminution of the piano at T_5. Subsequent answering voices suggest other rhythmic relationships, one in mirror inversion, although not in consistent rhythmic proportions.[21]

The separation is still more acute in the mensuration canon of *Largo Risoluto No. 2*. Example 2.7 shows the opening of this piece, with the *dux* in the piano answered by the *comes* in the strings.[22] The primary responsibility for the separated effect is carried by two familiar aspects of Ives's experimental work. One is the rhythmic proportions in the canonic structure: the rhythm of the *dux* is enlarged by half in the *comes,* so that the *comes* continually lags further and further behind. The other is tonal opposition, recalling the *Variations on "America"* interlude (Ex. 2.1). Here the canonic voices support tonal centers a tritone apart— A major in the *dux,* E♭ major in the *comes.* Dynamic contrast also plays a role in the separation, as the *dux* at *forte* is answered by the *comes* at *piano* (which is then reversed when the entire structure is repeated). Thus the rhythmic differentiation, tonal opposition, dynamics, and instrumentation all contribute to the stratified effect, even while the canonic aspects keep the passage securely unified.

Example 2.7. *Largo Risoluto No. 2*, mm. 1–3

Ives has taken to heart both of his father's admonitions quoted in *Memos:* the requirements to put "some sense behind" tonal juxtaposition (p. 46) and to "know what [you're doing] and why you're doing it" in extending contrapuntal conventions (p. 47; Kirkpatrick's interpolation).[23]

Ives creates a still more intricate web of canonic relationships and oppositions in the Trio of his Scherzo for string quartet (1903/1914); the complete Trio is given in Example 2.8.[24] The structure is set up as a double canon subdivided into scales that differ in content and direction: descending chromatic scales in canon 1 in the first violin and viola, and ascending C-major scales in canon 2 in the cello and second violin. Articulation also plays a role, as the notes of the chromatic scales are connected with bowings, whereas the notes of the major scales are not. As the Trio progresses, however, the original canonic pairings begin to break down, not because of changes in the scales themselves—which remain consistent throughout—but because of changes in the rhythmic relationships.[25] Starting with m. 24, each measure of the canon 1 *dux* uses slightly shorter values than the previous measure, while each measure of the canon 1 *comes* uses progressively longer ones. Conversely, in canon 2 the *dux* gradually augments, measure by measure, while the *comes* gradually diminishes.

As a result, there is a reasonable basis for making any pairing of voices. First there are the initial canonic pairings—first violin/viola, cello/second violin—based on scale content, articulation, and rhythmic relationships whose gradual changes are mirrors of each other. Another set of pairings associates the voices that start together—first violin/cello, second violin/viola—suggesting that the

Example 2.8. Trio from Scherzo for string quartet (mm. 22–28)

simultaneous chromatic and major scales are distorted mirrors, or perhaps ana-
logues, of each other. These pairings exhibit the same rhythmic divergences
seen in the first pairings. Finally, a third set of pairings associates voices that
have no similarity of scale content, direction, or articulation, but that display
identical rhythmic structures. These are the two diminishing voices (first violin
and second violin) or the two augmenting voices (cello and viola). In effect,
these pairings establish relationships of canonic rhythm: starting in m. 24, the

durations in the viola stop echoing canon 1 and begin to echo the durations of the *dux* of canon 2, and the durations in the second violin stop echoing canon 2 and begin to echo the durations of the *dux* of canon 1.

In this Trio Ives attains his highest degree yet of canonic sense and organized opposition of pitch materials. He takes a conventional constructive tool and reworks and reorganizes it to produce a systematic design of strong inner logic and coherence. But we are only beginning to see the extent to which contrapuntal devices and systematic methods provide basic expressive resources. As these tools continually recur in music discussed in later chapters, we will see still further extensions and applications and more fully recognize their utility for presenting and developing musical ideas.

Fugue and Beyond

Canon is a more "systematic" technique than fugue and will therefore more often claim our attention in these pages. But the conventions of fugal structure and technique nevertheless have great relevance to Ives's systematic compositions. Often he introduces a theme or motive in the manner of a fugal exposition, before moving on to other textures that may or may not be contrapuntal. The entrances in the first *Harvest Home Chorale* shown in Example 2.3 somewhat illustrate this phenomenon, since the rest of the piece is not so consistently contrapuntal. Other pieces with exposition-like beginnings include the Hymn for string quintet (1904) and the late song "Aeschylus and Sophocles" (1922).[26] As expected, Ives takes great care in these works to write "the wrong way—*well*."

Generally, Ives scorns fugal conventions. He calls fugal structure "unreasonable" and "a rule-made thing" (*Memos*, 49). But of course he has fugal studies to thank for his skills in thematic transformation and development, calculation of pitch relationships, and large-scale formal design.[27] He wrote few actual fugues in his mature period but often incorporated techniques that resemble, or perhaps mimic, fugal conventions.[28] In the next chapter we examine Ives's most conspicuous attempt to present systematic ideas in the framework of a fugal model, the *Tone Roads No. 1* (1911).

3 Analysis I: *Tone Roads No. 1*

ves explains that his *Tone Roads No. 1* was written "half serious, half in fun, but carefully worked out" (*Memos,* 63). Even as he wrote these words in the 1930s, and in the compositional attitudes he recalls from when the work was written—the period of his greatest productivity—he pays homage to his father's teachings about sensible experimentation, or "serious fun." Scored for small orchestra, *Tone Roads No. 1* is a lucid illustration of basic facets of his systematic writing, both in its contrapuntal and technical details and in its incorporation of these details into a coherent overall design.

Tone Roads No. 1 extends contrapuntal conventions along the lines of the procedures discussed throughout the previous chapter, as first seen in the three trend-setting aspects of *From the Steeples and the Mountains.* First there is the pervasive use of a contrapuntal model: in *Steeples* it was the continuous presence of canon, in *Tone Roads No. 1* it is fugue. Second, *Tone Roads No. 1* expresses a program that is still more detailed than the one in *Steeples,* giving the structure an extramusical sense in addition to the fugal one. Finally, rhythmic manipulations similar to those seen in *Steeples,* and in the *Largo Risolutos* and the Trio from the Scherzo for string quartet, also play a role in the "careful working out" of *Tone Roads No. 1.*

Let us first look at the work's program. The contrapuntal lines represent roads converging in the center of a town. Above a sketch for the piece Ives writes, "All Roads lead to Rome and to F. E. Hartwell & Co. Gent's Furnishings."[1] On another page he writes, "Over the rough & Rocky roads are ole Forefathers strode on their way to the steepled village church or to the farmers Harvest Home Fair or to the Town Meetings, where they got up and said whatever they thought regardless of consequences!"[2] Ives's description of the work in *Memos* emphasizes the variety of roads traveled and people traveling them, as a metaphor for the diversity of American society:

> The *Tone Roads* are roads leading right and left—"F. E. Hartwell & Co., Gents' Furnishings"—just starting an afternoon's sport. If horses and wagons can go sometimes on different roads (hill road, muddy road, rocky, straight, crooked, hilly hard road) at the same time, and get to Main Street eventually—why can't different instruments on different staffs? The wagons and people and roads are all in the same township—same mud, breathing the same air, same temperature, going to the same place, speaking the same language (sometimes)—but not all going on the same road, all going their own way, each trip different to each driver, different people, different cuds, not all chewing in the key of C—that is not all in the same key—or same number of steps per mile. (*Memos*, 63)

Ives's program brings to mind two images that are fundamental to his world view and to the subject matter of his most important artistic efforts. One is the image of the center as a key destination, as a goal of a spiritual journey: "All Roads lead to Rome."[3] A city may itself reflect these themes in its design around a central sacred or official place—as Ives says, "the steepled village church" or the farmers' Harvest Home fair or the town meetings. Humanity's challenge is in the journey to arrive at such a shrine, to earn and be worthy of its spiritual rewards. In the words of Mircea Eliade: "The road leading to the center is a 'difficult road,' and this is verified at every level of reality: difficult convolutions of a temple (as at Borobudúr); pilgrimage to sacred places (Mecca, Hardwar, Jerusalem); danger-ridden voyages of the heroic expeditions in search of the Golden Fleece, the Golden Apples, the Herb of Life; wanderings in labyrinths; difficulties of the seeker for the road to the self, to the 'center' of his being, and so on. The road is arduous, fraught with perils, because it is, in fact, a rite of the passage from the profane to the sacred, from the ephemeral and illusory to reality and eternity, from death to life, from man to the divinity."[4]

The second key image is that of different "wagons and people and roads" coexisting in "the same township." The portrait Ives paints is no mere provincial scene but a symbol of a diverse society bound together by a common understanding of the human condition—indeed, of the arduous path they all must follow in their journey toward the center. The image also raises musical ques-

Example 3.1. *Tone Roads No. 1,* bassoon, mm. 1:1–3:2. Road A

tions, since the diverse contrapuntal lines that depict the various roads must somehow achieve unity, depict commonality, while maintaining their individuality and eluding a common language of tonality.

The lines depicting the various roads, as they are restated, varied, and developed, resemble subjects in a multisubject fugue. The modeling process is fairly loose, however; there is not, for example, a standard exposition of all the voices. Ives's adaptions and extensions of fugal conventions include main roads that occasionally branch off into side roads and other roads without direct connections to their surroundings. At the end the lines suddenly adhere to a common purpose, adopting unified rhythmic gestures and melodic-harmonic structures to symbolize the arrival of the roads at their common destination.[5]

There are two main roads, both of which are stated in the opening five measures. The first one, labeled here road A and notated in Example 3.1A, is presented by the cello part unaccompanied, using several wide melodic intervals, a staccato articulation, and considerable rhythmic energy; surely, it is a "rough and rocky road." Immediately in road A we see the structural principles that bind much of the piece together, that become musical metaphors for shared societal values: emphasis on members of interval classes (ic's) 1 and 5. To illustrate this aspect of road A, the music of this road in Example 3.1A is aligned with a summary of its voice-leading structure in Example 3.1B. In the first five notes there is an ascent of a fifth, from A2 to E3, with a half-step double-neighboring of the latter pitch. This presages a longer-range movement from the initial A2 to the E2 at m. 2:2, also preceded by its upper and lower half-step neighbors, though in a different octave. The beamed downstems in Example 3.1B illustrate the chromatic stepwise voice-leading that fills in this long-range progression. Then in the rest of the excerpt the road moves away from and then returns to E via a largely chromatic rising line (m. 2:3–4) that restates the D♯ lower neighbor. Thus does the interaction of foreground chromatic lines with middleground fifths establish a musical environment for the subsequent tone roads.

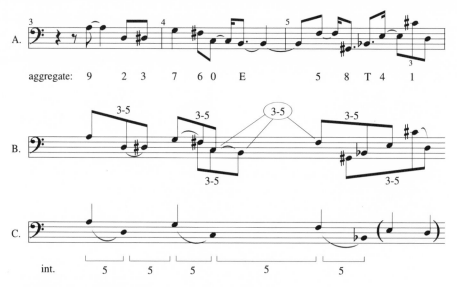

Example 3.2. *Tone Roads No. 1*, bassoon, mm. 3–5. Road B

The other main road, labeled B and shown in Example 3.2A, is quite different from road A. Its note values are longer and intervals wider; perhaps it is hillier than A, but smoother underfoot and with fewer twists and turns. And yet road B makes a structural connection with road A that confirms their coexistence in the same township and society. As road B completes the aggregate without duplication, it brings out members of ic's 1 and 5 to form set class (sc) 3 – 5s (016) as shown by beamings in Example 3.2B. (Interval class 1's are highlighted by slurs.) The first 3 – 5 is formed when the initial fifth A–D is followed by the half-step neighbor D♯. Then in m. 4 two 3 – 5s result from an interlocking of the fifths G–C and F♯–B. Common-tone 3 – 5 formations continue into the next measure, as this trichord is formed again by the last two notes of m. 4 plus the first of m. 5. Finally, in m. 5 the 3 – 5 occurrences and ic 1 and 5 relationships are mostly between nonadjacent notes: F in beat 1 relates by ic 5 to the B♭ on beat 3, and by ic 1 to the E on beat 4, altogether forming 3 – 5. This skips over the G♯ that associates by ic 5 with the penultimate C♯, which in turn relates by ic 1 to the D at the end of the bar; these three notes also form 3 – 5. Overall, as road B winds down and up, many of the higher notes can be combined into the voice-leading pattern reflected in the stemmed notes in Example 3.2C, a stepwise descent down a fifth to the final D. Each of the first three members of this descent is followed by its lower fifth, amassing a sequence of interval 5 <A–D–G–C–F–B♭> over the course of the road.

The first statement of road B overlaps with a restatement of road A at T1 in

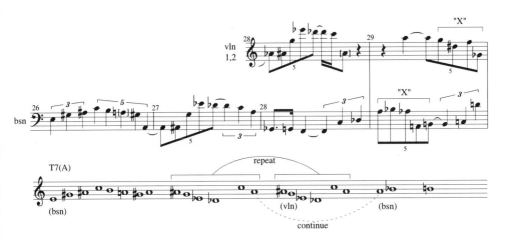

Example 3.3. *Tone Roads No. 1,* bassoon, mm. 26–29; violins, mm. 28–29

the flute and a stretto of road B in parallel fourths (T0, T5, T7) in the upper strings. The roads have thus set their courses and will continually reappear in various guises throughout the piece. The various entries of road A in particular are easily detected within the texture and therefore offer the strongest analogy with subject entries in a fugue. Passages without A material, to continue the analogy, often resemble episodes. The most noticeable forms taken by A are transposed fragments (m. 15, upper strings, T7; m. 19, flute, T4; m. 25, violins, T9) and inverted forms (m. 6, bassoon, T9I fragmented; mm. 17:1–20:1, bassoon, T6I complete; m. 20, violins, T10I varied and fragmented).

Certain restatements of A are less easily detected. Example 3.3 displays excerpts from the bassoon and violin lines in mm. 26–29, aligned with the ordering of pitch classes from a nonrhythmicized portion of T7(A) notated below the score. In the first two measures of the bassoon line, the pitch classes of T7(A) are simply stated in different rhythms—an inexact rhythmic augmentation. Then in m. 28 the bassoon abandons any direct relation to road A, while the violins repeat the six pitch classes just stated by the bassoon. Finally, m. 29 becomes yet further removed from A, as both parts freely develop the motive from the beginning of the second measure of road A, bracketed and labeled X in Example 3.1A. The bassoon's version of X includes the notes A, B♭, and B, which continue T7(A) exactly at the place where X should occur, interrupted by a descending major seventh between A♭3 and A2, and recall the most conspicuous interval in the original motive. The subsequent variant of X in the violins recalls its echoing relationships with the bassoon between mm. 27 and 28. The version of X in the violins in m. 29 is T2(X) except for the D♯, which is a half step lower than the corresponding note in X.

Example 3.4. *Tone Roads No. 1,* clarinet, mm. 7–12

If this appearance of the road A material is suggestive of a subject entry in varied augmentation, other appearances could represent episodic development of motives from A. In the clarinet line shown in Example 3.4, for example, motives from the beginning and end of A provide material for manipulation. Measure 7 is a rhythmic variant of six notes from the material stated by the cello in mm. 3–4, after the bassoon has entered with road B; this relationship is illustrated above the clarinet part in Example 3.4. At the end of m. 9 the clarinet begins to recall the beginning of road A. In m. 9:4 the rising major third of the first beat of the original is filled in; the first note then comes back at 10:2. From this point through m. 12 the clarinet continues to present intervallic sequences reminiscent of the first two beats of road A. The rising third and falling whole step stated by the last three notes of m. 10 recall the D♯–F–E of m. 1:2. This would be a consistent (T5) relationship if the B♮ at 10:4 were a half step lower, as it is when the figure returns in m. 12.[6] Measure 11 begins with a return to the exact pitch classes of beat one of A, and concludes with the rising whole step B♭–C, hinting once again at the first two notes of m. 1:2 (now at T7).[7]

At first glance, it is difficult to follow the path of the B material through the piece as we can that of road A. The only appearances of B in its original, transposed, or inverted forms are the two mentioned earlier: the initial bassoon entrance (mm. 3–5; Ex. 3.2) and the stretto against the bassoon in the upper

Example 3.5. *Tone Roads No. 1*, low strings, mm. 9:4–12:4. Road BD1

strings in parallel fourths (mm. 4–6). Upon closer inspection, however, a certain path taken by B does emerge, with a contrasting basis of continuity. Once we have recognized this we can say that both road A and road B unfold according to the same basic plan: the establishment of an original idea followed by a series of changes in that idea to depict the progress of the road. The difference is that as it progresses, A employs operations that are familiar (and systematic), whereas B does not.

The road B transformations assume a different conception of thematic structure than those of road A. Whereas the beginning of road A establishes a particular rhythm and contour for the pitch classes of this road, the beginning of road B (Ex. 3.2A) establishes only an ordering of pitch classes. Subsequently, the transformations of B involve manipulations of the relations between these pitch classes, with the intent of emphasizing ic's 1 and 5 in different ways. Example 3.5A illustrates the first transformation of road B as it appears in the music—in parallel fourths similar to the earlier statement of B (mm. 4:4–6:4).[8] The upper voice is extracted in Example 3.5B; it is labeled "BD1" to indicate that it is the first B-derivative. Then Example 3.5C renotates B itself for comparison with BD1. Like B, BD1 completes the aggregate without duplication.

The brackets and labels in Example 3.5B illustrate the manner in which ic's 1 and 5 are emphasized in BD1: ic 1 is "enclosed" within ic 5 in each of the first

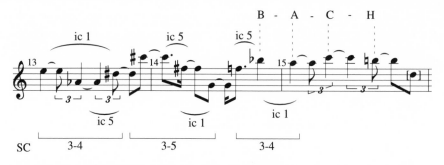

Example 3.6. *Tone Roads No. 1,* flute, mm. 13–15. Road BD2

three nonoverlapping trichordal segments. This establishes very specific connections to the structure of B. First, the first two adjacent intervals from B (ic 5 and ic 1) are formed between the first note and each of the next two in BD1 (F–F♯, F–C). Because the other interval in both trichords is ic 6, both B and BD1 begin with sc 3–5. Then, the second trichord of BD1 is a precise inversional mirroring of the second trichord of B, also therefore forming 3–5s. (This is a T10I relationship, whereas the initial trichords are in a T3 relationship (B → BD1).) Next, the third trichord of BD1 is another 3–5, recalling the trichord in B that overlaps one note with the aforementioned second trichord. Finally, the last trichord of BD1 abandons the emphasis on the germinal intervals to state 3–2 (013), recalling the trichord formed by the E, C♯, and D at the end of road B. (The D technically occurs just after road B ends.)

Immediately following the first full statement of BD1, road B branches off yet again. Example 3.6 shows this second B-derivative, BD2. Again, the derivation of a new road from road B makes extensive use of ic's 1 and 5 in completing the aggregate. The first three nonintersecting trichords of BD2 emphasize ic's 1 and 5 much as do B and BD1, but here only the second one forms sc 3–5; the first and third form 3–4 (015). Then, beginning with the B♭ in the center of the third trichord, Ives spells out B-A-C-H. He often does this in a passage involving systematically conceived musical details, paying homage to the master of contrapuntal calculation while affirming the connection between counterpoint and systematic methods.[9]

A closer look at the texture underlying this first statement of BD2 reveals just how extensive is the calculation signaled by the B-A-C-H. Example 3.7 gathers together selected parts from the passage where BD2 first appears. After its initial statement in the flute (mm. 13–15), BD2 appears again in the flute (mm. 16:1–18:2) and is then fragmented in the same instrument (end of m. 18). Two complete statements and a partial statement of BD1 appear throughout the excerpt in the low strings in parallel fourths. Meanwhile, the retrograde of BD2 appears in two complete statements followed by an almost complete statement in the clarinet, joined by the upper strings in m. 17. The retrograde forms apparently help to depict the "roads leading right and left" (*Memos,* 63). Further, the rhythm of each line is controlled by durational patterns that are different in length from the pitch-class patterns, an isorhythmic technique Ives uses elsewhere.[10] There are two durational patterns, labeled X and Y below and within the score, each associated with a different pitch source. (The patterns are subject to slight variation.) Pattern X, which has eight attack points, determines the rhythm of BD2 and R(BD2), the latter beginning with the second measure of X to avoid lining up with the X in the flute. Pattern Y, which determines the rhythm of BD1, contains fourteen attack points and begins in the second measure of BD1.[11]

The subsequent progress of road B includes additional occurrences of BD1, BD2, and R(BD2) in various rhythms and usually at their original pitch levels. The single exception is mm. 20–25, in which T4(BD1) appears several times in the bassoon, accompanied by repetitions of BD2 and R(BD2) in the flute and violins, respectively, similar to the flute-clarinet retrograde pairing in the passage shown in Example 3.7. Toward the end of the work, BD2 is continually present while BD1 is reduced to incomplete statements and motivic fragments.

Example 3.8 summarizes the overall form of *Tone Roads No. 1* up until the roads reach their common destination (m. 33).[12] The chart includes all the previously mentioned occurrences of A and B and their various transformations, variations, derivatives, and fragmentations. Also charted are several passages that have not been identified as direct transformations of or derivations from the main roads; most of these are, nevertheless, somehow related to a main road. For example, the material in the lower strings in mm. 4:4–9:3 begins at the same time as the statement of road B in parallel fourths in the upper strings. The lower strings also move in parallel fourths, and the first chord formed by all the string parts (at m. 4:4) combines the fourths from the upper and lower parts to form a larger stacking of fourths, from bottom to top <C♯3–F♯3–B3–E4–A4–D5>. So the parts begin together and at first seem to be engaged in an interplay, but they soon begin to move off in different directions, with the upper parts stating road B and the lower stating material that continues in parallel fourths but is not road B. The diverging process suggests that all of the material in the lower strings starting in m. 4:4 is a gradual branching off of road B that reaches its new pathway when BD1 begins in m. 9:4.

There are also passages of free motivic development, as might occur in an episode within a fugue. In some cases that object of development is clear, as indicated by bracketed symbols in the chart. Other passages, labeled episodes, exhibit free development in the style of one road or another without employing specifically recognizable elements of either.

Example 3.7. *Tone Roads No. 1*, B-derivatives in mm. 13–19

m.   1   2   3   4   5   6   7   8   9   10   11   12   13   14   15   16   17   18   19   20   21   22   23   24   25   26   27   28   29   30   31   32

fl   T1(A) —— [B] —————— T0(BD2) —————— T4(A)||(BD2)
                    y   y   y

cl   [A] —————— R(BD2) ——— 3/2 rhythmic acceleration, piano-drum chords
                          y   y   y

bsn   T0(B) — T9I(A)|| [A] ——— T6I(A) ——— T4(BD1) ——— ~T7(A)|| episode
                                     x   x

vln I   T5(B) —— episode   T7(A)|| R(BD2) ——— ~T10I(A)|| ~R(BD2) ——— ~T9(A)|| ~T7(A) episode
                            y|| y

vln II   T0(B) —— episode   T7(A)|| R(BD2) ——— ~T10I(A)|| ~R(BD2) ——— ~T9(A)|| ~T7(A) episode
                            y|| y

vla   T7(B) —— episode   T7(A)|| R(BD2) ——— 3/2 rhythmic acceleration, piano-drum chords
                            y|| y

VC   T0(A) —— [B] ——— T0(BD1) ——— 3/2 rhythmic acceleration, piano-drum chords
                (veer toward side road)   x   x

bass   [B] ——— T0(BD1) ——— 3/2 rhythmic acceleration, piano-drum chords
                (veer toward side road)   x   x

key: for melody Q, Q|| = Q truncated   ~Q = truncated   =Q = variation on Q   [Q] = development of Q   x y = rhythmic patterns

Example 3.8. Tone Roads No. 1, chart of overall form

Example 3.9. *Tone Roads No. I,* clarinet, viola, cello, bass, mm. 20:1–26:2

Beginning in m. 20, the clarinet, viola, cello, and bass introduce contrasting material that could only be considered a third road. From m. 20 through m. 31 these instruments state only dissonant chords in a unified rhythm, with occasional rhythmic embellishment in the clarinet. Example 3.9 shows the first six and a half measures of this road in condensed score.[13] Throughout, the chords are constructed to highlight intervals 11 and 13, thus resembling chords Ives describes as simulations of drum sounds on a piano.[14] As indicated in the score, almost every simultaneity contains at least one instance of both intervals, though not in any sort of regular arrangement. Almost every chord also contains at least one instance of ic 5, thus linking this road with the others. The most systematic aspect of the passage is the rhythm in the lower voices, graphed below the excerpt in the example, which falls into a pattern of four whole notes followed by a fifth whole-note duration stated as dotted quarter/eighth note/half rest. In subsequent measures, decreases in the number of sustained chords in each grouping enact a kind of rhythmic acceleration.

Example 3.10A shows the beginning of the first ending, where the roads arrive at their common destination. Now the texture is saturated with the principal intervals, stated as ic 5s related by ic 1. In tremolo chords in the low strings,

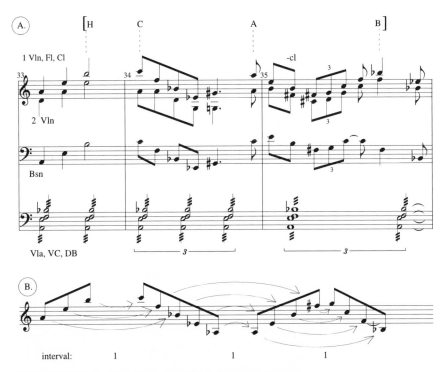

Example 3.10. *Tone Roads No. I,* mm. 33–35, condensed score

these intervals are expressed by <A–E> and <F–Bb>. In the upper parts, series of ic 5s are interrupted three times by half steps to subdivide the material into four groups. Example 3.10B shows the result: the groups (highlighted by beamings) contain individual notes that relate to notes in subsequent groups by interval 1. Meanwhile, the highest notes in each group, as highlighted above Example 3.10A, make one last reference—this one spelled backwards—to the master architect of the type of tone roads that served as the model for these.

Earlier we quoted Ives's description of the ultimate destination of the diverse journeys: "All Roads lead to Rome and to F. E. Hartwell & Co. Gent's Furnishings" (Kirkpatrick, *Catalogue*, 50). As the work concludes, this seemingly offhand comment looms as a veiled reference to a very specific musical destination. Though it is hard to tell whether Ives has some specific musical event in mind when he mentions Rome, the reference to F. E. Hartwell can be translated, using the significant first letters in the spirit of B-A-C-H, into the musical configuration F-E-B-C shown as Example 3.11. The piece's two primary intervals (ic's 1 and 5) are formed adjacently within the tetrachord, and ic 5 is also formed between the outer pitches. In effect, one ic 5 (E–B) is enclosed within another (F–C) at a half-step distance.

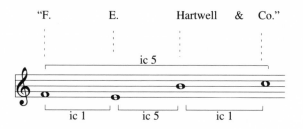

Example 3.11. *Tone Roads No. 1,* clue to intervallic structure

Indeed, this is the place to which all roads lead. The tremolo chords in the low strings present the same tetrachord type as that of F-E-H-C, sc 4–8 (0156). (This tetrachord type earlier appeared within road B—see Ex. 3.2A, m. 4.) Appropriately, the notes of these chords are T5 of those of F-E-H-C. Further, the notes of the chords combine with the two highest notes of the passage—the H and C of H-C-A-B—to make two other important associations. First, the upper H and C combine with the outer notes of the chords (A and B♭) to form yet another B-A-C-H. Second, the H and C also combine with the inner notes of the chords (E and F) to form yet another F-E-H-C. Thus do the roads converge. In this final unified arrival, we are reminded of the goal at the spiritual center and of the travelers' common humanity.

4 Structural Models

ves depends on structural models to give his systematic music continuity and goal orientation, to provide a framework within which a particular systematic idea may be presented, developed, and completed. He thinks in these terms because he recognizes the essential role played by such a framework in the systematic music he is typically writing—music that is dense, complex, unfamiliar, and lacking any tonal guideposts. George Perle speaks of similar procedures that supply what he calls "normal harmonic continuity" in music of European composers of Ives's generation.[1] Perle emphasizes the *extracontextuality* of such models—their reliance on a universally recognizable process or shape rather than a principle of continuity operating only within the boundaries of a given piece. Any true substitute, or at least analogue, for tonality must, in Perle's view, have some kind of global salience. Extracontextuality is basic to the two models we discuss here: the wedge and the palindrome.

The Wedge

It is possible to define the wedge model broadly as not only a gradual divergence or convergence of voices moving in opposite directions but also as any pattern of graduated increases or decreases, such as a series of gradually augmenting or

53

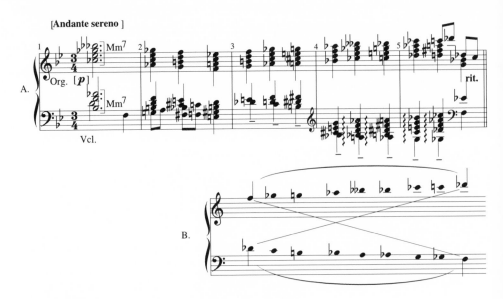

Example 4.1. *The Celestial Country,* Interlude before No. 4

diminishing durations.[2] We will not adopt such a definition, although there is certainly merit in recognizing broad compositional principles common to diverse phenomena. The broader definition will be useful in later chapters; for now we confine our discussion to instances in which the wedge shape is realized in pitch space, effecting a specific registral symmetry. In Ives's mature writing, wedges generally bring together several organizational strategies, influence form on several levels, and do so in a manner that is both artistic and original.[3]

Indeed, it was artistry and originality that offered the greatest room for growth in the wedge realizations mentioned in Chapter One. From these crude beginnings—the triad wedge (Ex. 1.4A) and the wedge "Amen" (Ex. 1.4B)— Ives expands in profound and distinctive directions. In music written slightly later, but still in a relatively early developmental phase, for example, he begins to refine the harmonic component of a wedge unfolding so that it has a more unique flavor that relies less on conventions of the sort found in the wedge "Amen." One such realization is the organ Interlude from the cantata *The Celestial Country* (1898–1902), shown in Example 4.1A.

The distinctive harmonic principle Ives applies in this Interlude is again based on an idea handed down from his father. Ives's recollections of this father-son lesson are part of another passage in *Memos* where he mentions both the felicitous and the rational sides of his father's teachings, illustrating the duality through technical details: "Father used to let me, half in fun and half seriously, make chords up of several 3rds, major and minor, going up on top of themselves."[4] The first sonority of the Interlude in Example 4.1A is such a chord, in effect a stacking of two Mm7 chords with roots a minor ninth apart, or pitch intervals (from bottom to top) <4 – 3 – 3 – 3 – 4 – 3 – 3>. The chord contains eight notes with no pitch-class duplications, as do chords formed from these intervals in other organ interludes in *The Celestial Country* and in a short organ interlude inscribed by Ives in his father's copybook.[5]

In the first two measures of the Interlude Ives writes descending parallel chords similar to several other instrumental passages in the cantata.[6] These chords continue to form the harmonic component in the expanding chromatic wedge of mm. 2 – 5; the outer-wedge voices are extracted in Example 4.1B. In these voices an exact mirroring of chromatic lines takes place between the (compound) M3 at m. 3:1 and its inversion, a (compound) m6, at m. 5:3, to enact a voice exchange. The final chord (m. 5:3) then implies a dominant function that is subsequently resolved when the next movement (Intermezzo for String Quartet) begins with a B♭-major triad.[7] Meanwhile, the chords between the wedge voices do not actually show a contrary motion between the hands, but rather state parallel lines, as if continuing the progression from mm. 1 and 2. Every note in the last three measures, except for the lower wedge voice, participates in a parallel chromatic ascent of chords structured exactly like those in mm. 1 and 2 (pitch interval <4 – 3 – 3 – 3 – 4 – 3 – 3>), with the left hand providing only those notes which will fit above the lower wedge note. Thus the chord at m. 3:1 contains a complete Mm7 chord in the right hand (the upper note is also a member of the upper wedge voice) but only one note in addition to the wedge note in the left hand—this pitch (E4) would be the upper left-hand note if two Mm7 chords were stacked as before. This trend continues thereafter: the sonorities at mm. 3:2 and 3:3 contain two apparent extractions from Mm7 chords in the left hand in addition to the wedge notes, and the sonority at m. 4:1 similarly contains three notes in addition to the wedge note. Then from m. 4:2 to 5:2 the complete eight-note chords—still ascending in half steps—fill the space between the wedge voices.

In sum, two aspects of the Interlude reflect advancement over earlier practices. First, the Interlude has a tonal basis, as does the earlier wedge "Amen" (Ex. 1.4B), but its suggestions of B♭ major and of a voice exchange are more a mimicry of tonal procedures than applications of them. The "Amen," in contrast, is very much controlled by principles of harmonic progression, albeit somewhat distorted ones. Second, the chord structures in the Interlude are more interesting and more interestingly developed than the sonorities in the earlier triad wedge (Ex. 1.4A). That wedge simply contrasts opposing streams of triads; its overall structure is defined by completion of the octaves in the streams. In the Interlude the chords themselves are more distinctively structured, and the musical shape is defined by the interaction of the chords with the wedge voices and by the voice exchange.

One aspect of Ives's wedge conceptions to which he gives increasing attention over the years is the size of the melodic intervals in the wedge voices and the resulting vertical intervals between the voices. Thus far we have seen only chromatic wedges, or mirrorings of melodic half steps. In this type of wedge the vertical intervals change by increments of two. Chromatic wedges of this type are also used in *A Yale-Princeton Football Game* (?1898), where the converging voices depict a wedge formation in a football game.[8] But during his formative years Ives also begins to investigate other choices for melodic intervals, creating wedge designs with more rapid rates of expansion. And this introduces the new problem of wedge voices with actual ranges wider than the performing medium will accommodate.

Ives first confronts these issues in the choral *Psalm 24* (1898–1902). Each verse of the *Psalm* is a realization of a wedge model, with the sizes of the melodic intervals gradually changing, verse by verse: verse 1 is based on an expanding wedge mirroring intervals 1 and 11, verse 2 is based on an expanding wedge mirroring intervals 2 and 10, verse 3 similarly mirrors intervals 3 and 9, verse 4 mirrors an upper voice that alternates intervals 3 and 4 against a lower voice that alternates intervals 9 and 8, verse 5 mirrors intervals 5 and 7, verse 6 mirrors an alternation of 5 and 6 (upper voice) against an alternation of 7 and 6 (lower voice), and the progression ends with a mirroring of intervals 5 and 7 in verse 7. After this, the wedge models switch to the contracting shape and the intervals in successive realizations gradually decrease in size. Thus the entire verse-to-verse progression exhibits a wedge-like expansion and contraction of intervallic bases, a kind of macrocosm of the procedures within each verse.[9]

Of course, Ives must use octave displacements to realize some of these wedges in a choral setting. He is able to do this while preserving some semblance of wedge shapes by breaking the wedges up into segments. Example 4.2 shows one instance of a wedge segmentation, the setting of verse 5 that is based on a wedge of interval 5. The verse is divided into two parts (mm. 22–24 and 25–27), each a wedge that projects interval 5s as far upward and downward as is practical for the vocal ranges. Actually, Ives makes some sacrifices to achieve the desired registral effect: the outer voices are not exact mirrors of each other (the upper consists of more notes than the lower), the two expansions do not both begin on unisons, and the voices stop short of presenting complete interval-5 sequences, and thus of unfolding complete aggregates.

The realization of the interval-5/interval-7 wedge in verse 5 contains only one octave displacement, the one that separates the first miniwedge from the second. But whereas this displacement is necessary, in other verses displace-

Example 4.2. *Psalm 24*, mm. 22–27, verse 5. © 1955 Mercury Music Corporation. Used by Permission.

ments are used even though they are not required in order to accommodate the vocal ranges. The half-step wedge in verse 1, shown in Example 4.3, is such a case, suggesting the wide-jumps treatment of the chromatic scale discussed earlier (Chapter One). At first the outer voices mirror each other exactly: the soprano line from the initial C4 to the F4 at the end of m. 2 mirrors the concurrent bass line (C4 through G3) in pitch space. But then at the beginning of m. 3 the soprano leaps up to the F#5 while the bass keeps its half-step movement, in order to stay within a reasonable range. Mirrorings continue to be mixed with nonmirrorings thereafter.

Example 4.3. *Psalm 24*, mm. 1–6, verse 1. © 1955 Mercury Music Corporation. Used by Permission.

Another verse that could easily project a registral wedge shape but does not is verse 2, whose interval-2/interval-10 wedge realization is shown in Example 4.4. Measures 6:3–9:2 state all the wedge notes, with unpredictable octave displacements; subsequently the same wedge begins again but stops short of completion at the end of the verse. What is more notable about verse 2, however, is the activity in the inner voices. In verse 2 the wedge intervals determine not only the outer voice-leading, but also the content of the vertical sonorities at almost any given point. With the exception of the fleeting last chord of m. 7 and the E♭ in the tenor in m. 11—a kind of appoggiatura—every note in every voice in verse 2 is a member of the whole-tone collection that is projected in the interval-2/interval-10 wedge model.[10] Thus this particular wedge model not only prescribes the outer voice-leading, but also the referential collection for the passage.

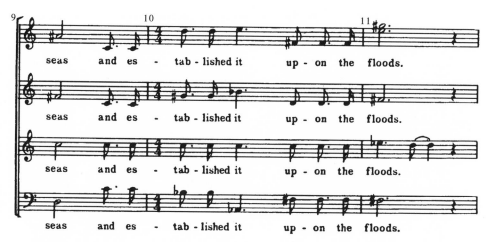

Example 4.4. *Psalm 24,* mm. 6:3–11:4, verse 2. © 1955 Mercury Music Corporation. Used by Permission.

Comparing verse 2 with verses 1 and 5, just shown, we can see the two different options as we attempt to unify horizontal and vertical phenomena. Since the wedge voices in verse 2 contain mainly just six different pitch classes (the members of the "even" whole-tone collection), they define a distinctive and appropriately limited referential collection from which the notes in the inner voices may be extracted. But in verses 1 and 5, where the models contain all twelve pitch classes, the outer voices cannot define satisfactory referential collections. These verses could project a horizontal-vertical unity only by retaining the generating intervals as vertical adjacencies. Ives does not do this in verse 1, and, in fact, often forms consonant structures. He does do it in verse 5, where all of the simultaneities are quartal.

Example 4.5. *Study No. 20*, mm. 21–24. © 1981 Merion Music, Inc. Used by Permission.

It is this concern for vertical and horizontal relationships that plays an ever greater role in some of Ives's later wedge realizations. Example 4.5 shows a passage from the piano *Study No. 20* (?1908) in which a mirroring of outer voices moves mostly to adjacent white keys, and occasionally to black keys. The vertical space between the voices is filled in with clusters of keys that are the same color as those of the outer voices. Example 4.6 shows verse 9 from the choral *Psalm 90* (around 1923). Here the upper voice-leading by interval 2, mirrored in the

Example 4.6. *Psalm 90*, mm. 60–65, verse 9. © 1966, 1970 Merion Music, Inc. Used by Permission.

A. vocal line, mm. 2–4. © 1933 Theodore Presser Co. Used by Permission.

B. model

Example 4.7. Soliloquy, compound wedge

lowest voice by interval 10, presents the same intervals that occur in the space between the wedge voices, producing a whole-tone cluster wedge that expands and then contracts. (Only the outer voices at the midpoint, setting the word *wrath,* disrupt the intervallic consistency.) Rhythm also plays a role, as we might expect in a more advanced realization. The durations of the sonorities decrease by one sixteenth up to the midpoint and then return to their starting point. Ives keeps track of this process with numbers, indicating number of sixteenths per duration, placed above the score.

Ives has several ways of developing and extending the wedge model in his later work; the remainder of this section discusses three of them. The first way is to create a wedge using successive but not necessarily adjacent notes within the same melodic line, as voices in a compound melody. Example 4.7A illustrates an application of this idea in the opening vocal phrase (following the initial recitative) of the song "Soliloquy" (1907).[11] The basis of the melody could be the model shown in Example 4.7B, which is a wedge of the two compound voices moving chromatically in opposite directions, recalling the subject of Bach's E-minor organ fugue (the "wedge fugue," BWV 548) or anticipating the tone row in Nono's *Il Canto sospeso*.[12] Ives's realization of this model, however, includes octave displacements to obscure the literal registral wedge. The lower wedge voice begins with all the notes in the first measure of the excerpt (m. 2)—F, E, and a leap up to D♯ (respelled E♭ in the model)—and then concludes with the D–D♭ at the end of m. 3 and the C–B–B♭–A at the beginning of m. 4. The upper wedge voice can be started from the same initial F, which then connects with the G♭ (respelled F♯ in the model) and the leap down to G in m. 3, and then with the final G♯ and the leap down to A in m. 4.

A second way of expanding the wedge concept is apparent in "Like a Sick Eagle," a song Ives originally composed as a movement of the *Set No. 1* for small orchestra and later arranged for voice and piano.[13] Here he constructs a kind of wedge between two voices that proceed not in contrary motion but in the same direction, in intervals of different sizes: an upper voice in whole steps moves in stride with a lower voice in half steps. Example 4.8A shows a note-for-note alignment of descending chromatic and whole-tone scales, the latter occurring twice over a two-octave span in order to state the same number of notes as the former. The wedging effect is spelled out by the vertical intervals notated between the staves, which change in increments of one.[14] We might consider this matrix a more complete version of the actual model used in the song, which is boxed in the example and labeled song model. Throughout much of the song Ives places the chromatic portion of the song model in the vocal line and both the chromatic and whole-tone lines (the entire song model) in the right hand of the piano part. Example 4.8B shows the song's introduction and first two vocal phrases. The model comes into play on the fourth vocal note, at the word *is*. From there the wedge voices (vocal line and piano right hand) move through the complete song model to effect an intervallic contraction up through the final syllable of the word *mortality*—vertical intervals $10-9-8-7-6-5-4$. After a short reprise of the contraction ("weighs heav - i'"), the voices go backward through the model to unfold an intervallic expansion starting on the last syllable of the word *heavily* and ending on the second syllable of the word *unwilling*—vertical intervals $4-5-6-7-8-9-10$. Subsequently, much of the rest of the vocal line, in tandem with the right-hand piano part, continues this movement back and forth through the model, depicting the sluggish flight of a sick eagle.[15]

Our third and last way of expanding the wedge concept involves large-scale projections of wedge properties. A simple example appears in the piano accompaniment to the brief song "Luck and Work" (?1913), which begins with a short pattern that is subsequently transposed by tritones upward in the right hand and downward in the left hand, so that the distance between the hands gradually widens, suggesting an expanding wedge, over the course of four measures.[16] Still more extended is the elaborated wedge in the first eight measures of the piano part of *Hallowe'en* for piano quintet (1906), a work, we recall, that Ives describes as "one of the most carefully worked out (technically speaking), and one of the best pieces (from the standpoint of workmanship) that I've ever done."[17] Example 4.9 shows the piano part of these measures in line A, accompanied by analytical graphs on lines B, C, and D.

This passage is based on a series of transpositions of a pattern established

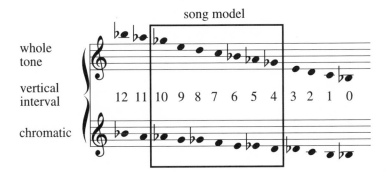

song model

A. model

B. first two vocal phrases. © 1933 Merion Music, Inc. Used by Permission.

Example 4.8. "Like a Sick Eagle," excerpt and analysis

first in mm. 1–2. The pattern consists of a widely spaced sonority in the low register (in m. 1, octave Cs) answered by two higher and denser structures (end of m. 1 and beginning of m. 2). Starting in m. 3 (after a repetition of m. 1:1 at the end of m. 2), this three-element pattern—low chord/high chord/high chord—is repeated five more times; the six occurrences are labeled with Roman

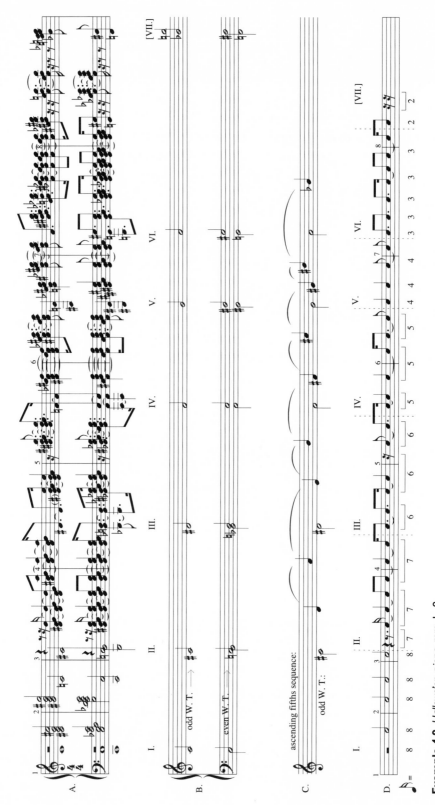

Example 4.9. *Hallowe'en*, piano, mm. 1–8

numerals I through VI below the score. Line B shows the pitches in the low chords that constitute the unfolding wedge: ascending lines (stems up) of parallel whole-tone scales, one odd and the other even, and a single descending line (stems down) of half steps. (The passage ends with the fleeting suggestion of a seventh occurrence.) Meanwhile, the high chords unfold the sequence summarized in line C. In each pattern repetition, the right hand is transposed up a fifth from the first high chord to the second, while the left hand stays where it is in both high chords. And since the entire pattern moves up by whole steps along with the whole-tone ascent in the upper voice of the low chords, the highest voice unfolds the sequence of ascending fifths shown with upward stems in line C. Finally, line D illustrates a concomitant rhythmic pattern, in which the durations in each successive repeated pattern decrease by one sixteenth. The resulting durational acceleration contributes to the general growth and intensification of the overall wedge expansion. This simple structural model unites diverse structural forces.

The Palindrome

We have seen how certain pitch and rhythmic procedures provide new rules for Ives to use in place of the old ones. He thereby rejects the traditional rules themselves but does not deny that rules of some sort are necessary. Ives's use of palindrome follows a similar logic: like Bartók and others of his contemporaries, he turns to symmetry for new principles of form. His realizations of palindromic structural models affect form on a range of levels, from brief appearances within otherwise diverse structural plans to expansive determinations of large-scale structure, and including various levels in between.

The palindromic model is intimately connected with the wedge: both rely extensively on symmetry and are capable of generating structural designs based entirely on this extramusical principle. Indeed, Winters chooses not to separate the two, conflating them as the "wedge-palindrome."[18] And the wedge and palindrome certainly are connected when a particular wedge is paired with its retrograde to create a palindromic contraction-expansion or expansion-contraction. Ives does often present wedges in this way, as we saw in the passage from *Psalm 90* in Example 4.6. But we treat wedges and palindromes separately here because they also have important differences. The wedge, as we have defined it, is a particular contour realized in pitch space; the palindrome is a principle of compositional ordering. In separating them, we recognize that a wedge may or may not be paired with its retrograde to create a palindrome, just as a palindromic structure may or may not include a wedge realization.[19]

We will define and discuss three types of realization of the palindromic model

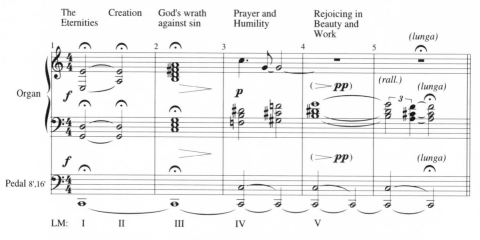

Example 4.10. *Psalm 90*, mm. 1–5. © 1966, 1970 Merion Music, Inc. Used by Permission.

in Ives's music, designated the *arch form,* the *unit palindrome,* and the *event palindrome.* The three are distinguished by the scope of their palindromic arrangements: the arch form involves whole sections of music, the unit palindrome relates smaller musical groupings, and the event palindrome organizes individual musical entities.

In an *arch form,* the principal musical ideas in the first half of a structure, such as themes, textures, or other structural delineators, reappear in the second half in reversed positions relative to each other. As in other music of this period, such as the outer movements of Bartók's Fifth Quartet, Ives's arch forms may include sectional variation and a general but not exhaustive unfolding of symmetrical relationships. One of Ives's arch forms is the song "The Cage" (1906), which has a palindromic structure based on the scalar content of the vocal line and a concluding reprise.[20] Another is the piano *Study No. 20,* in the score of which Ives adds section labels to identify an overall structure of 4B–3B–2B–1B–Trio–1B–2B–3B–4B–Coda.[21]

The whole-tone cluster wedge in *Psalm 90* mentioned above (Ex. 4.6) is the center of a large-scale arch form articulated by recurrences of the chordal structures from the first five bars shown in Example 4.10. In the inscriptions above the score Ives associates each chord with a religious concept, beginning with "The Eternities" and "Creation" in m. 1, followed by "God's wrath against sin" in the chord of m. 2, and ultimately "Prayer and Humility" and "Rejoicing in Beauty and Work" in mm. 3 and 4. As Donald Grantham explains, Ives continues throughout the piece to associate these chords with the concepts as they arise in the text, so that the chords become "harmonic leitmotifs."[22] Grantham numbers the five leitmotifs (LM I through V) as shown below the score in Example 4.10.

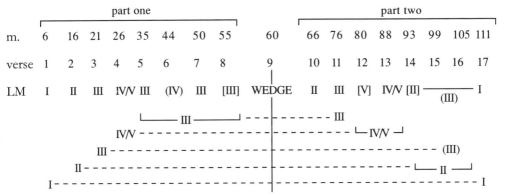

Example 4.11. *Psalm 90,* diagram of formal structure

Example 4.11 charts the various appearances of the LMs throughout the *Psalm* to define the arch form.[23] Roman numerals show the prominent use of an LM in a particular verse, parenthesized Roman numerals indicate brief or otherwise relatively inconspicuous uses of LMs, and Roman numerals in brackets refer to passages where some characteristics, though not the original forms, of an LM predominate.[24] The relationships do not articulate a precise palindromic arrangement—every usage in the first part is not reflected in reverse order in the second part—but they nevertheless unfold a significant number of symmetrical associations: the piece starts and ends with LM I, uses LMs II and III in the next positions inward, arranges LMs IV and V as well as III about the center, and places the expanding-contracting wedge (Ex. 4.6) in the exact center. Generally, a greater presence of LM III in the first half (verses 3, 5, 7, 8) is counterbalanced by more references to LM II in the second half (verses 10, 14, 15, 16). As LM III represents God's wrath against sin and LM II Creation, this shift reflects a change in the text from greater negativism in part one, especially in verses 5–9, to words of rejoicing in part two.

The *unit palindrome* displays retrograde relationships on a more local level. In realizations of this type, relatively brief musical units, such as measures or groups of beats, reappear without substantial change but in reversed positions relative to each other. Although it might be argued that the unit palindrome and the arch form are simply the same phenomenon on different scales—that the arch form is essentially a unit palindrome in which the units are whole sections—there are other distinguishing differences. In the arch form, the units that are rearranged are complete and self-contained, with clearly articulated beginnings and endings. Some difference in musical effect may occur, owing to the reordering and to any variation in the material, but for the most part the sections within themselves will be similar and will play similar, or at least analogous, roles with respect to the form as a whole. In the unit palindrome, conversely, the units are not complete and self-contained but are segments of some larger musical entity. When the units reappear in reverse order in the second half, this continuity is dramatically disrupted, and wholly new meanings and effects may emerge.

In the previous chapter we observed that the bell parts in *From the Steeples and the Mountains,* in addition to being canonic and in tonal conflict, are rhythmically organized according to a symmetrical pattern. When the pitch pattern changes at the midpoint, the durational pattern helps to highlight the center by beginning its palindromic reversal. We can now consider the brass parts as well: the midpoint of the bell parts is also the hinge of a unit palindrome in the trumpet and trombone. The brass parts are canonic in the first half of the structure, but they break the canon shortly before the palindromic center; then, just after the bell parts start to change pitch patterns (m. 27:4 in the first bell part), they begin to state the previous measures in reverse order: m. 28 is the same as m. 26, m. 29 is the same as m. 25, and so on. (Occasional adjustments are necessary at the beginning or end of a measure to make the connections smooth.) As a result, measures that are canonically derived in the first half recur in the second half completely separated from any canonic context.[25]

Ives uses the unit palindrome to great effect in *Calcium Light Night* (1911), a work for winds, percussion, and piano (four hands).[26] This composition is a reminiscence of his college days, intended, according to Kirkpatrick, to evoke "the torchlight parades at the time of student society elections."[27] The parade image is conveyed by piano-drum chords suggesting a march in the piano and percussion and a collage of tunes from college fraternity songs in the winds. To depict the gradual approach and then retreat of the parade, Ives constructs a unit palindrome that grows in volume and density up to the center and gradually fades thereafter.

The units in this unit palindrome are always groupings of measures, ranging in length from one measure in the center of the structure (m. 34) to nine measures just before and after the center (mm. 25–33, returning as 35–43). Other units are two, three, four, or five measures long.[28] Part of the way the palindrome contributes to the program has to do with relationships between the units and the musical ideas. In their initial presentations both the piano-drum material and (especially) the fraternity songs cross unit boundaries, so that when the units reappear in reverse order in the second half, the original musical ideas are fragmented. This fragmentation contributes, along with the textural thinning and overall diminuendo, to the depiction of the dissipation and withdrawal of the parade.

To get a clear idea of how this works, let us follow the path of one tune through the structure of *Calcium Light Night*. Example 4.12 traces a tune Ives

Example 4.12. *Calcium Light Night,* "Psi U. Marching Song." © 1964 Merion Music, Inc. Used by Permission.

identifies as "Psi U. Marching Song."[29] First, Example 4.12A gives the tune in its standard form. Then Examples 4.12B and 4.12C show two of the many variations on the third phrase of this tune that appear in the piece, these in the bassoon and trombone respectively. In the bassoon version (Ex. 4.12B) the first measure is actually the end of one palindromic unit, and the next two measures are the beginning of another. The place where the bassoon version returns in the second half of the palindrome is shown in Example 4.12D. Indeed, Ives not only fragments the tune according to units, but also rearranges measures within units: m. 6 returns as m. 62, obeying the unit boundaries, but mm. 7–8, which would be expected to appear in order, appear in reverse as mm. 59–60. The trombone version (Ex. 4.12C) is similar: its first measure, m. 8, is the last measure of a unit and thus recurs after the other measures in the second half, at m. 59, as shown in Example 4.12E. Ives actually adds two notes in m. 55:4 that connect to the next measure in the same way that the displaced notes did—a deviation from the palindromic plan. As a result, the phrase does not seem fragmented until the displaced notes arrive in m. 59.

These versions can also help demonstrate the structural role played by all the versions of this tune in the piece. The two versions shown in Example 4.12 B and C participate in a pattern of rising half steps created by the implied tonal centers of successive versions: the bassoon version (Ex. 4.12B) suggests A♭ major, and the trombone (Ex. 4.12C) begins on A major and shifts to suggestions of B♭ and subsequently B major. This pattern pervades the first half of the piece as graphed in Example 4.12F, beginning with an initial statement in G major, moving upward through A♭, A, B♭, and B in the two versions we have been looking at, and continuing with a wandering chromatic ascent up to E♭ at the center of the form. There the trombone presents a more extensive version of the tune (mm. 28–34). The fragmented reversal of these versions in the second half creates an even more wandering chromatic descent to support the final effect of dissipation and retreat.

The *event palindrome* operates on the smallest level of detail, reordering individual events so that the second half of the structure is an exact mirror of the first half. Ives typically applies this treatment to harmonies, rhythms, and instrumentations, in addition to pitches. We have already seen hints of an event palindrome in the precise mirrorings of certain wedge realizations, such as those in *Study No. 20* (Ex. 4.5) and *Psalm 90* (Ex. 4.6). On a larger scale, we also mentioned *Psalm 24*, where the verses in the second part employ converging wedges that mirror the earlier diverging ones. This is hardly an exact mirroring, however, as the converging wedges are somewhat condensed and set differently than are the diverging ones. This unsystematic relation of mirrored events is more like an arch form—we could say that *Psalm 24* is an arch form enriched by features of an event palindrome. In music written later than this relatively early work, Ives explores both the arch form and the event palindrome more thoroughly, but separately.

Indeed, in his later work he seems to seize on the idea of the event palindrome in a variety of contexts. On one end of the spectrum is the brief retrograde-symmetrical line in the left hand of the passage from *Study No. 21* (?1909) for piano shown in Example 4.13. The E2 at the end of m. 4 is the center of a palindromic line comprising mostly rising fifths or fourths and stating every pitch class except pc 9 on both sides of the center. (Only pc 4 is repeated, both as the axis and elsewhere in the line.) At the other end of the spectrum are entire pieces structured as event palindromes. Ives's best-known large-scale realization of this structural model, like his oft-cited realization of the wedge model in *A Yale-Princeton Football Game,* is a depiction of a scene from a sporting event. The strict realization of event palindrome in a major portion of the chamber work

Example 4.13. *Study No. 21,* mm. 4–5. © 1949, 1975 Mercury Music Corporation. Used by Permission.

All the Way Around and Back (1906) represents the movement of a base runner in a baseball game running from first to third base on a long fly ball but then returning to first when the ball is ruled foul.[30] The midpoint of the form corresponds to the runner's arrival at third base, and the reversal of material after this point symbolizes his return to his starting point over the same path but in the reverse direction. Not surprisingly, the rhythm of the mirrored material displays carefully organized patterns of duration.[31]

Ives's most sophisticated event palindrome is the accompaniment to the song "Soliloquy." Example 4.14 gives the complete song. The text (by the composer) presents a dichotomy between simplicity and complexity: "Nature" is first seen as "a simple affair" (m. 1) and then as a force that "can't be so easily disposed of!" (mm. 8–10).[32] In the sketches, Ives also writes a second verse:

When a man is sitting
on a nice cushion, he says,
"All great things are simple."
But when he loses the cushion
and stands up and considers something,
he may think that
"Great things are not so simple!"[33]

The "cushion" is, of course, part of the easy chair in which the ears are tempted to recline, according to Ives's comments about beauty in music. (See Chapter One.) But the dichotomy in the second verse, which echoes Ives's familiar preference for progressive ideas over traditional ones, is stated broadly to apply to virtually anything. Ives thus draws an analogy between the hidden inner complexity of nature, as explained in verse 1, and the deeper sophistication of intellectual enlightenment extolled in verse 2. It is a notion that is central to his philosophies of art, and that we will return to later.

The text's dichotomies are clearly portrayed in the song's straightforward

Example 4.14. "Soliloquy." © 1933 Theodore Presser Co. Used by Permission.

binary structure: in the first measure, a chantlike recitation of the simple perspective, and then in the rest of the song a dissonant, active declaration of the complex perspective. And as the text reminds us of the hidden complexities of nature and society, so do various musical details represent a level of sophistication lying well below the musical surface. This is first apparent in the initial vocal phrase of this part, as we have already observed, with octave-displaced chromatic lines realizing an underlying wedge progression (see Ex. 4.7). But the more pervasive inner logic of the song is the entirely palindromic accompaniment starting in m. 2, in which pitches, rhythms, and articulations are mirrored exactly between mm. 2 and 11, 3 and 10, 4 and 9, 5 and 8, and 6 and 7. Similar to the center of the arch form in *Psalm 90,* the center of this event palindrome is a contracting-expanding wedge (mm. 6–7). But unlike the strictly regulated whole-step cluster wedge in *Psalm 90,* the outer-wedge voices are not inversions of each other, and the vertical intervals are organized into a pattern of gradual change starting with interval 10 (first chord of m. 6, last chord of m. 7) and moving inward through vertical stackings of intervals 7, 5, 4 alternating with 3, and 2, with a half-step cluster in the center.

In the measures leading up to the central wedges (and assuming the same observations apply in reverse on the other side of the center) the accompaniment consists of wide-jumps arpeggios of pitch intervals 11 and 13.[34] Ives refers to these, as well as to the octave displacements in the vocal line, in his subtitle for the song, "A Study in 7ths and Other Things." Four arpeggios occur before the central wedge: the first and third use interval 13 (mm. 2 and 4), and the second and fourth use interval 11 (mm. 3 and 5). Each arpeggio is one note longer than its predecessor—hence the meter changes in mm. 2–5—and spans ever greater amounts of pitch space. The arpeggio pattern discontinues just when there is no room left on the standard piano keyboard for a fifth one.[35] Their registral spans suggest pairings of the first with the second, and the third with the fourth; the first pair unfolds complementary chromatic segments <12345> in m. 2 and <ET9876> in m. 3. (The second pair completes the aggregate but necessarily contains pitch-class duplications.)

The vocal line in the second part also contains a hint of a symmetrical structure, as its last five pitch classes (<890ET>, mm. 9–10) are RT_3I of its first five (<54367>, mm. 2–3). This suggestion of retrograde-inversional symmetry, however, does not carry through to the rest of the vocal line, and instead the material after the first phrase offers hints of additional compound wedge structures. Example 4.15A shows phrase 2 and a partial wedge model. This phrase starts with a diverging wedge of upper-voice F–G♭ and lower voice F–E–E♭–D and concludes on B♭–A. This is similar to the model of phrase 1 shown in Example 4.7B, which begins with upper-voice F–F♯–G and lower-voice F–E–E♭, then

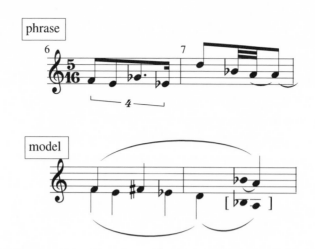

A. phrase 2 (mm. 6–7)

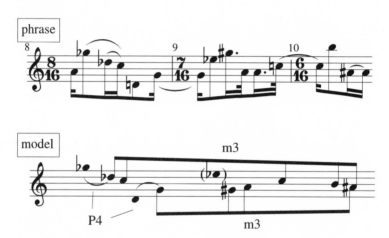

B. phrase 3 (mm. 8–10)

Example 4.15. "Soliloquy," structure of vocal line. © 1933 Theodore Presser Co. Used by Permission.

concludes, in the lower voice, on B♭ and A. Phrase 2 is a kind of capsule of phrase 1. The third phrase, shown and modeled in Example 4.15B, contains compound voices of half-step convergences moving by distances of minor thirds, with slight variations, and preceded by perfect-fourth leaps. This final converging wedge mirrors the diverging wedge at the beginning of phrase 1 to call attention to the retrograde-inversional relationship.

"Soliloquy" was composed around the same time as several other works we have been discussing, including *All the Way Around and Back, Hallowe'en,* the *Largo Risolutos,* and "Like a Sick Eagle." Kirkpatrick explains the flurry of progressive compositional activity during this time as a reaction to Ives's first years of courtship with his future wife.[36] Whatever the inspiration, it is obvious that this time period, when Ives was in his early thirties and just starting to gain a foothold in the insurance business, marked the development of a core of systematic procedures and compositional ideals that would stay with him throughout his mature work.

5 Transformational Techniques

With this chapter and the analysis in the next chapter we round out our discussion of basic tools and materials in Ives's systematic music. The techniques described thus far—contrapuntal devices and the structural models of wedge and palindrome—represent the most rudimentary aspects of his systematic catalogue. In Part Two, we will explore tools and procedures that are more complex and unique. First, though, as a transition to that later discussion, we examine principles common to a wide range of compositional procedures: techniques of musical transformation.

Canonical Transformations

To characterize the first category of transformation, we will adopt the notion of *canonical transformation*.[1] Most generally, a canonical transformation is one operation in a group of operations known as a canonical group.[2] Two pc sets are canonically equivalent if there is some operation in the group that will map one set onto the other.[3] Then, a given analytical or compositional application determines exactly which operations will constitute the canonical group for the purposes at hand. Some theorists have used only transpositional operations in their canonical groups.[4] The more standard group consists of transposition or of inversion followed by transposition.[5] Starr and Morris have defined a group of TTOs ("twelve-tone operators") that includes transposition, inversion followed by transposition, and the circle-of-fifths transform (M).[6]

In this study the canonical group consists either of transposition or of inversion followed by transposition; our canonical transformations are Tn and TnI. As Morris explains, Tn and TnI make up a strong and musically meaningful group because sets related under these transformations have equivalent interval-class content.[7]

A composer is first exposed to these canonical transformations in studies of counterpoint, when calculating pitch levels of voices in a canon or subject entries in a fugue. Chapter Two mentions transpositional relationships in canonic writing in the *Variations on "America"* interlude (see Ex. 2.1), the canon in C and E♭ (Ex. 2.2), *From the Steeples and the Mountains* (Ex. 2.5), *Central Park in the Dark* (Ex. 2.6), the *Largo Risolutos* (Ex. 2.7), and the Second String Quartet. It describes canonic voices related by inversion in the first *Harvest Home Chorale* (Ex. 2.3). The analysis of *Tone Roads No. 1* in Chapter Three highlights melodic transformations by Tn and TnI that evoke the procedures by which subject entries may be related in a fugue. As one component of the calculation process in contrapuntal writing, these operations contribute strongly to the systematic tools Ives is developing and help to solidify the linkage in his mind between contrapuntal devices and systematic composition.

In Ives's mature work the most intensive applications of our canonical transformations are those we will discuss in Part Two. In part to prepare for that discussion, we now mention a few applications of these operations that appear in other contexts. Ives often transforms large chunks of material with little or no variation. This is an economical approach to composition we have seen before—for instance, in the reuse of material in the second half of a palindromic form. Some of these transformations adapt a contrapuntal device, such as when three measures of the piano *Study No. 20* are repeated at T7 with the hands exchanging material, as in invertible counterpoint.[8] Otherwise, a transposition or inversion may simply generate a thematic variation. In another portion of this same study, a melody is repeated in the same voice at T4I, with slight changes in the rhythm of the melody, but with wholesale changes in the accompaniment.[9] Similarly, the *Three-Page Sonata* for piano (1905) begins with a long phrase that immediately recurs at T4 and then, after an interlude, at T4I.[10] Both the invertible counterpoint section of *Study No. 20* and this passage of the *Three-Page Sonata* invoke the B-A-C-H motive, calling our attention—as do portions of *Tone Roads No. 1* shown in Examples 3.6 and 3.7—to the presence of calculation and carefully worked-out compositional details.[11]

These canonical transformations are used extensively to generate the thematic structure of the *Robert Browning Overture* (1908–1912). In recalling his initial feelings about this orchestral work in *Memos*, Ives at first remembers thinking that it relied "perhaps too much . . . [on] the academic, classroom habits of inversion, augmentation, etc. etc., in the development of the first theme and related themes" and that it seemed "somewhat too carefully made, technically." But then he adds, "looking at it now, [al]most twenty years after, it seems natural and worth copying out" (*Memos*, 76). His comments surely refer to several passages in which a transposition of the main theme is paired with an inversional form. Three of these pairings are given in Example 5.1.[12]

Example 5.1A shows the theme as it first appears. Only the placement of pc 4 (m. 48:4) prevents the theme from presenting a complete series of fifths; such a series would be formed without disruption if the pc 4 were moved from its penultimate position to the fourth position in the sequence, just after the pc 9 in m. 46. Example 5.1B shows an inversional form of the theme in parallel fifths in the flute and oboe that is answered in canon two measures later by a transposition of the theme in the tuba. The particular operators seem carefully chosen, as both the upper inverted line and the transposed line begin with pc's [70] and have retrograde-equivalent segments in the center: <3816E4> in the upper inverted line (mm. 71:3 – 75:1) answered by <4E6183> in the transposed line (mm. 73:3 – 77:1). By contrast, the pairing shown in Example 5.1C, an inversion of the theme line in the tuba answered one measure later by a transposition in the clarinet, contains few such invariances. Finally, the pairing shown in Example 5.1D illustrates the rhythmic augmentation to which Ives apparently refers: an inverted line in the bassoon, trombone, and tuba is answered one measure later by a transposed line with longer rhythmic values in the horn and trombone. The lines have retrograde-equivalent opening hexachords (<705381> answered by <183507>).

Ives also writes inversionally equivalent lines that unfold not in canon but simultaneously. The principle is similar to that of a wedge, but without the intervallic repetition in the mirrored lines. One passage with this type of writing appears in the piano *Study No. 22* (?1909), where two mirrored lines are answered canonically by two other mirrored lines (mm. 3 – 5). Another instance is in *Varied Air and Variations* (?1923) for piano, which is a series of variations on the theme shown in Example 5.2A. The first variation (mm. 20–28) restates the theme in something close to its original form, but subsequent variations preserve only the theme's pitch-class ordering. Example 5.2B shows variation 2. Here the right hand restates the pitch classes of the theme in new rhythms, with a few lapses, while the left hand mirrors the right in identical rhythms.[13] The pitch-class sequence of the theme is completed on the second note of m. 39, and it occurs

A. original theme: bassoon, trombone, mm. 46:1–49:1

B. flute, oboe, tuba, mm. 70–77

C. clarinet, tuba, mm. 82–86

D. bassoon, low brass, mm. 96–101

Example 5.1. *Robert Browning Overture,* inversional thematic pairings

A. theme, mm. 6–14. © 1947, 1971 Merion Music, Inc. Used by Permission.

Example 5.2. Excerpts from *Varied Air and Variations*

again up through the E5 of m. 41, as the rhythmic values diminish. In the next variation the melody from the right hand of variation 2 is restated in the right hand, with no changes, while the left hand follows in canon at T5 two beats later.

All the principles we have looked at so far in this chapter have involved ordered transformations of a theme—one-to-one mappings between corresponding notes in a pc series and its transformation. But we should also take note of canonical transformations of pitch-class sets that are unordered. The relevance of pitch-class set analysis to the music of Ives is of course a large and complex issue, and we will not take the time here to explore all its aspects.[14] Instead, we will get a sampling of some pertinent materials and procedures by narrowing our focus to one specific procedure: the formation of aggregates by combining smaller unordered pc sets that are equivalent under one of the canonical transformations. We have already discussed some transformations of aggregate structures, as we will again later; now we focus not on transformation of the whole structure but on transformational relationships among subsets within it. Given Ives's abiding interest in pitch-class variety, this narrow orien-

* beginning of pc sequence

B. variation 2, mm. 34–41. © 1947, 1971 Merion Music, Inc. Used by Permission.

Example 5.2. (continued)

tation will nevertheless provide a useful perspective on some of his most favored structures and techniques.[15]

Ives is especially fond of whole-tone collections, and he frequently forms aggregates in which these collections supply the equivalent subsets. At the beginning of *Central Park in the Dark* and of the song "A Farewell to Land" (1909), he simply states a complete whole-tone collection vertically and then transposes it by an odd number of semitones to state its complement.[16] In both cases the individual chords subdivide into augmented triads, drawing parallels with a portion of the second movement of the Fourth Symphony (1909–1916) in which aggregates are formed from complementary augmented triads that are more texturally separated.[17] Ives also addresses the issue of augmented-triad complementation in his article on quarter-tone composition, speaking about music for two pianos tuned a quarter tone apart: "An interesting effect . . . may be obtained by striking a chord on both pianos, made of a series of whole-tone [augmented] triads on, say C C♯ D D♯, distributing them upward through three or four octaves. In this way all the twenty-four tones are caught, and in a chord not especially harsh."[18] Augmented triads combine in somewhat this manner in the first of his *Three Quarter-Tone Pieces* for two pianos (1923–1924), though no single verticality illustrates a chord of this exact description.

In the passages from the Second String Quartet shown in Example 5.3, whole-tone collections that are not triadically partitioned are combined to complete the aggregate. Example 5.3A, from the second movement, shows whole-tone complementation between two chords (circled) displaying a sudden moment of rhythmic unity amidst a passage in which the parts are generally rhythmically independent. The first verticality presents all the even pitch classes, the second all the odd. Example 5.3B, from the first movement of the quartet, illustrates a three-chord rising whole-step sequence in the viola and cello (circled) that is transposed by T_3 to generate, and complete the aggregate with, the three-chord rising whole-step sequence in the violins (circled). Again, the even pitch classes are answered by the odd.

In addition to triads of augmented quality, Ives also forms aggregates from triads of major and minor qualities, thus combining subsets that are inversionally equivalent. It is possible to build an aggregate from major and minor triads without any overlapping notes; in portions of the *Ode to Napoleon,* for example, Schoenberg partitions the aggregate into two major and two minor triads (in one instance, G–B–D, F–A–C, E♭–G♭–B♭, C♯–E–G♯).[19] Ives never forms an aggregate this way within a piece, although he does notate such an aggregate formation on a sketch page relating to the Third Violin Sonata and the *Universe Symphony,* combining A-major, B-minor, E♭-major, and F-minor triads.[20] But more typically he combines triads that share some notes, as in the final sonority from the piano piece *Rough and Ready* (1906–1907) shown in Example 5.4.[21] The bottom two triads, DM and D♭M, contain no overlappings, but the treble notes are variously distributed among E♭M, Cm, and Em triads.

A portion of the vocal line in the song "On the Antipodes" (1915–1923) forms an aggregate from four equivalent subsets that are not triadic. As shown in Example 5.5, the four trichords are members of set class 3–3 (014); the structure calls to mind Webern's use of this same trichord type in nonoverlapping subsegments in the row of his op. 24 Concerto.[22] As shown in the interval sequence notated below the pitch-class integers, Ives constructs the series to emphasize "thirds," or members of ic's 3 and 4, between adjacencies. Webern, by contrast, emphasizes ic's 1 and 4.

Finally, Example 5.6 shows a thematic aggregate from the *Three-Page Sonata* saturated, as is much of the work, with transformations of B-A-C-H. The theme begins with eleven different pitch classes in mm. 62:1–64:2; the arrival of the twelfth, pc 0 at m. 68:1, is delayed by the repetition of pc's 5 and E in

A. String Quartet No. 2, 2nd mvt., m. 84

B. String Quartet No. 2, 1st mvt., mm. 69–71

Example 5.3. Complementary whole-tone collections

Example 5.4. *Rough and Ready,* final sonority

Example 5.5. "On the Antipodes," vocal line (upper notes), mm. 28–34. © 1935 Merion Music, Inc. Used by Permission.

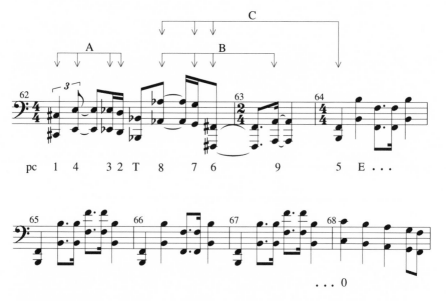

Example 5.6. *Three-Page Sonata*, mm. 62–68. © 1949, 1975 Mercury Music Corporation. Used by Permission.

mm. 64–67. The three tetrachords highlighted as A, B, and C in the example are transposed rotations of B-A-C-H.[23] Tetrachord A (pc <1432>) is T4 (B-A-C-H) = <2143> with the first pc rotated to the end; tetrachord B (pc <8769>) is T9(B-A-C-H) = <7698> with the last pc moved to the beginning; and tetrachord C (pc <8765>) is T8(B-A-C-H) = <6587>, with the adjacent dyads switching places. Thus Ives incorporates three of the four rotations of the motive, saving the normative B-A-C-H ordering for other places in the piece.[24]

Order Transformations

Order transformations can be either closely or distantly related to the canonical transformations. Those which are closely related are the two commonly linked with canonical transformations in much twelve-tone writing: retrograde and rotation. Those which are distantly related are less easily categorized and defined but are generally based on some contrived operation that produces a new ordering quite different from the result of any of the more familiar transformations. Both categorizations raise basic theoretical questions about the nature of these operations and their compositional utility. We will discuss them in turn.

The close association between canonical transformations and the standard order operations of retrograde and rotation is reflected in the interval content of the objects being transformed. To investigate this, we adapt Morris's INT function to list all the adjacent intervals in a pitch-class segment (which is ordered, by definition).[25] The INTs of segments transformed via Tn, TnI, or R are related as follows: segments related by Tn have identical INTs, segments related by TnI have inversionally equivalent INTs, segments related by R have INTs equivalent by retrograde inversion, and segments related by RI have INTs equivalent by retrograde.[26] These INT relationships help explain the musical sensibility of the four transformations in Schoenberg's twelve-tone method; as Morris points out, "it is the INT by which people (without absolute pitch) can compare" segments that are equivalent under the canonical transformations.[27] We can also include rotation as a close relative, since a rotation of a segment yields a rotated INT that preserves most of the original adjacent intervals.[28]

Most of Ives's applications of retrograde operations are in the second halves of event palindromes, such as the central wedge expansion and contraction in *Psalm 90* (Ex. 4.6) or the accompaniment of "Soliloquy" (Ex. 4.14). Our earlier analysis of *Tone Roads No. 1* showed one use of retrograde not in a palindromic context (Ex. 3.7). More common in Ives's work is a technique of dividing a

Example 5.7. *The Fourth of July, selected parts from m. 119*

larger segment into subsegments and applying retrograde or rotation or some combination thereof individually on the subsegments. Examples 5.7 and 5.8 illustrate this process in one measure from *The Fourth of July* (1911–1913).

This measure is part of a surge of dense contrapuntal activity depicting the explosions of fireworks. Ives says, "In the parts taking off explosions, I worked out combinations of tones and rhythms very carefully by kind of prescriptions,

			W		X			Y			Z		
A.	flute	= <	8	3	9	6	1	7	4	E	5	0	T	2 >
	$OM_A A$	= <	0	1	2	3	4	5	6	7	8	9	T	E >

W,X,Y : 3–5 (016)

Z : 3–6 (024)

			W			X			Y			Z		
	$OM_A B$	= <	2	1	0	5	4	3	8	7	6	E	T	9 >
B.	piccolo/trumpet	= <	9	3	8	7	1	6	5	E	4	2	T	0 >
	$OM_B B$	= <	0	1	2	3	4	5	6	7	8	9	T	E >

			W			X			Y			Z		
	$OM_A C$	= <	1	2	0	4	5	3	7	8	6	T	E	9 >
C.	oboe	= <	3	9	8	1	7	6	E	5	4	T	2	[0] >
	$OM_C C$	= <	0	1	2	3	4	5	6	7	8	9	T	E >

cf. segment C

			W			X			Y			Z		
	$OM_A D$	= <	0	2	1	3	5	4	7	8	6	T	E	9 >
D.	clarinet	= <	8	9	3	6	7	1	E	5	4	T	2	0 >
	$OM_D D$	= <	0	1	2	3	4	5	6	7	8	9	T	E >

			W	X	X	X	Z	Y	Y	Y	Z	Z	W	W	Y
E.	cornet	= <	8	1	7	6	2	5	4	T	0	9	3	E >
	$OM_E E$	= <	0	1	2	3	4	5	6	7	8	9	T	E >

Example 5.8. *The Fourth of July, segments in m. 119*

in the way a chemical compound which makes explosions would be made" (*Memos,* 104). The rhythmic elements of his compound, evident in Example 5.7, are various subdivisions of the measure, into sixteenth notes in the flute, fifteenth notes in the clarinet, fourteenth notes in the piccolo, twelfth notes in the cornet, eleventh notes in the oboe, and tenth notes in the trumpet. In *Memos* (p. 105) Ives points out that he used a similar rhythmic scheme in a sketch for an orchestral work named *The General Slocum* (1904) but that *The Fourth of July* "is much better musically, as each group has a phrase of musical sense."

Again he invokes his father's words of advice in reference to principles of systematic organization. The musical sense of the pitch element of his compound arises from order operations relating to the trichords circled and labeled W, X, Y, and Z in the trombone and violin parts of Example 5.7. The trichords define an ordering of the aggregate that is linearized (bottom to top in each trichord) in the flute, as shown in Example 5.8A. Trichords W, X, and Y are members of sc 3–5 (016), and Z is a whole-tone segment, a member of sc 3–6 (024). The analytic notations throughout Example 5.8 include Morris's "order mapping" symbols to compare the order of different segments.[29]

Segment A, the ordering of the aggregate in the flute—reflecting the trombone and first violin—can be seen as the progenitor for many of the other segment orderings in the measure. The ordering in the piccolo and trumpet, shown in Example 5.8B, is produced by retrograding each individual trichord in segment A: the first trichord is <839> in A, but <938> in B, the second trichord is <617> in A, <716> in B, and so on. More precisely, $OM_B B<012> = OM_A B$ $<210> = R(OM_A A<012>)$; $OM_B B<345> = OM_A B<543> = R(OM_A A<345>)$; etc. In segment C, the oboe line broken down in Example 5.8C, each trichord of A is rotated: <839> (in A) becomes <398> (in C), <617> becomes <176>, and so forth.[30] More precisely, $OM_C C<012> = OM_A C<120> = r_2(OM_A A$ $<012>)$, $OM_C C<345> = OM_A C<453> = r_2(OM_A A<345>)$, etc.[31] Segment D, the clarinet line analyzed in Example 5.8D, ends with two trichords rotated exactly like the corresponding trichords in segment C, but begins with trichords that are both retrograded and rotated: $OM_D D<012> = OM_A D<021> = r_1 R$ $(OM_A A<012>)$, and $OM_D D<345> = OM_A D<354> = r_1 R(OM_A A<345>)$. Finally, segment E, taken from the cornet part and shown in Example 5.8E, keeps trichord X intact but breaks up trichords W, Y, and Z.

We can see a more intensive application of the subsegmentation-permutation technique in one of Ives's most ambitious systematic pieces, the chamber work *Chromâtimelôdtune* (?1919). Ives sketched this piece out in its entirety but also left open certain performance-related aspects and made some ambiguous markings on the manuscript. This has permitted no fewer than three different versions of the work to be produced, performed, and recorded in recent years.[32] The title communicates the essence of Ives's conception: the chromatic scale, or the aggregate (the "chromatic collection") is the basis for melodies and tunes. In other words, *Chromâtimelôdtune* is a study in aggregate formation and transformation.

We will confine our attention just to one of the four surviving sketch pages, the one that Ives apparently composed first and that is of greatest relevance to the study of order transformation.[33] Example 5.9 is a transcription of that page, exactly replicating the composer's musical notations and visual layout.[34] Only the arabic numerals 1–29 within the staff have been added to the transcription; all other notations, including the uppercase letters above and below the staffs, are the composer's. The first three measures are an introduction mocking tonality. Then a melodic line, in the top stave of each system, presents a wide-jumps chromatic scale that ascends one octave (mm. A–I) and returns to its starting point (mm. I–Q). It is joined by a second wide-jumps line (top stave, stems down) in the second half, starting in m. I. Of greatest relevance for our purposes are the chords accompanying the melodic lines in the bottom two staves of each system. The chords are grouped into four-bar phrases, each of which has three measures of chords in half-notes followed by one measure of a chord in whole notes, excepting the first ending. The chords in mm. F and L are arpeggiated.

Ives's placement of the letters A and B below the chords points out pitch-class equivalences between all chords labeled with the same letter. Collections A and B alternate strictly throughout, so that all odd-numbered chords contain the pc's of the A collection and all even-numbered chords contain the pc's of the B collection. (There are occasional exceptions; for example, chord 11 needs a pc 0 to complete the A collection.) And the six pc's of A, [789012], plus the seven pc's of B, [TE03456], combine to complete the aggregate, with pc 0 shared. But while the content of the chords is fairly consistent, their presentations are not; no two appearances of the same collection distribute the pc's in the same way. Instead, Ives structures the chords to produce specific order relationships among various chords. In order to investigate these relationships we must first identify a reference ordering, or source ordering, to which all others may be compared.

Chord 27 offers a clue to a basic structure that Ives might have thought of as a source ordering. Its six notes, expressing collection A, are segmented into three perfect fifths: C#–G# on the bottom, C–G in the middle, and D–A on the top. Another statement of A, chord 21, exactly inverts chord 27 to present the same adjacent dyads as perfect fourths. Collection B could also be organized this way, but no B derivative states purely fifths or fourths, although chord 8 states both fifths and fourths (respelled): Eb–A# on the bottom, C–F in the middle, and Gb–B–E at the top. On the basis of this evidence, we might organize all the notes in A and B according to a regular relationship between the ic-5 dyads. Chord A may be arranged to unfold a series of fifths rising by half steps—C–G, C#–G#, D–A—and B picks up where A leaves off, with D#–A#, E–B, F–C, and F#. The note C occurs twice in the sequence, as the first and penultimate notes; this explains why it appears in both collections.

Let us use this sequence as the basis of source orderings. Example 5.10A subdivides the half-step-related fifths sequence into collections A and B and shows the order mappings for each collection separately. When we compare this source with the various orderings of the chords in the music, it seems reasonable to believe that Ives thought of the collections in this way. The intervallic pattern makes them easy to remember and to distribute in a chord during the process of

Example 5.9. *Chromâtimelôdtune,* first sketch page, transcription. CHROMÂTIMELÔDTUNE by Charles Ives (reconstructed & completed by Gunther Schuller). © 1963 (renewed 1991) by MJQ MUSIC, INC. All Rights Reserved. Used by Permission.

A. source   A $= < 0\ 7\ 1\ 8\ 2\ 9 >$ $B = < 3\ T\ 4\ E\ 5\ 0\ 6 >$

$OM_A A$ $= < 0\ 1\ 2\ 3\ 4\ 5 >$ $OM_B B = < 0\ 1\ 2\ 3\ 4\ 5\ 6 >$

B. chord 3 $= < 2\ \ \ 8\ \ \ 1\ \ \ 7\ \ \ 2\ \ \ 9\ \ \ 0 >$

$OM_A 3$ $= < 4\ \ \ 3\ \ \ 2\ \ \ 1\ \ \ 4\ \ \ 5\ \ \ 0 >$

                       ⌞_⌟   ⌞_⌟   ⌞_⌟   * 5-sums

                        *   *   *

C. chord 15 $= < 0\ \ \ 2\ \ \ 1\ \ \ 7\ \ \ 9\ \ \ 8 >$

$OM_A 15$ $= < 0\ \ \ 4\ \ \ 2\ \ \ 1\ \ \ 5\ \ \ 3 >$

                     ⌞___⌟   ⌞____⌟ $T1(X) = Y$

                       X   Y

D. chord 9 $= < 2\ \ \ 1\ \ \ 0\ \ \ 7\ \ \ 8\ \ \ 9 >$

$OM_A 9$ $= < 4\ \ \ 2\ \ \ 0\ \ \ 1\ \ \ 3\ \ \ 5 >$

                     ⌞___⌟   ⌞____⌟ $T5I(X) = Y$

                       X   Y

E. chord 25 $= < 7\ \ \ 9\ \ \ 1\ \ \ 8\ \ \ 0\ \ \ 2 >$

$OM_A 25$ $= < 1\ \ \ 5\ \ \ 2\ \ \ 3\ \ \ 0\ \ \ 4 >$

                     ⌞___⌟   ⌞____⌟ $R(T5I(X)) = Y$ [mod 6]

                       X   Y

F. chord 23 $= < 8\ \ \ 2\ \ \ 0\ \ \ 1\ \ \ 9\ \ \ 7 >$

$OM_A 23$ $= < 3\ \ \ 4\ \ \ 0\ \ \ 2\ \ \ 5\ \ \ 1 >$

                     ⌞___⌟   ⌞____⌟ $r_1 R(T5I(X)) = Y$ [mod 6]

                       X   Y

Example 5.10. *Chromâtimelôdtune,* structure of selected chords

composing. In addition, constant reference to the source helps to bring out structural similarities between different chords, as we have already seen with chords 27, 15, and 8. We might summarize the common origin of these three chords as a step-through of the source by two's, to preserve order positions *<01>*, *<23>*, and *<45>* as adjacencies (*<456>* as adjacencies in chord 8).

Another process of derivation exhibited by several chords preserves reciprocal pairs from the source as adjacencies: the first pc of the source is paired with the last, as are the next two inward and the two in the center (or, in the case of collection B, the two surrounding the center). In the A collection, the resulting order-position pairs will sum to 5: *<05>*, *<14>*, *<23>*. (In pc notation the pairs sum to 9.) These pairs are adjacent in chord 3, excluding the redundant pc 2 at the bottom: *<50>* on the top (pc *<90>*), *<14>* in the lower treble clef (pc *<72>*), and *<32>* in the upper notes of the bass clef (pc *<81>*). Example 5.10B summarizes this chord. Other chords with reciprocal pairs as adjacencies are numbers 13, 17, and 19, all derived from the A collection. In the B collection there is no 5-sum partner for order position (op) *6*, so this note (pc 6) often disrupts complete structural regularity. Chords 2 and 4, for example, can be partitioned into reciprocal pairs only if pc 6 is overlooked.

The most common method of chord formation in the piece is to subdivide the source into two groups of notes, placing one group in the treble and the other in the bass staff. If collection A is the source, both groups will usually be trichords; if B is the source, the partitioning will usually be four plus three. The trichordal groupings of chord 15, labeled X and Y below the order mappings in Example 5.10C, are derived by stepping through the source in strides of four, or a plus 4 (modulo [mod] 6) sequence of order positions: X = *0* (+4 mod 6 =), *4*, (+4 mod 6 =), *2*, and Y = *1* (+4 mod 6 =), *5*, (+4 mod 6 =), *3*. The op's of Y are T1 of those of X; the source is thus parsed into even and odd op's.

In chord 9 the two trichords arise from an enclosure process: OM_AA<*01*> in the center is surrounded by OM_AA<*23*>, which is in turn surrounded by OM_AA<*45*>, thus placing <*420*> in the bass staff and <*135*> in the treble—another parsing of the source into even and odd op's. As illustrated in Example 5.10D, members of reciprocal (5-sum) pairs occur in corresponding locations in each trichord, so that the order positions of the treble trichord (Y) are T5I of those of the bass trichord (X). (It is a T9I pc mapping.) Other enclosure processes are not so clean. Chord 1, for instance, has a duplication of pc 0 and a pc 4 borrowed from chord B. Nevertheless, the derivation of its top six notes shows an interesting twist on the scheme of chord 9. Instead of keeping the even op's on the bottom and the odd op's on the top, chord 1 takes the same enclosure pattern as chord 9 and alternates the registral dispositions: the first dyad (OM_AA<*01*>) is C above G, the second one (OM_AA<*23*>) is C♯ below G♯, and the third one (OM_AA<*45*>) is D above A. A similar "down-up" enclosure pattern is apparent in chord 18, expressing the B collection, if we ignore the pc 6.

What all the enclosure derivations have in common is that they distribute members of 5-sum pairs into different staffs. Chord 25, shown in Example 5.10E, demonstrates another way of doing this. Whereas chord 9, for example, places dyads that are adjacent in the source in symmetrical arrangements to effect the enclosure (<*01*> surrounded by <*23*> surrounded by <*45*>), chord 25 arranges 5-sum dyads symmetrically: <*23*> surrounded by <*50*> surrounded by <*14*>. In chord 25, Y is RT5I of X (mod 6). (As a pc mapping, RT9I.) And the 5-sum dyads in chord 23, analyzed in Example 5.10F, would also be symmetrically arranged but for a rotation. The symmetrical relationships could be restored by rotating X to read <*403*>. Some other chords (for example, chords 5 and 7) exhibit similar separations of members of 5-sum pairs and rotational equivalences.

In addition, a thorough examination of the chord sequence reveals that Ives is not only concerned with vertical structures when he derives the various arrangements of the A and B collections. His choices of top and bottom notes show that he is also unfolding significant melodic lines in the outer voices. The first six representations of collection A, for example, all have different top notes, so that the entirety of collection A is unfolded atop these chords. The highest notes are op *4* in chord 1, *0* in chord 3, *1* in chord 5, *3* in chord 7, *5* in chord 9, and *2* in chord 11. And these notes alternate with a similar unfolding of every note of collection B in chords 2, 4, 6, 8, 10, and 12, reserving the shared pc *0* for the top of chord 14. Thus the first twelve notes of the top voice (chords 1–12) unfold a complete, nonduplicative aggregate. Though such an unfolding does not occur in the lowest voice of these measures, both upper and lower voices execute unfoldings of this nature in the second half of the passage (mm. I–P).

Further, the order in which these outer-voice notes are presented draws connections with the chords themselves and the source. For example, the lower-voice unfolding of collection A in mm. I–N presents <*024531*>, an even-odd trichordal distribution recalling chord 15 (compare with Ex. 5.10C). This arrangement is based on a +2 mapping with the second trichord reversed: X = *0* (+2 mod 6 =), *2*, (+2 mod 6 =), *4*, and Y = R(*1* → *3* → *5*). Since chord 15 begins the passage where this unfolding starts—its lowest note is the first note of the lower voice in the second half—the outer voice "composes out" its initiating chord. Meanwhile, the lower-voice unfolding of collection B in these same measures (I–P) presents op *6* and then a similar odd-even arrangement, <*531240*>. This arrangement has closest ties to chord 28, the B-derivative at the end of the passage, which is <*04215636*>, if we can ignore the peripatetic op *6* and the two boxed notes in the score in m. P, which do not belong to their respective collections.

In the other pages of *Chromâtimelôdtune* Ives explores a number of melodic structures to accompany this chord sequence, apparently as replacements for the wide-jumps chromatic scale notated on the first page (Ex. 5.9). At one point, for example, he creates a separate melodic line by selecting notes from the chords, just as he did in the outer voices of the chords themselves.[35] All along, his compositional choices look back to the aggregate as the source collection, whether represented as a series of half steps, a sequence of half-step-related fifths, a combination of the two chords, or an outer-voice unfolding. Indeed, it is not just the aggregate but the chromatic scale that is the ultimate progenitor, the source ordering from which all other structures in the work may be systematically derived.[36] The title says it all.

We turn now to the second category of order transformation, the procedures that are more distantly related than are retrograde and rotation to the canonical transformations. The essence of these techniques is *scrambling*—nonsystematic reordering of selected pitch classes to highlight properties of a segment that might not emerge from other operations. The notion of scrambling covers a wide range of ordering changes, from the displacement of a single pitch class to rearrangements of isolated subsegments to more substantive redistributions. To examine these, we again turn to the INT: if the INT can illustrate close relations under retrograde or rotation, it can also reveal distant relations resulting from scramblings. For example, take the pc segment $Q = $ <T1430>. The INT(Q), <33E9>, emphasizes "thirds"—three of its four intervals are members of ic 3. And as we have already seen, any of the conventional transformations would yield an INT exhibiting similar characteristics: INT(Tn(Q)) = <33E9>, INT(TnI(Q)) = <9913>, INT(R(Q)) = <3199>, INT(RI(Q)) = <9E33>. Further, any rotation of one of these transformations would generate an INT containing three of these intervals plus the wraparound interval (10 or 2). But a scrambling of Q might bring out intervals that would never appear as adjacencies otherwise; the degree of difference would depend on the degree of scrambling. For example, a scrambled version could completely obscure "third" relations: if we scramble Q to produce $Q_1 = $ <10T43>, then the INT(Q_1) = <ET6E>. Another scrambling could saturate the INT with intervals 2 and 1: if $Q_2 = $ <T0134>, INT(Q_2) = <2121>. A minimal scrambling, resulting in no substantive change, could just reverse the last two pc's, yielding a complete saturation of thirds: if $Q_3 = $ <T1403>, INT(Q_3) = <3383>.

Thus scrambling opens up a host of new possibilities. Yet it also raises some critical issues about its nature and use, and about a composer's motivations for employing it. One concerns pitch-class content. Ives's scramblings are pitch-class oriented; they are intended to preserve the pitch-class content of a transformed object while varying its order. They are not, in other words, equivalent to composition with unordered pitch-class sets—a topic addressed earlier in this chapter—since that approach also involves canonical transformations. It is instructive to compare the three approaches to transformation we have been discussing in this chapter, using interval content as a barometer: unordered pc sets under canonical transformations preserve only the total (unordered) interval-class content (as do the others), pc segments under canonical transformations or retrograde or rotation preserve the INT or a close relative thereof, and Ives's scramblings preserve pitch classes while disrupting the INT.

A second issue concerns set sizes and set-class relations. It is easy to see how a scrambling, no matter how extensive, of a relatively small pc segment could establish close relations with any other permutation of that same segment. The result is a set-class relation of the strongest kind: not just equivalence, as with members of a Tn/I set class, but also pc identity. But with larger segments, the significance of equivalence or identity diminishes. It is usually less desirable to identify larger segments as members of the same set class, or as sets with equivalent large subsets, since their contents alone are not distinctive enough. Larger pitch-class groupings are distinguished by order, not content.[37] Thus a composer using scrambling techniques for large segments such as aggregate orderings—as we now expect to find in Ives—must take care to preserve at least some subsegmental orderings and other identifiable structural properties.

Finally, we should note a pertinent difference between the scrambling approach and the other techniques discussed in this chapter: a scrambling does not uphold all the principles of systematic composition. It can be motivated by a variety of unity-producing concerns, but usually not by an interest in self-generating patterns or structural models. Nevertheless, scrambling is an essential topic in the study of Ives's systematic language, first, because scramblings do often address the other systematic concerns—calculation, transformation, and pitch-class variety—and second, because they often interact with techniques that exemplify all the systematic criteria.

There are examples of scrambling throughout Ives's music. In *Psalm 25* (1898–1902), another progressive choral work from the immediate post-Yale years, he even draws our attention to the technique in a diagram inscribed in the margin of a sketch page:[38]

8	12	11	9	5	7	10	6	4	3	2	1
F♯	F	B	E♭	C	G	D	B♭	E	C♯	A	G♯
1	2	3	4	5	6	7	8	9	10	11	12

The aggregate ordering defined by the note names on the middle line, accompanied by order positions on the bottom line, actually appears in reverse (op's *12,11, . . . 2,1*) in the soprano part of mm. 17:1–20:1. This is labeled segment A in the score excerpted in Example 5.11. (The second note (F5) inexplicably deviates from the diagram.) The next segment of the soprano line (segment B, mm. 20:2 – 24:1), which includes "nonessential tones," circled in Example 5.11, presents the ordering prescribed in the top line of the diagram. The alto joins the soprano in unison, while the lower voices answer the upper in canon at a distance of one measure. This canonic arrangement continues throughout the excerpt.

The diagram suggests that segment B is derived from A, and yet there is only a tenuous musical connection, given the extent of scrambling. Both segments start with the same tetrachord, but B skips around, moving *5* and *8* far later than their original positions, and *10* far earlier. Of op's *5–12*, only *11* and *12* appear in direct numerical sequence. In other words, the diagram simply provides a listing of all the remaining pitch classes after the initial tetrachord, to facilitate com-

Example 5.11. *Psalm 25,* mm. 17:1–36:2. © 1979 Merion Music, Inc. Used by Permission.

Example 5.11. (*continued*)

pletion of the aggregate, rather than a musically meaningful transformational scheme. Indeed, if Ives had not left behind the diagram it would be difficult to justify making much of a connection between segments A and B; the diagram itself is the connection.

In subsequent segments of the melody, however, the scrambling technique creates much closer correspondences between consecutive segments. Though Ives gives no more diagrams, it is clearly his intent to create an extended melodic line in which successive segments are related via minor scramblings, with each new segment becoming more and more different from segments further back in the series. Thus the structure of the line slowly evolves from one state to another.[39] Example 5.12 organizes the Example 5.11 melodic line into segments in this chain of derivations.[40] Each segment is identified by an uppercase letter corresponding to the labels above the soprano in Example 5.11.

The order mappings in Example 5.12 show that not every note in a given segment reappears in the next one. For example, OM_BB *4* and *6* do not appear in segment C, although these pc's (0 and 7) do return in segment D. And there are some duplicated pc's, shown in parentheses. But these factors do not obscure the basic derivational chain, as revealed in the order mappings indicated directly above the segments. Each segment begins with a signal G♯ and with few

A (sopr. mm. 17:1–20:1)   = < 8 9 1 4 T 2 7 0 3 E 5 6 >
OM_AA   = < *0 1 2 3 4 5 6 7 8 9 T E* >

OM_AB   = < *0 1 2 3 7 4   6 E   8 5   9 T* >
B (sopr. mm. 20:2–24:1)   = < 8 9 1 4 0 T (9) 7 6 (7) 3 2 (0) E 5 >
OM_BB   = < *0 1 2 3 4 5   6 7   8 9   T E* >

OM_BC   = < *0 1 2 3 5 7 8 9 T E* >
C (sopr. mm. 24:1–26:2)   = < 8 9 1 4 T 6 3 2 E 5 >
OM_CC   = < *0 1 2 3 4 5 6 7 8 9* >

OM_CD   = < *0   1 2 3 5   4 6 8 7   9* >
D (sopr. mm. 26:2–30:2)   = < 8 0 9 1 4 6 7 T 3 E 2 (0) 5 >
OM_DD   = < *0 1 2 3 4 5 6 7 8 9 T   E* >

OM_DE   = < *0 1 5 4 2 3 7 6 8 9 T E* >
E (sopr. mm. 30:3–36:2)   = < 8 0 6 4 9 1 T 7 3 E 2 5 >
OM_EE   = < *0 1 2 3 4 5 6 7 8 9 T E* >

Example 5.12. *Psalm 25*, melodic structure of mm. 17:1–36:2

reorderings in the initial positions. In the remainder of each segment, order-position numbers close to each other in numerical sequence are usually bunched together, perhaps with slight ordering adjustments; dramatic shifts of the type seen in the diagram are rarely used after segment B.

The resulting subsegments shared between consecutive segments are often built around triads. In a way, the entire melodic line is a kind of evolving exploration of aggregates with triadic subsets, a topic explored earlier in this chapter. Segment A contains A major (OM_AA<*123*>) followed by an overlapping of G minor (OM_AA<*456*>) with C minor (OM_AA<*678*>). Segment B attempts to involve more pitch classes in triads: the shift of pc 2 from op *5* in A to op *9* in B forms a diminished triad at the end of B (OM_BB<*9TE*>), while the movement of pc 6 from the end of A to op *7* in B forms E♭ major/minor (OM_BB <*5678*>) to contrast with the preceding A major/minor tetrachord (OM_BB <*1234*>). Segment C discontinues major/minor formations by excluding pc 0 (isolating A major at OM_CC<*123*>), and by excluding pc 7 (isolating E♭ minor at OM_CC<*456*>). Thus the ten notes of segment C display nonintersecting major, minor, and diminished triads, plus the initial G♯. The excluded pitch classes return in segment D, again forming major/minor tetrachords (OM_DD<*1234*> and <*5678*>). Finally, segment E dissociates the minor thirds from the two tetrachords by moving them to the beginning (OM_EE<*12*>), thereby forming two major triads and a diminished triad after the first three notes: A major (OM_EE<*345*>), E♭ major (OM_EE<*678*>), and B diminished (OM_EE<*9TE*>).

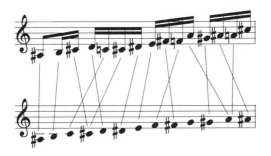

A. violin, m. 38

B. C trumpet, mm. 39–42

Example 5.13. *Robert Browning Overture,* derivations from chromatic scale

Segment E comes closest to a complete triadic partitioning; indeed, a structure of four nonintersecting triads could be achieved in E simply by exchanging the positions of pc's 6 and 5, to yield Fm–AM–E♭M–Bm.

Ives uses scrambling in his later work to make musical connections that are more substantive and inventive than those examined so far. He includes scrambled segments in a portion of the piano *Study No. 6* (1907–?1908) within a dialogue between fragments of a borrowed tune in one hand and angular lines of sixteenth-note quintuplets in the other.[41] And in the *Robert Browning Overture,* scramblings associate materials derived from the chromatic scale. In this respect the overture anticipates *Chromâtimelôdtune,* although it is otherwise more conventionally conceived. For long passages in the overture, chromatic wedges move by half-step transpositions, and many other structures in the piece also project half-step relations.[42] There are also melodic lines with substantial chromatic subsegments, often including wide jumps.[43] In this environment, a melodic line such as that shown in Example 5.13A comes across as a derivative of the chromatic scale. As demonstrated by the lines connecting the segment on the upper stave with notes of the chromatic scale on the lower stave, this wandering chromatic ascent includes several slight rearrangements and occasional repetitions, and concludes with three of the scale's pitch-class pairs in reversed positions.

Example 5.13B shows one of the main themes of the overture. This theme is based on the model of a full chromatic ascent and return, as shown on the lower stave, with only the circled notes not present in corresponding portions of the theme. The initial ascent reorders two individual subsegments, <78T> and <E012>. Thereafter, the seven pitch classes in the center are preserved in order, with one wide jump at the beginning of m. 41. The final descent includes more wide jumps and states the notes in order, skipping some.[44] As this theme assumes prominence in the piece, it relates strongly to the other important theme, the mild reordering of a complete cycle of fifths that we examined at the beginning of this chapter (Ex. 5.1). Ives exploits and highlights the similarities between the two sources—the ability of both to generate the aggregate by repeating the same interval. Ultimately, we might use multiplicative operations to show both the materials with chromatic features and the theme based on the cycle of fifths emanating from the same chromatic source.[45]

Ives's most extensive exploration of scrambling is in the piano *Study No. 5* (1907–?1908). In the next chapter we see how this work is held together through scrambling techniques working in collaboration with many of the other procedures we have been discussing.

6 Analysis II: *Study No. 5*

The piano pieces Ives calls studies are in some sense performance études in the tradition of Chopin or Liszt. But even more they are compositional études—studies in particular compositional techniques. And if a performance étude is often focused on the development of a single technical skill, Ives's compositional études often concentrate on the exploration of a specific systematic idea. They are studies "in" this idea, just as *Psalm 24* is a study in the wedge, *Tone Roads No. 1* is a study in the fugal model, and the *Three-Page Sonata* is a study in the B-A-C-H motive.

This emphasis on compositional over performance technique helps explain why *Study No. 5* is so user-unfriendly. It is composed more as an abstract combination of musical events than as a work for a particular instrument and consequently makes few concessions to pianistic exigencies. At times the score resembles not a piano piece but a short score for an ensemble of at least four instruments. At one point Ives writes a note that is to be sustained for more than nineteen beats.[1] One wonders about the legitimacy of an arrangement of the *Study* for separate instruments. Ives's only advice regarding the difficulties is to suggest that "a friend with 2 more hands may join in."[2]

The topic of study in *Study No. 5* is the aggregate transformed by scrambling. As in the passage from *Psalm 25* we examined in Chapter Five, different aggregate orderings grow directly out of structures that precede them and in turn serve as source orderings for aggregates that follow (see Exs. 5.11, 5.12). But *Study No. 5* elevates the technique to a higher level of sophistication. One purpose of this analysis is to explain the nature of this advancement and the manner in which Ives integrates the scrambling technique with other systematic procedures as he aspires toward ambitious compositional goals.

There are some textural changes and other possible formal demarcations in the *Study*, but for the most part the form of the piece is difficult to pin down because it so frequently thwarts conventional expectations—it contains no thematic returns and makes only rare distinctions between expositional, transitional, and developmental material. Its dense, complex texture is the product of a relentless spinning out of diverse polyphonic lines. The resulting effect calls to mind the persistence and rhythmic constancy of *Chromâtimelôdtune*, which reminds Kenneth Singleton of the "immediacy" and "constant drive" of a rock tune.[3] Ultimately, an analysis of the piece's form must depend as much on minute details as on larger gestures. We will therefore divide the work into large sections according to the most extreme changes in texture and material, and subdivide the large sections into subsections according to subtler differences in techniques and systematic patterns.

Example 6.1 charts the two levels of formal division that will provide a backdrop for this analysis.[4] Section I features chromatic lines, often stated in octaves in one hand and set against contrasting material in the other hand that recedes into the background. Then section II, the longest of the piece, presents dense contrapuntal activity in which single voices rarely assume prominence over others. The remaining three sections each begin with falling quarter-note triplets in the right hand. In section III the triplets are mirrored by rising triplets in the left hand, and together the hands present a rhythmic acceleration from beats 217 through 226. Section IV begins with triplets in the right hand only, accompanied by sustained tones in the inner voices. Sections III and IV both conclude with passages that recall the texture of section II (beats 229–244 in section III, 264–288 in IV). Finally, section V starts with the same kind of triplet mirroring as did section III and briefly suggests another rhythmic acceleration before concluding with a cadential flourish.

Segmental associations begin in the first few beats of the piece. Example 6.2A shows the first subsection, and Example 6.2B breaks down beats 1 through 7 into voices, numbered 1 through 4, and subsegments, labeled a through d. The four subsegments together complete the aggregate within each hand (in voice pairings 1–2, 3–4) in the first five beats. There is one inconsistency, however: pc 7 appears predictably in subsegment b in both hands but is then duplicated in

section:	I				II								III		IV		V
subsection:	a	b	c	d	a	b	c	d	e	f	g	h	a	b	a	b	
beat:	1	8	22	38	55	82	101	119	133	157	180	197	217	229	245	284	289

Example 6.1. *Study No. 5,* diagram of form

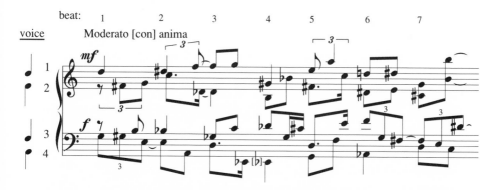

A. beats 1–7. © 1978, 1988 Merion Music, Inc. Used by Permission.

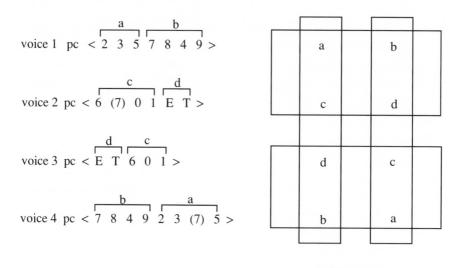

B. segmental relationships

Example 6.2. *Study No. 5,* subsection Ia

subsegment c in the right hand and in subsegment a in the left hand (these duplications appear in parentheses in Example 6.2B). Another difference between the hands is the order in which the subsegments are presented: voice 1 has a before b but voice 4 has b before a, and voice 2 has c before d but voice 3 has d before c. Thus in addition to the aggregates formed within the hands, aggregates are formed by the four subsegments in vertical alignment, as diagrammed in Example 6.2B. These first five beats, in this and other subsegmentations, will prove important as the structure of the piece becomes clear.

The next two subsections are dominated by wide-jumps chromatic ascents in octaves, first in the right hand (subsection Ib, beats 8–21) and then in the left (Ic, 23–38). Example 6.3A shows the score of subsection Ib, with the octave-displaced chromatic ascent starting on pc 11 at beat 8, digressing briefly in beats 17–18, and reaching octave completion at beat 20. Meanwhile, the accompanying material in both this subsection and the next begins to unfold derivational relationships that will bind the structure together. This first appears in the lower notes of the parallel fifths in voice 4 of subsection Ib; these notes are bracketed and labeled A in Example 6.3A, and listed as a pc segment in Example 6.3B. Segment A completes the aggregate without duplication. Although this segment essentially represents a new theme, it also forges the first link in a derivational chain by recalling the structure of the opening aggregate. Example 6.3C shows a subdivision of the right hand of beats 1–5 (see also Ex. 6.2) into subsets that reappear as adjacencies in segment A (see Ex. 6.3B). Subsets v and x are contiguous within a single voice, w is taken from a single voice but omits the pc 7 that is duplicated (pc 7 also appears in x), and y and z are notes taken from different voices that are close neighbors in the presentation. Only pc 4 is excluded. These subsets appear in the order z-x-w-y-v in segment A, as indicated in Example 6.3B.

When the left hand takes over the wide-jumps scale in subsection Ic, given here as Example 6.4, the right-hand accompanying material moves in parallel fourths. It is not, however, an inversion or some other close relation to the left hand of the previous subsection. Rather, some notes of the parallel fourths are unsystematically chosen to form members of ic 1—the piano-drum intervals— with the left hand's wide-jumps scale. These intervals can be located throughout Example 6.4: for instance, the first note of the wide-jumps scale, the left-hand F in beats 23–24, forms ic 1 with the upper F♯; the left-hand G at beat 25 does this as well; the left-hand A♯ in beats 28–29 forms ic 1 with the A♮ in voice 1; the left-hand D♯ in beats 33–34 forms ic 1 with the upper-voice E; and so on. Members of ic 1 are also often formed in other right-hand notes; for example, voice 2 has B♭–A at beat 24, D♭–C at 25 and 26, C–B at 27–28, and so forth. (And these notes will often form ic 1's with the fourths above or the scale tones below, or

A. beats 8–21. © 1978, 1988 Merion Music, Inc. Used by Permission.

$$A = < T\ 9\ E\ 7\ 5\ 4\ 0\ 6\ 8\ 1\ 2\ 3 >$$

z   x   w   y   v

B. segment A

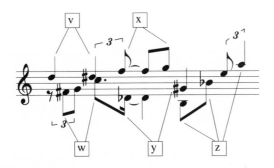

C. connection to subsection Ia

Example 6.3. *Study No. 5,* subsection Ib

Example 6.4. *Study No. 5,* subsection Ic. © 1978, 1988 Merion Music, Inc. Used by Permission.

both.) The writing brings to mind the road saturated with ic 1 in *Tone Roads No. 1* (see Ex. 3.9).

In the first three subsections, then, are both the tools and the materials that Ives has set out to study. The tools are the techniques of order transformation we examined in the previous chapter—either scrambling or more systematic means of revising order without changing content. The materials, which are typically constructed and associated through the use of transformational tools, immediately separate into two branches of structural evolution. The first branch associates the aggregate in the first five beats (Ex. 6.2) with the left-hand aggregate of subsection Ib (segment A, Ex. 6.3). This branch generally emphasizes conventionally dissonant melodic intervals but avoids any particular intervallic structure. The other branch consists of the chromatic lines first presented in wide jumps in the right hand of subsection Ib, subsequently echoed in the opposite register in subsection Ic, and additionally developed by specific intervallic combinations in the accompanying hand in Ic (Ex. 6.4). We will call the latter the chromatic branch, and the former the nonchromatic branch. As the work unfolds, most subsections will continue one of the branches by either manipulating chromatic lines or adding a link to the nonchromatic chain.

The streams and branchings of sections I and II are graphed in Example 6.5. The diagram includes the most important material in the derivational structure

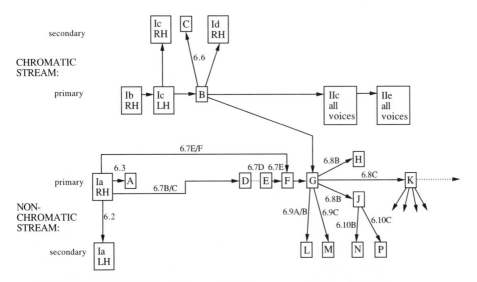

Example 6.5. *Study No. 5*, network of segmental derivations in sections I and II

but does not purport to account for all the musical ideas in a given section. Each important event is identified either by its location (for example, "IbRH [right hand]") or by a segment label (A–P). The arrows connecting the symbols illustrate structural connections, either segmental derivations, as is usually the case in the nonchromatic stream, or reflections of a common scalar source, as is usually the case in the chromatic stream. (Broken lines represent weak or obfuscated connections.) Further, each stream is itself subdivided into two parts: these are a primary branch, comprising the most important segments and the strongest derivations, and a secondary branch, consisting of less prominent ideas derived from some aspect of the primary branch. Connections in the primary branch unify the section on a deeper level, while more localized activity in the secondary branch binds together individual subsections. The chart shows the connections we have just observed as follows: in the chromatic stream, the primary branch in IbRH and IcLH begins with wide-jumps scales, which then branch off secondarily to the ic 1's in IcRH; and in the nonchromatic stream, IaRH is shown as the source both for segment A in the primary branch and for the rearrangement of subsegments in IaLH as a secondary branching. The graph will provide a useful overview as we work our way through the center of the *Study;* to facilitate orientation, arrows in the graph are cross-referenced to the example where the connection is illustrated.

The final subsection of section I (Id, beats 38–54) extends the chromatic stream. As shown in Example 6.6A, the left hand continues in octaves, first presenting a wide-jumps chromatic descent that begins and ends on G (beats 38–42), roughly recalling the wide-jumps chromatic ascent in octaves in the previous subsection. We will call this particular form of the chromatic scale segment B because of its subsequent connection to the ten-pc pattern bracketed and labeled C. Segment C begins on the pc 7 that completes segment B and subsequently presents chromatic subsegments as if rearranging the preceding scale. This is illustrated through order mappings in Example 6.6B: first segment C states the initial pc 7, then pc <3120>, which is OM_BC<4657>, then pc <456>, which is OM_BC<321>, and finally pc <98>, the same dyad with which B concludes. Segment C occurs three times in subsection Id, meanwhile presenting a rhythmic pattern in which successive beats are subdivided into three, four, five, three, and two parts. This pattern, which is a different length than the pc segment and thus is not coordinated with it, appears three times: beats 40–44, 45–49, and 50–54.

Meanwhile, the right hand contributes to the chromatic stream by forming more piano-drum intervals. Unlike in the treatment of these intervals in the right hand of subsection Ic, however, the sonorities here are organized into a four-chord pattern. Each repetition of the pattern begins with an accented chord and is marked with a bracket above the score in Example 6.6A. The chords in the pattern are trichords that are consistently constructed of intervals (bottom to top) <E3>, <85>, <85>, <85>. Only the intervallic structures are consistent—the transpositional relationships between the chords themselves vary from one occurrence to the next.

Beat 55 marks a substantial change in the *Study*. As is apparent in the score shown in Example 6.7A, the new section begins with a texture that is no longer dominated by one hand moving chromatically in octaves, but instead is characterized by four seemingly independent contrapuntal voices interacting in vigorous and often directionless rhythmic motion. (The lowest voice is at first presented in parallel fourths, giving the appearance of two separate voices for a total of five.) But there are many systematic plans within the chaotic texture. In subsection IIa, the plan encompasses aggregate completion and a continuation of the nonchromatic derivational stream. This occurs in the lowest voice, in the upper notes of the parallel fourths, as circled in segments labeled D, E, and F in Example 6.7A.[5] Ives roughly separates the segments with a rare use of barlines.[6] The remainder of Example 6.7 shows derivational relationships among these segments.

To find the source for segment D we again look to the first five beats of the *Study*. This time the linking subsets are those shown in Example 6.7B: s, t, and u are dyads sounding between the voices, and v is the last dyad of the upper

A. beats 38–54. © 1978, 1988 Merion Music, Inc. Used by Permission.

$$B = < 7\ 6\ 5\ 4\ 3\ 2\ 1\ 0\ E\ T\ 9\ 8 >$$
$$OM_BB = < 0\ 1\ 2\ 3\ 4\ 5\ 6\ 7\ 8\ 9\ T\ E >$$

$$OM_BC = < 0\ 4\ 6\ 5\ 7\ 3\ 2\ 1\ T\ E >$$
$$C = < 7\ 3\ 1\ 2\ 0\ 4\ 5\ 6\ 9\ 8 >$$

B. segmental relationships

Example 6.6. *Study No. 5,* end of subsection Id

[poco marcato in bass, through 81]

A. beats 55–80. © 1978, 1988 Merion Music, Inc. Used by Permission.

Example 6.7. *Study No. 5,* nonchromatic branch in subsection IIa

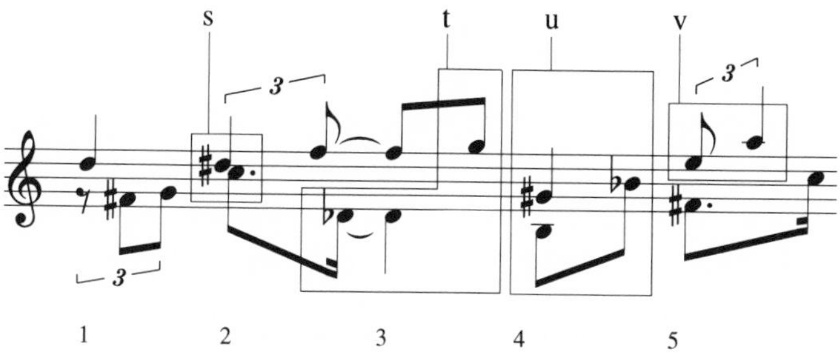

B. comparison with subsection Ia

C.

u t v s rep.

D = < 2 T 5 8 E 7 1 4 9 0 3 6 T 7 8 >

$OM_D D$ = < *0 1 2 3 4 5 6 7 8 9 T E* >

triad qualities: M d d d M d m m

D.

ic: 3 2 4 6 1

$OM_D E$ = < *2 0 7 4 6 8 E 9 3 5 T 1* >

E = < 5 2 4 E 1 9 6 0 8 7 3 T >

$OM_E E$ = < *0 1 2 3 4 5 6 7 8 9 T E* >

E.

$OM_E F$ = < *3 2 0 4 5 6 7 9 8 E T 1* >

F = < E 4 5 1 9 6 0 7 8 T 3 2 >

q p r o

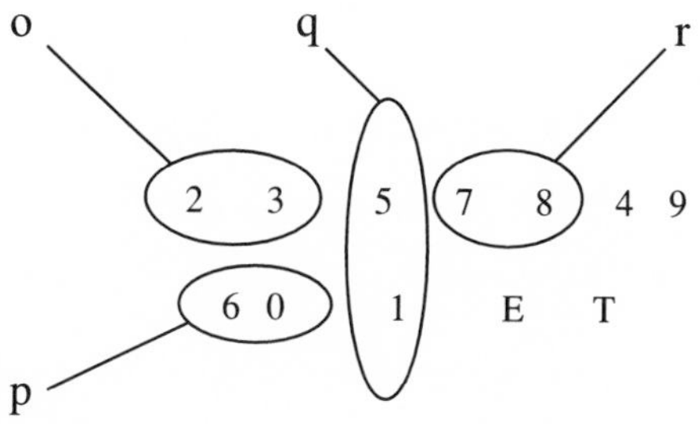

F. comparison with subsection Ia

Example 6.7. (*continued*)

voice. Example 6.7C illustrates how segment D is formed from these dyads: the first dyad of the source, s = <03>, appears as $OM_DD<9T>$, the second, t = <17>, is reversed as $OM_DD<56>$, the third, u = <E8>, is reversed as $OM_DD<34>$, and the last, v = <49>, is $OM_DD<78>$. In contrast to the linear emphasis on ic's 1 and 2 within the voices of the source, these dyads are ic's 3, 6, 3, and 5, respectively. The brackets and quality labels below segment D in Example 6.7C show that every note in this aggregate is part of at least one triad formed by adjacent notes.

The next aggregate of the subsection, segment E, both establishes and obscures a connection with segment D. The connection is established by the derivational pattern illustrated in Example 6.7D. As bracketed, many op's that are separated by one op in D appear as adjacencies in E, specifically $OM_DE<20>$, <46>, <68>, <E9>, and <35>. But this really discourages making a strong connection between the two, because the resulting structures are so different—triads are as conspicuously absent from segment E as they are prominent in D. The dyads introduce a great deal of intervallic variety in segment E: $OM_DE<20>$ is ic 3, <46> is ic 2, <68> is ic 4, <E9> is ic 6, and <35> is ic 1.

Then the last aggregate of the subsection, segment F, continues the primary branch of the nonchromatic stream by making a strong connection with segment E. As shown in Example 6.7E, only op 1 of segment E is shifted to a substantially different location in F, and many of the op's remain as they were in E or are moved only slightly (for example, $OM_EF<4567>$, <98>, <ET>). This structure also allows us to draw yet one more connection with the original source for the nonchromatic stream, as shown in Example 6.7F, by retaining as adjacencies the dyads labeled o, p, q, and r.

Activity in the nonchromatic stream predominates in section II, just as connections within the chromatic stream permeate section I. To complete our discussion of section II we will look first at the primary branch of the nonchromatic stream, then at the secondary subsections that branch out from it, and finally at the continuation of the chromatic stream. All the derivations we are observing are illustrated in Example 6.5.

Example 6.8 compiles segments from different subsections that are part of the primary nonchromatic branch: voice 4 at the beginning of subsection IIb (segment G, Ex. 6.8A), voices 1 and 4 at the beginning of subsection IId (segments H and J, Ex. 6.8B), and voice 4 at the beginning of subsection IIf (segment K, Ex. 6.8C). The first segment, segment G, serves as a kind of pivotal event for this section and for the piece, as it grows out of earlier segments and generates new ones. But before examining these relationships, we should note that segment G is also closely linked to the chromatic branch. It is actually a fairly simple reordering of segment B, the chromatic descent starting on pc 7 that influenced material in subsection Id (cf. Ex. 6.6). Segment G starts with pc <67>, reordering the first dyad of B, then states <45>, reordering the second dyad (the whole first tetrachord is T4I(BACH)), then <132>, scrambling the next three scale tones, and so on. But at the same time, the connections from segment G back to F from the end of the preceding section (Ex. 6.7E) are equally significant. The <67> dyad at the beginning of G presents pc's that are nonadjacent in the middle of F, but next G has <451>, which are the second, third, and fourth notes of F, and <32>, the last two notes of F. Segment G also has <T8> near the end, a reversal of F's penultimate dyad.

Thus segment G is an important hinge that momentarily associates both derivational streams while advancing the nonchromatic stream. In the subsections that follow, G becomes a direct or indirect source for all the material in section B's nonchromatic stream. The remainder of Example 6.8 illustrates the use of segment G to generate material for both subsections IId (Ex. 6.8B) and IIf (Ex. 6.8C). Segment H, the upper voice at the beginning of subsection IId, preserves several subsegments of segment G: it begins with pc <45> (OM$_G$H<*23*>), has pc <T98> (OM$_G$H<*9ET*>) in the center, and pc <67> (OM$_G$H<*01*>) just after this. Segment J, the lowest voice at the beginning of this subsection, also has pc <T98>, but near the beginning, and pc <67>, but at the end, and additionally scrambles OM$_G$G<*45678*> in the center (pc <*230E1*> = OM$_G$J<*65874*>). Thus the upper and lower voices at the beginning of subsection IId (H and J, respectively) relate almost as complements: the subsegments extracted from G and placed in the middle of H appear at the beginning and end of J, while many of H's outer notes appear in J's center. Later, segment K in subsection IIf (Ex. 6.8C) adds another link to the chain by again recalling segment G: the second and third notes of segment K are pc <98>, which is OM$_G$K<*ET*>; the last three notes are pc <0ET>, which is OM$_G$K<*879*>; and the hexachord in the center is a scrambling of G's first hexachord (pc <*615734*> = OM$_G$K<*043152*>).

Having taken an overview of this primary branch, let us now look at some of the secondary branches in these same subsections. As we can see in Example 6.8A, the important G segment in subsection IIb is answered canonically in varied inversion two beats later in the top voice. Example 6.9A gives the INT(G) for comparison with the canonic answer, segment L, in Example 6.9B. The comparison shows that L is an inversion of G except for the circled intervals. The first noninverted interval may have been necessitated by range considerations, and the two noninversions at the end reflect changes required, as a consequence of the earlier change, to complete the aggregate. Another secondary branch in subsection IIb is the segment in voice 3 of beats 82–89 (again, see Ex. 6.8A). Example 6.9C labels this segment M and compares it with G. As the

$$G = < 6\ 7\ 4\ 5\ 1\ 3\ 2\ E\ 0\ T\ 8\ 9 >$$
$$OM_G G = < 0\ 1\ 2\ 3\ 4\ 5\ 6\ 7\ 8\ 9\ T\ E >$$

A. subsection IIb, beats 82–89. © 1978, 1988 Merion Music, Inc. Used by Permission.

$$OM_G H = < 2\ 3\ 5\ 7\ 9\ E\ T\ 0\ 1\ 6\ 4\ 7 >$$
$$H = < 4\ 5\ 3\ E\ T\ 9\ 8\ 6\ 7\ 2\ 1\ E >$$

$$OM_G J = < 3\ 9\ E\ T\ 2\ 6\ 5\ 8\ 7\ 4\ 0\ 1 >$$
$$J = < 5\ T\ 9\ 8\ 4\ 2\ 3\ 0\ E\ 1\ 6\ 7 >$$

B. subsection IId, beats 119–132. © 1978, 1988 Merion Music, Inc. Used by Permission.

Example 6.8. *Study No. 5,* section II, primary nonchromatic branch

$$OM_GK = < 6\ E\ T\ 0\ 4\ 3\ 1\ 5\ 2\ 8\ 7\ 9\ >$$
$$K = < 2\ 9\ 8\ 6\ 1\ 5\ 7\ 3\ 4\ 0\ E\ T\ >$$

C. subsection IIf, beats 156–179. © 1978, 1988 Merion Music, Inc. Used by Permission.

Example 6.8. (*continued*)

OM_GM indicates, M is a kind of scrambled retrograde of G, starting with $OM_GM<ET098>$ before stating three notes from the beginning of G (OM_GM $<431>$) and concluding with three notes from the middle of G ($OM_GM<657>$). It is a structure with eleven different pc's (pc 8 repeated) that concatenates three $3-2$ (013) trichords and a $3-3$ (014).

The remainder of subsection IIb continues to uphold the initial aggregates as sources for reorderings and derivations. Because these relationships do not pro-

$$\text{INT(G)} = <\ 1\ 9\ ①\ 8\ 2\ E\ 9\ 1\ T\ Ⓣ\ ①\ >$$

A.

$$L = <\ 9\ 8\ E\ 0\ 4\ 2\ 3\ 6\ 5\ 7\ T\ 1\ >$$
$$\text{INT(L)} = <\ E\ 3\ ①\ 4\ T\ 1\ 3\ E\ 2\ ③③\ >$$

B. voice 1, beats 84–89

$$\text{OM}_G M = <\ E\ T\ 0\ 9\ 8\ 4\ 3\ 1\ T\ 6\ 5\ 7\ >$$
$$M = <\ 9\ 8\ 6\ T\ 0\ 1\ 5\ 7\ 8\ 2\ 3\ E\ >$$

$$\quad\quad\quad\; \underbrace{}_{3\text{-}2}\ \ \underbrace{}_{3\text{-}2}\ \ \underbrace{}_{3\text{-}2}\ \ \underbrace{}_{3\text{-}3}$$

C. voice 3, beats 82–89

Example 6.9. *Study No. 5,* relationships in subsection IIb

mote any new insights into the piece or into Ives's methods, it will not be necessary to investigate them in detail. We might simply observe that Ives uses a
particular pc dyad, {89}, to signal segment beginnings. We have already seen this
in segments L and M; other instances include subsequent reorderings of this
material in voice 1 at beats 90 and 94–95, as well as voice 3 at beat 90 and voice
4 at the beginning of the next subsection (beat 101).

The secondary branches of subsection IId explore retrograde transformations, following up on the earlier hints of this operation in subsection IIb (segment M, Ex. 6.9C). As is apparent in Example 6.8B, the retrogradings occur in
the inner voices and use segment J as a source, while the outer voices exchange
material—segment H shifts to voice 4 and segment J shifts to voice 1 in beats
126–131. Example 6.10A renotates segment J (see Ex. 6.8B) and uses its order
mappings as a basis for understanding the inner voices: Example 6.10B is segment N, taken from voice 2 (beats 126–131), and Example 6.10C is segment P,
taken from voice 3 (beats 126–132). The order mappings $\text{OM}_J N$ and $\text{OM}_J P$
show both inner voices winding their way imprecisely through segment J in
reverse, much as other segments in the piece skip around within but generally
step through the chromatic scale (segment G, Ex. 6.8A) or other segments (see,
for example, the derivation of segment F from segment E in Ex. 6.7E).

In subsection IIf, the final secondary branching from section II's chromatic
stream applies more of the same procedures, as we can see by returning to
Example 6.8C. Segment K in voice 4 is at first answered canonically at T7 one
beat later in voice 1 (beats 157–163); at beat 169 this material shifts to the inner
voices, where it is presented in the same kind of varied retrograde we just saw in

$$J = <\ 5\ T\ 9\ 8\ 4\ 2\ 3\ 0\ E\ 1\ 6\ 7\ >$$
$$OM_J\ J = <\ 0\ 1\ 2\ 3\ 4\ 5\ 6\ 7\ 8\ 9\ T\ E\ >$$

A. voice 4, beats 119–125

$$OM_J\ N = <\ T\ E\ 9\ 8\ 7\ 6\ 4\ 5\ 2\ E\ 0\ 1\ 3\ 0\ >$$
$$N = <\ 6\ 7\ 1\ E\ 0\ 3\ 4\ 2\ 9\ 7\ 5\ T\ 8\ 5\ >$$

B. voice 2, beats 126–131

$$OM_J\ P = <\ E\ T\ 7\ 8\ 9\ 5\ 6\ 4\ 1\ 9\ 3\ 0\ >$$
$$P = <\ 7\ 6\ 0\ E\ 1\ 2\ 3\ 4\ T\ 1\ 8\ 5\ >$$

C. voice 3, beats 126–132

Example 6.10. *Study No. 5*, relationships in subsection IId

subsection IId (voice 2, beats 168–173, is a varied retrograde of voice 4, beats 156–162; voice 3, beats 170–174, is a varied retrograde of voice 1, beats 157–160). What is new about this subsection is the slower rhythmic values that begin in the inner voices and complementarily shift to the outer voices as the outer-voice material moves inward. Voices 2 and 3 begin, at beat 157, with perfect-fifth leaps that are precisely mirrored between the voices, up until beat 166, where voice 3 states A3–E3 instead of B3–E3; the change ensures completion of the aggregate. When this material shifts to the outer voices in beats 168–179, both lines are transposed at T7.

The final two subsections of section II also continue the nonchromatic branch without presenting any substantially new materials or techniques. Subsection IIg (beats 180–196) actually overlaps three beats with IIf, using the final pitch classes of the earlier segments as the beginnings of segments that are paired with their exact retrogrades in voices 1 and 4 and in voices 2 and 3 in beats 177–186. Then the entire complex (all voices) is restated at T4 with minimal rhythmic variation in beats 190–196. Finally, the material in subsection IIh (beats 197–216) recalls some aspects of the nonchromatic branch but generally draws more indirect derivational connections.

In our tour of section II we have skipped only subsections IIc and IIe, the only portions of this section that lie outside the nonchromatic stream. And although it is true that subsections IIc and IIe advance the chromatic stream, we should also note that the material in either branch can bear a superficial resemblance to the other during this part of the piece. We first saw this in the primary segment at the beginning of subsection IIb (segment G, Ex. 6.8A), which is both a direct derivative of the preceding segment and a close relative of a chromatic scale. Also, though we did not pause to point them all out, other portions

Study No. 5   117

of the nonchromatic stream likewise inch close to the chromatic one. What distinguishes subsections IIc and IIe as sole purveyors of the chromatic branch is that first, they do not exhibit the other branch's self-contained aggregate orderings and their canonical or order transformations, and second, the structures they do display are more directly and obviously affiliated with chromatic segments and subsegments than with the orderings in the other subsections.

One portion of subsection IIc will illustrate the nature of the distinction. Example 6.11 shows six beats from IIc that associate chromatic sets in a manner typical of the writing in this subsection. The boxed groupings highlight chromatic clusters formed by notes in several proximate voices. Again displaying the piano-drum-chord approach, Ives is interested in maximizing dissonance and avoiding intimations of tonal structures. The clusters are all trichords (3–1 (012)), except for one tetrachord (4–1 (0123)) in beat 111; when this technique is used elsewhere in the subsection and in the piece, the sizes of the clusters are more varied. (For example, subsection IId, in the nonchromatic branch, similarly associates chromatic clusters more varied in size.) In addition, in this particular case the clusters are organized to unfold contiguous subsegments of a descending chromatic scale, as shown through brackets and connections below the score. The scale thus serves as a source ordering that controls the content and presentation of the chromatic materials.

Thus we come to the end of our discussion of section II and to the dramatic textural change that marks the beginning of section III at beat 217, shown in Example 6.12. Because of the contrasts between sections III, IV, and V and sections I and II, as well as between the final three sections themselves, these concluding passages have the effect of three final divergent bursts of musical energy bringing the *Study* to a close. Accordingly, the beginning of section III marks the end of the chromatic and nonchromatic branching we have been following up to now. When section III begins, there is little doubt that something new is happening: the hands are suddenly rhythmically similar, if not identical; they cooperate to present a rhythmic acceleration of quarter-note triplets (beats 217–218), eighth notes (219–221), quintuplets (222–223), eighth-note triplets (224), and sixteenth notes (225–226); and this rhythmic pattern is coordinated with a wedging pitch pattern transposed up by whole steps, a pitch distance rarely emphasized heretofore, from beats 217–221 to 222–224 to 225–226. The second and third chords in this repeated pattern complete the aggregate from a complementation of sc 6–31 (013589) (for example, in beats 217–218, the second chord of the quarter-note triplet is, bottom to top, <6T4192> and the third is <7E4805>).

Subsequently, the contrast at the beginning of section IV (beat 245 and following) is provided by a sudden textural thinning. While the outer voices begin

Example 6.11. *Study No. 5,* beats 110–115 (excerpt from section IIc). © 1978, 1988 Merion Music, Inc. Used by Permission.

Example 6.12. *Study No. 5,* beginning of section III (beats 217–226). © 1978, 1988 Merion Music, Inc. Used by Permission.

in contrary motion—the top voice in quarter-note triplets—to draw a parallel with the beginning of section III, the inner voices offer only sustained tones, with voice 3 sustaining for eight beats and voice 4, impractically, for almost twenty. But what this section also accomplishes is a recollection, a sort of last gasp, of the transformational procedures *Study No. 5* has set out to explore. Example 6.13 separates the voices in the first part of the section to illustrate this last network of order associations.

The bracketed subdivision of the voices in Example 6.13 into segments Q through Y represents the most logical structural segmentation of the voices, based on segmental relations and pitch-class variety, often aggregate formation, within and among voices. In Example 6.14 each segment from Example 6.13 is notated with pc integers and order mappings. Similarities in ordering among successive and simultaneous segments create a latticework of connections between and among the voices, just as the earlier segmental relationships created derivational streams running from subsection to subsection. The first segment in voice 1, labeled segment Q, becomes the progenitor for the network. First, Q is the basis for the next segment, segment R, in voice 1: as shown in the order mappings in Example 6.14A, R retains as adjacencies $OM_QQ<23>$ and $<9T>$ and scrambles $OM_QQ<45678>$ in the middle (pc $<45E80>$ = $OM_QR<58746>$). Segment R becomes the basis for the subsequent one, labeled S; the order mappings accompanying segment S in Example 6.14B show it to be only a slight variation on the ordering of R.

Segments T, U, V, and W of voice 4 relate both to voice 1 and to each other. First, segment T presents ten pitch classes, combining with the two sustained tones in voices 2 and 3 (pc's 7 and 9) to complete the aggregate. Structurally, T is most closely affiliated with Q, the segment with which it is paired on either side of the sustained notes. As the order mappings in Example 6.14C demonstrate, pitch classes $<840>$ are moved from the center of Q to the beginning of T ($OM_QT<546>$), pc's $<31>$ are moved from the beginning of Q to the end of T ($OM_QT<01>$), and pc's $<E52T>$ from near the end of Q reappear in the second half of T ($OM_QT<7798>$). Then the second segment of voice 4 (U) anticipates the structure of the second segment of voice 1 (R), as illustrated in Example 6.14D. U begins with pc $<694>$, which is $OM_RU<103>$, and then presents a hexachord from the center of R (pc $<2108E5>$) in reverse ($OM_RU<987654>$). But in the next two segments of voice 4, the affiliation with voice 1 stops, and the derivations take place horizontally within the same voice, echoing what happens in voice 1. Example 6.14E shows that the next segment in voice 4 (V) connects with the previous segment in the same voice (U) by retaining the same opening trichord (pc $<649>$ = $OM_UV<021>$) and the same last note (pc 7) but scrambling the notes in between (pc $<50218E>$ = $OM_UV<853467>$).

Example 6.13. *Study No. 5,* section IV, beats 245–268. © 1978, 1988 Merion Music, Inc. Used by Permission.

A.	Q	=	< 3 1 6 7 8 4 0 E 5 2 T 9 >
	$OM_Q Q$	=	< *0 1 2 3 4 5 6 7 8 9 T E* >
	$OM_Q R$	=	< *E 2 3 5 8 7 4 6 1 9 T 0* >
	R	=	< 9 6 7 4 5 E 8 0 1 2 T 3 >
	$OM_R R$	=	< *0 1 2 3 4 5 6 7 8 9 T E* >
B.	$OM_R S$	=	< *0 2 3 1 4 5 7 6 5 8 T 0 E* >
	S	=	< 9 7 4 6 5 E 0 8 E 1 T 9 3 >
C.	$OM_Q T$	=	< *5 4 6 T 7 9 2 8 0 1* >
	T	=	< 4 8 0 T E 2 6 5 3 1 >
	$OM_T T$	=	< *0 1 2 3 4 5 6 7 8 9* >
D.	$OM_R U$	=	< *1 0 3 9 8 7 6 5 4 2* >
	U	=	< 6 9 4 2 1 0 8 E 5 7 >
	$OM_U U$	=	< *0 1 2 3 4 5 6 7 8 9* >
E.	$OM_U V$	=	< *0 2 1 8 5 3 4 6 7 9* >
	V	=	< 6 4 9 5 0 2 1 8 E 7 >
	$OM_V V$	=	< *0 1 2 3 4 5 6 7 8 9* >
F.	$OM_V W$	=	< *5 0 1 3 5 4* >
	W	=	< 2 3 6 4 5 2 0 >
G.	$OM_R X$	=	< *0 1 E 9 T 3 2 6 5* >
	X	=	< 9 6 3 2 T 4 7 8 E >
	$OM_X X$	=	< *0 1 2 3 4 5 6 7 8* >
H.	$OM_X Y$	=	< *0 1 5 4 7 3 2 6 8 1* >
	Y	=	< 9 6 4 T 8 2 3 7 E 6 5 1 0 >

Example 6.14. Segments from Example 6.13

And the final, brief segment in voice 4 of this excerpt (W) connects with its predecessor, segment V, by stating $OM_V W$<*01354*>, as illustrated in Example 6.14F.

Voice 3 also develops structural relationships within itself and with other voices. Its first segment (X), starting with the sustained note, is derived from segment R, which is sounding concurrently in voice 1. The order mappings in Example 6.14G illustrate X beginning with the same dyad as R (pc <96>), stating the last trichord of R (pc <32T> = $OM_R X$<*E9T*>), and finishing with dyads <47> and <8E> from the center of R ($OM_R X$<*32*> and <*65*>, respectively). Segment X then becomes the source for the next segment in this voice (Y). As demonstrated in Example 6.14H, Y retains three dyads from the first hexachord of X: <96> ($OM_X Y$<*01*>), <4T> ($OM_X Y$<*54*>), and <23> ($OM_X Y$<*32*>).

Thus this penultimate section is a kind of microcosm of the segmental rela-

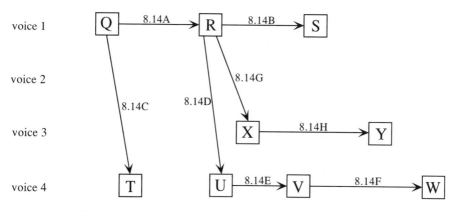

Example 6.15. *Study No. 5, derivational network in subsection IVa*

tions that permeate the *Study*. Example 6.15 graphs the derivational network of this passage, using the same typography as the previous diagram (Ex. 6.5). A single segment, segment Q, acts as a starting point for branches of derivations that extend through all three active voices. In voice 1 alone, Q initiates a *Psalm 25*–like chain, where each successive segment is derived from the one just before. Segment Q also serves as the source for voice 4, directly influencing segment T and leading indirectly to U, given that U's source, segment R, is a derivative of Q. The remainder of voice 4 extends the chain from U to V and V to W. Voice 3 starts with X, which is also an indirect descendant of Q (via R), and which then becomes the source for Y.

Inversionally mirrored quarter-note triplets starting at beat 289 herald the final section (V) and a flamboyant cadential flourish. There are some recollections of earlier ideas—for example, chromatic wedges in beats 300–301 recall earlier chromatic materials—but even more, there are sounds that are quite uncharacteristic of the *Study* in general. This is never more true than in the final gesture of the piece, shown in Example 6.16, where a quiet juxtaposition of A major and A♭ major triads resonates in the wake of a harsh fortissimo chord. That the piece should end so differently from its beginning is utterly consistent with the trend of growth and evolution that has characterized its overall design. An important melody, such as an aggregate ordering or wide-jumps chromatic scale, or some other important derivational source, such as segment Q in section IV, is not a "theme" in the sense of a pervasive musical presence but is merely a starting point for a series of operations that may progress through a derivational chain to arrive at a new and quite different form. When we hear the final juxtaposed triads emerge from the dissonant sounds that precede them, we are reminded one final time of the paths we have traveled and of the disparity between our place of departure and our point of arrival.

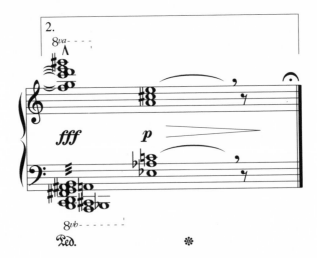

Example 6.16. *Study No. 5,* final gesture. © 1978, 1988 Merion Music, Inc. Used by Permission.

PART II

Cyclic Substance

7 Transposition Cycles

George Ives's advice about compositional sense inspired his son in a number of ways. Up to now we have examined the sense of contrapuntal devices, structural models, and transformational techniques that characterize Charles Ives's systematic music. Now, in the second and final part of this study, we investigate that aspect of Ives's systematic work that most intensely seized his interest: the phenomenon of interval cycles and the methods he uses to realize cyclic models of pitch structure. As a systematic tool, cycles are an ideal coalescence of calculation, modeling, patterning, transformation, and pitch-class variety. They are the closest Ives comes to finding a compositional sense that is both substantive and original.

Part of the appeal of cycles is their extracontextuality. That is one reason Ives is among several composers of the period who explored their possibilities as a novel pitch resource, including Debussy, Bartók, Stravinsky, and Berg.[1] As George Perle points out, interval cycles emerge "in the most natural way" in music of this period, evolving from "a long prehistory in the tonal progressions that symmetrically partition the octave in the music of Schubert and Chopin and Liszt and Wagner."[2] Cycles can provide the necessary constraints for an artist, define the creative boundaries. As the structural norms supplying the listener with points of orientation and the artist with points of departure, cycles can be "windows of order" on post-tonal music.[3]

In these final four chapters we take a slightly nonstandard approach to the subject, in part to highlight the ways in which Ives's uses of cycles are distinctive, and in part to situate better this facet of Ives's technique within all of his systematic writing.[4]

Transposition Cycles Defined

The approach outlined here focuses not on intervals per se but on the operation that is the generator of an interval cycle—transposition. We have already seen the importance of this operation in Ives's systematic writing as one of the canonical transformations of Chapter Five. The theoretical premises are as follows. The operation of transposition by n semitones (Tn), when applied to an operand of any size—from a single pitch class to entities as large as musical circumstances will allow—produces a one-to-one mapping between the element(s) in the operand and the element(s) in the result. A *transposition cycle*, (Tn cycle) is a series of transpositions in which each result is treated as a new operand and transformed by the same Tn, up until some result is equivalent to the operand that began the series. At that point the cycle is considered complete. The "length" of a Tn cycle is the number of applications of the operation required to achieve cyclic completion. Cyclic lengths vary with the value of n: T1, T5, T7, and T11 cycles are of length 12, T2 and T10 cycles are of length 6, T3 and T9 cycles are of length 4, T4 and T8 cycles are of length 3, and T6 cycles are of length 2. Note that the *cycle* under this definition is the series of transformations (transpositions), not the things being transformed. As a convenience, however, and following custom, we will often use the word *cycle* to refer to both the process and the product.

When an operand in a Tn cycle contains only a single pitch class, the process will yield a series of equidistant notes that resembles the interval cycle as it is customarily defined. In such cases the conventional label will reflect the value of n in our terminology: an interval 1 cycle is a T1 cycle, an interval 2 cycle is a T2 cycle, and so forth. But since our definition also encompasses larger operands, such as whole chords or phrases or other musical entities that might be transformed through the stages of a cycle, we also recognize and emphasize the fundamental similarity between the conventional interval cycle and any cyclic compositional process. This approach, especially its emphasis on process over product, has a conceptual basis in several recent studies of transformational processes, and particularly in the work of David Lewin.[5] I am also indebted to Richard Cohn's notion of "transpositional combination," applicable to transpositional structures in a variety of musical settings.[6]

We can learn more about transposition cycles by examining the customary definitions and applications of the concept of interval cycle. In other words, we focus for a moment only on Tn cycles in which the operands are single notes. In common usage the interval cycle is a structural model that is susceptible of a variety of realizations. In some cases music that is said to realize this model is simply a direct statement of the notes of the model in their original ordering and without embellishment. But there will also be times when music traced to cyclic roots does not display obvious cyclic features. This is often the case, for example, in music said to be based on a whole-tone collection (cycle of interval 2 or 10), where the pitch classes of the model are permitted to appear in any order and register and in any number of vertical or horizontal combinations. The music may resemble the model at some point, but this is not a necessary condition; indeed, very few surface features may be literally cyclic.[7] It will be useful to distinguish between the two usages. We will refer to the former usage—for cases where the model's ordering is preserved—as a *sequence*, and to the latter as a *referential collection*.

A second issue that arises in cyclic realizations concerns the limitations of the conventional cyclic resources. An interval 2 or 10 cycle provides fertile material for a referential collection or sequence, but many of the others do not. Models generated by cycles of smaller lengths—intervals 3 or 9, 4 or 8, or 6—do not make useful referential collections but can have some value as sequences. Cyclic models containing all twelve pitch classes—those generated by intervals 1, 5, 7 and 11—may also be realized as sequences but do not have the distinctive content required of a referential collection. The twelve-element cycles are sometimes viewed as sources for referential collections when they are abbreviated—and therefore no longer literally cyclic—as where a segment of a 5 or 7 cycle generates a diatonic collection.

These two issues—the *ordering* of the original model and the *limitations* of the standard cyclic resources—relate to our broader definition of cycles in varying degrees. For the most part, if a model is to be realized as a referential collection, the operand must be a single note. The notion of a Tn cycle does not shed significant new light on this usage but rather expands the possibilities for the size of the operand in sequential applications. At the same time, the availability of various sizes of operands, which certainly enhances the compositional palette, can also magnify a composer's limitations. The infinite expansion in the possibilities for transformational objects is not accompanied by an analogous increase in the number of transformational operations.

We will examine Ives's response to the problem of limitation in Chapter Nine. In this chapter we explore his work within the compositional boundaries defined by the conventional cyclic resources. Given his preoccupation with cal-

Example 7.1. *Largo Risoluto No. 1*, mm. 24–25, strings

culation, transformation, and patterning, it should come as no surprise that most of his realizations of cyclic models favor the sequential approach. His operands range in size from single notes to large blocks of music.

Single-Note Operands

Ives's projections of single-note operands take several forms. We start with the simplest, where the notes of the model are presented without decoration, as a bare unfolding of basic intervallic relationships. Example 7.1 illustrates such a procedure in the string parts of the first ending of *Largo Risoluto No. 1*, a passage that is quite out of character with the surrounding music.[8] The violins unfold two complete T5 cycles, stated in parallel pitch interval 5s; the viola, beginning one beat later and doubled an octave lower in the cello, unfolds one complete T5 cycle and a portion of another one, as bracketed in the example. The basis of the passage could be a structural model in which three T5 cycles move together, in vertical distances of interval 5 between both the top two and the bottom two voices. The model is realized here by delaying the entrance of the lower cycle by one beat and displacing its first two notes by an octave. (In the octave doubling in the cello these two notes would be in the correct octave.) Ives accents every other note in the cycles, thereby highlighting the notes of a T10 cycle. We will often see him emphasizing this kind of embedding of one cycle within another, in this case revealing a 2:1 proportional relationship between T5 and T10.

Some of Ives's most musically effective projections of complete cyclic sequences occur in the conclusion to the Second String Quartet, in music closely related to the Finale of the Fourth Symphony. The four measures shown in Example 7.2 begin a final section that aspires to bring together the work's musical and extramusical themes. As ostinato patterns begin repeating in the upper three

Adagio maestoso

Example 7.2. String Quartet No. 2, 3rd mvt., mm. 123–126

parts, a T10 cycle unfolds in quarter notes in the cello, spanning an octave over seven beats and then repeating, as if in continual cyclic revolution. It is a perfect illustration of what Robert P. Morgan calls spatial form, in which the music denies a sense of sequence and temporality while encouraging "spatial," simultaneous, and nontemporal qualities. The circularity and stratification in this passage are two of the features of Ives's music that Morgan cites as causes for this kind of effect.[9]

Ives says that at the end of the quartet four men, personified by the instruments, "walk up the mountainside to view the firmament."[10] He seems to have in mind a spiritual transcendence something like the end of the Fourth Symphony, where he aspires to capture "the reality of existence and its religious experience."[11] In other words, the four men ascend a sacred mountain, seeking enrichment and enlightenment at the place where heaven and earth meet.[12] The passage's spatial features support the imagery by transcending the ordinary sense of musical progression, as if ascending to a higher spiritual plane where time stands still. The repeating T10 cycle also contributes, by evoking the image of a circle and its historic connotations of cosmic order and universal oneness.[13]

Actually, it is not that common in Ives's oeuvre to find this type of clarity of cyclic presentation, where the model's intervallic structure and circularity are so readily visible. Ives is much more inclined to create sequences from fragments of cyclic models, as, for instance, where he links rising fourth motives (from "Taps") into sequences in *From the Steeples and the Mountains*.[14] Another method

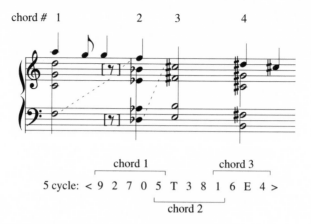

Example 7.3. "Song in 5's" (Kirkpatrick *Catalogue,* #7E38)

of fragmentation subdivides a presentation of one of the longer cycles into two
or more separate melodies or chords. Example 7.3 illustrates Ives's application
of this technique in a short sketch entitled "Song in 5's" that appears on a page
of materials relating to the "Thoreau" movement of the *Concord* Sonata.[15] The
chords are stackings of interval 7s, and they are connected via common tones:
pc 5 is common between the bottom of chord 1 and the top of chord 2, and pc
1 is similarly shared by the bottom of chord 2 and the top of chord 3. Thus all
three chords may be integrated into a cyclic model generated by a T5 cycle, as
shown beneath the score. The chords realize the complete model in three parts.

A similar procedure underlies the one-measure string quartet introduction to
In Re Con Moto Et Al (1913), Example 7.4. The rhythms relate in the proportion
4:3:2:1 (cello:viola:second violin:first violin). The pitches are derived by stepping
through a T5 cycle, as shown through op numbers within the score that corre-
spond to the pc/op notation of the cycle underneath. The three statements of
the complete cycle appear enclosed in boxes in the example. Though notes
from the model sometimes appear slightly out of order, they usually occur in
close enough proximity to reflect the intervallic structure of the model; for
example, the first verticality is op <*0123*>, the last sonority of the first realization
is <*89TE*>, and op's <*567*> occur together in the second realization, as do
<*1234*> in the third. Although some melodic intervals also reflect the structure
of the model—<*345*> in the first realization, <*123*> and <*45*> in the second, and
<*45*> in the third—many melodic intervals are also formed by notes not adja-
cent in the model. Generally, the melodic lines are byproducts of the vertical
combinations.

Linkages between vertical sonorities also play important roles in portions of
The Fourth of July. Example 7.5 shows most of the string parts from mm. 8–13,

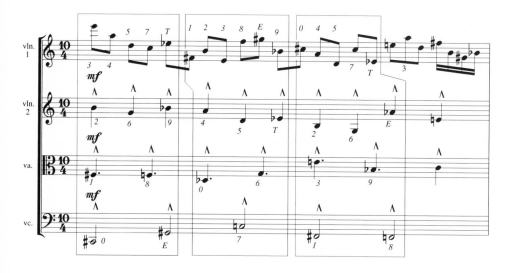

op *0 1 2 3 4 5 6 7 8 9 T E*

5 cycle: < 1 6 E 4 9 2 7 0 5 T 3 8 >

Example 7.4. *In Re Con Moto Et Al,* m. 1

in which are presented cyclic structures that become important sources of harmonic unity in the piece.[16] At first there are three intervallically repetitive chords: A, a stacking of interval 5 in m. 8, B, a whole-tone cluster in m. 9, and C, a stacking of interval 7 in m. 10. Then B is repeated as a stacking of interval 10 in m. 11, and A and C are repeated in mm. 12 and 13. Chords A and C are complementary segments of a T5 cycle, as notated beneath the score; their linkage suggests a progression of the cycle upward through chord A (pc <05T3816>), then downward through C (pc <E4927>) to achieve cyclic completion. Meanwhile, an analogous relationship exists between the two occurrences of chord B: five notes of the T2 cycle (pc <2468T>) progress upward through the voicing of B in m. 9, but downward through the voicing in m. 11. Simultaneously, the lowest part in mm. 8–12 presents a fragment of a patriotic song ("Red, White, and Blue") that becomes a primary source for melodic and harmonic structures in the piece.[17] The manner in which Ives weaves together systematic structures, such as the cyclic patterns shown here or the aggregate formations in the "explosions" section discussed in Chapter Five, with materials that are not systematically conceived, such as tune quotations or fragmentations, contributes substantially to the work's overall unity and offers one of the best examples in his work of an integration of compositional approaches.

Another model based on single-note-operand cycles links corresponding notes from two different cycles. We have seen some of this already, in the wedge-

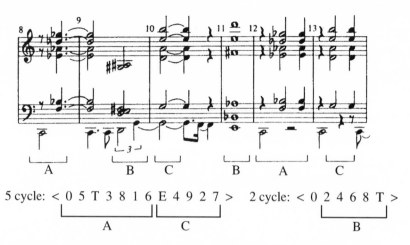

Example 7.5. *The Fourth of July,* mm. 8–13, 3rd and 4th violins, viola, cello, bass

like note-for-note presentation of T1 and T2 cycles in "Like a Sick Eagle" (Example 4.8). Example 7.6 shows another instance, a passage from Ives's song "From *The Swimmers*" (1915), in which a collaboration of these cycles does not unfold a wedge because the cycles move at different rates, in a 2:1 rhythmic proportion. As the text describes "windy waters rushing past me, through me," the T1 cycle ascends in the lowest voice of the piano left hand, rhythmically synchronized with a T2 cycle stated a fifth higher (the notes of the cycles are connected with downward stems). Each note of the T2 cycle occurs twice, so that two of the same notes appear in the T2 cycle for every two different notes in the T1. It is therefore an embedding of the T2 cycle in the T1—a 2:1 relationship not unlike the embedding of T10 within T5 displayed in *Largo Risoluto No. 1* (Ex. 7.1). Indeed, these two instances demonstrate that T2 or T10 is thus embedded in any of the twelve-element cycles. In "From *The Swimmers*" a second T2 cycle enters on offbeats (bass clef stems up), beginning a major third higher than the stems-down T2 cycle and repeating every note, starting with the second one.[18]

In yet another method of realizing a single-note-operand model, the notes of the cycle are treated as the primary structural line within a generally diverse texture. The cyclic presence gives the music a sense of direction and orientation, its completion providing a sense of closure. Example 7.7 illustrates a gradual unfolding of a T11 cycle in a passage from *Study No. 20*. The presentation begins with the C♯ circled in the highest voice of m. 6 and moves through the circled C, B, and B♭ in mm. 6–7. It skips A, which is the lowest note—a kind of pedal—of mm. 6–8, and then moves through A♭, G, and F♯, as circled in mm. 7–8. The line shifts to the bass clef, with the next two notes from the model, F and E, stated together in m. 9 and then separately as the lowest notes of m. 10. At this

Example 7.6. "From *The Swimmers*" (*114 Songs,* p. 63, last system). © 1933 Merion Music, Inc. Used by Permission.

Example 7.7. *Study No. 20,* mm. 6–17. © 1981 Merion Music, Inc. Used by Permission.

A. segment Y. © 1949, 1975 Mercury Music Corporation. Used by Permission.

$$X\ (=5\text{-cycle}\ ) = \ <\ 9\ \ 2\ \ 7\ \ 0\ \ 5\ \ T\ \ 3\ \ 8\ \ 1\ \ 6\ \ E\ \ 4\ >$$

$$OM_X X\ = \ <\ 0\ \ 1\ \ 2\ \ 3\ \ 4\ \ 5\ \ 6\ \ 7\ \ 8\ \ 9\ \ T\ \ E\ >$$

J   L   K

$$Y\ = \ <\ 2\ \ 9\ \ 2\ \ 7\ \ 0\ \ 5\ \ 6\ \ 1\ \ 4\ \ T\ \ 8\ \ 3\ \ 8\ \ E\ >$$

$$OM_X Y\ = \ <\ 1\ \ 0\ \ 1\ \ 2\ \ 3\ \ 4\ \ 9\ \ 8\ \ E\ \ 5\ \ 7\ \ 6\ \ 7\ \ T\ >$$

J   K   L

B. comparison of Y with segment X

Example 7.8. *Three-Page Sonata,* derivation of left hand, mm. 77–79

point the left hand begins a three-beat ostinato that includes the structural F and E in m. 10 plus the next note in the cyclic unfolding, the E♭, in m. 11. This pattern is then transposed by T11 twice, in order to state the remaining notes of the cycle: the first transposition is mm. 11:2–12:2, adding the note D (m. 12:2), and the second transposition is m. 13, arriving at the final C♯ (m. 13:3). With this return to the pitch class with which the unfolding began comes a sense of arrival, reinforced by the subsequent varied repetition of the final sequential measures (mm. 10–13) in mm. 14–17.

Ives applies a similar idea when he establishes cyclic relationships among tone centers. In a passage from the *Three-Page Sonata,* for example, each of five diverse phrases is clearly anchored on a single tone center, through repetition and a general oscillation between major and minor sonorities. These tone centers descend in whole steps from G (mm. 31–33) to F (mm. 34–35) to E♭ (mm. 36–38) to C♯ (mm. 39–40), and then arrive on B (mm. 41–42), which remains an important tonal anchor for the next large section of the piece.

To close this survey of Ives's use of single-note operands, let us recall his use of cycles as sources for order derivations, as discussed in Chapter Five. Example 5.1 displays melodic lines from the *Robert Browning Overture* formed by displacing one note in a T7 cycle, and Example 5.13 shows reorderings of T1 and T11 cycles. Of course, the cyclic aspects of the musical results of such derivations are widely variable; nonetheless, the cycle helps determine the line's primary structural features and organize the pitch-class exhaustion. Example 7.8 shows a melody from the *Three-Page Sonata* more diverse than the ones from the *Robert Browning Overture,* but which still betrays cyclic roots. The melody, labeled Y and shown in Example 7.8A, is closely associated with the T_5 cycle labeled X in Example 7.8B. As shown with brackets, three segments of X are contiguous (though possibly scrambled) in Y: OM_XY<*101234*>, OM_XY<*98*>, and OM_XY<*576*>, labeled J, K, and L, respectively. The connections between X and Y are extensive enough to ensure a strong presence of intervals 5 and 7 in the line and to achieve pitch-class exhaustion, yet there is also enough variety to avoid the sense of simple intervallic repetition.

Large Operands

Ives's treatment of large operands follows similar practices. As always, he is interested in the regularity and forward momentum provided by the cyclic repetition, and by the sense of closure provided when a realization reaches its cyclic completion. The particular cycles he selects to project large operands are mostly of moderate size: 3 or 9 cycles, and especially 2 or 10 cycles. The smallest cycles (4, 6, 8) seem not to provide enough transposition levels for full development of ideas, whereas the largest cycles are perhaps too large and require too much time to complete. Large cycles can, of course, be truncated, but doing so compromises the sense of arrival and closure.

We have already seen some cyclic projections of large operands, as a basic principle of certain of the large-scale wedge unfoldings discussed in Chapter Four. For example, the structure of the excerpt from *Hallowe'en* shown in Example 4.9 is dependent on the transposition of whole chunks of material in the upper wedge voice through a T_2 cycle. We also mentioned the piano accompaniment to the song "Luck and Work," where a short section of music is repeatedly transposed by T_6 with the hands going in opposite directions to enact a large expanding wedge. But there are also many examples in Ives's work of transposition cycles projecting large operands without any ancillary purposes, solely to exploit the distinctive qualities of the cycle.

Many of the early choral pieces include cyclic projections of large operands; this procedure seems to have become somewhat of a preoccupation for Ives in his early years. His efforts usually involve using cycles of T_2 or T_{10} to project some kind of triad. In a passage based on transposition cycles in *Psalm 54,* for example, the operand is simply an augmented triad, transposed through a T_{10} and a T_2 cycle. The score reduction of this passage in Example 7.9 illustrates the first of several instances of such a progression in the work. While the upper

Example 7.9. *Psalm 54,* mm. 1–6, piano reduction of vocal lines. © 1973 Merion Music, Inc. Used by Permission.

voices add doubling or embellishing tones, the lower voices state the basic progression, starting on a C augmented triad and moving through the transposition levels of a T10 cycle until their arrival on another C augmented triad at m. 4:1. Then a C♯ augmented triad at m. 4:2 (spelled as first-inversion A augmented) begins an ascent through the transposition levels of the T2 cycle. Thus the initial descent unfolds augmented triads comprising exclusively even-numbered pitch classes, and the ensuing ascent states the complementary odd-numbered ones.[19]

Ives does something very similar in *Psalm 135* (around 1902), a choral work with parts for trumpet, trombone, percussion, and organ that was written around the same time as *Psalm 54.* The work begins with a sequential pattern stated at four whole-step-related transposition levels (mm. 1 – 5). These opening bars are a harbinger of activity in a later passage where triads on whole-step-related roots form the basic harmonic structure. This latter passage is mm. 53 – 72; Example 7.10 shows its first half. Just above the trumpet part Ives writes a series of note names identifying the roots of minor triads that are presented with embellishment in the voice parts (doubled in the organ). Over a D organ pedal, the progression of roots descends through a T10 cycle of even pitch classes in mm. 53:1 – 57:2, starting with Dm and Cm in m. 53, continuing to B♭m and A♭m in m. 54, G♭m in m. 55, Em in m. 56, and returning to Dm at m. 47:1. Then the roots ascend through a T2 cycle of odd pitch classes in mm. 57:3 – 62:2. The basic sequential logic, then, is the same as the projection of augmented triads above a C pedal in *Psalm 54:* a T10 sequence descending, followed by a shift of collection and a T2 collection ascending. After this (mm. 62:3 – 72) the same root pattern is repeated but with major-quality triads.

Example 7.10. *Psalm 135*, mm. 53–62. © 1981 Merion Music, Inc. Used by Permission.

The trumpet and trombone parts of this passage emphasize the structure of the progression by approaching each cyclically projected chord root by interval 5, in dotted-eighth–sixteenth rhythms (usually resembling "Taps"). For example, the brass parts at the beginning of the passage emphasize the first four cyclically projected roots, D, C, B♭, and A♭, with motives stating <A–D>, <G–C>, <F–B♭>, and <D♯–G♯> (mm. 52:4–54:3). The remaining structural chord roots are similarly accentuated. One result of the accentuation pattern is the possibility of linking the complete dyads within a T5 cycle: for the dyads just mentioned, <A–D–G–C–F–B♭–D♯–G♯>. As the motives continue, eventually all the dyads connect in a T5 cycle that reaches completion at the same moment the progression of chord roots completes its T10 cycle. Once again Ives highlights the T10 cycle embedded within the T5, just as he did in the *Largo Risoluto No. 1* excerpt in Example 7.1

Yet one more example of triads on whole-step-related roots in an early choral work is the second *Harvest Home Chorale* (around 1902). Example 7.11 shows the piano introduction to the work, which establishes a harmonic progression that subsequently provides a harmonic framework for the entire piece. Measure 1 establishes a C♯ pedal, which will continue throughout, and also states a C♯–G♯ open fifth that combines with the E at m. 1:3 to form a minor-quality triad. Thereafter, every measure begins with a major triad (excluding the C♯ pedal) that becomes minor when the voice that has the third of the chord falls a half step on beat three. In m. 2, for example, a B-major triad becomes minor with the half-note movement of D♯ to D♮ in the upper voices of both staffs. The chord roots underlying these modal shifts, as indicated in the example, are related by whole step, first in a T10 cycle that descends to its completion in m. 7, and then in a repetition of the same roots in reverse to present a T2 cycle that ascends to completion in m. 13. At that point the tempo changes, the choral voices begin entering, and the root pattern starts over. The progression resembles the passages we just saw in *Psalm 54* and *Psalm 135*, except that in those pieces the music shifted collections (from even to odd) at the midpoint. It also resembles portions of the first *Harvest Home Chorale,* where the roots of triads of inconsistently different qualities are presented in various whole-step relations, although not through the transposition levels of a complete cycle.[20] The passage in Example 7.11 also calls to mind our discussion of palindromic form in Chapter Four, since equivalent measures are paired around m. 7: m. 8 duplicates m. 6, m. 9 duplicates m. 5, and so forth, with a few subtle exceptions.

Further, since the half-note modal inflections occur above the whole-step descent, the half notes themselves participate in a unified chromatic descent in mm. 1:1–7:1: E in m. 1, then <D♯–D> in m. 2, <C♯–C> in m. 3, <B–B♭> in m. 4, <A–A♭> in m. 5, <G–G♭> in m. 6, and <F–E> in m. 7, reaching com-

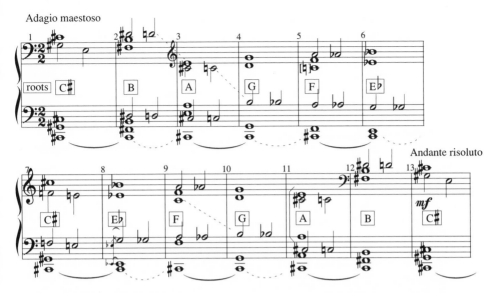

Example 7.11. *Harvest Home Chorale* No. 2, piano, mm. 1–13. © 1949 Mercury Music Corporation. Used by Permission.

pletion just as the whole-step root movement does. It is yet another 2:1 chromatic to whole-tone relationship, this one most closely resembling the one between T1 and T2 cycles in "From *The Swimmers.*" In the second half of the progression, where the roots are related by ascending whole step, the half notes connect with the roots of the ensuing chords to form three-note chromatic segments that rise by whole steps: <F–E> in m. 7 connects to E♭ in m. 8, followed by <G–G♭–F> in mm. 8–9, <A–A♭–G> in mm. 9–10, <B–B♭–A> in mm. 10–11, <C♯–C–B> in mm. 11–12, and <D♯–D–C♯> in mm. 12–13.

But the operands in these early works are only slightly larger than single notes. In Ives's later cyclic realizations the operands are substantially larger, their treatments significantly more complex. Further, they invite comparisons with harmonic sequences in tonal music. Setting aside the obvious distinction that Ives's transpositions are not adjusted to remain within a uniform key (they are real rather than tonal), the process is the same: a sequential unit is transposed through a repetitive pattern of pitch levels. The musical objectives are also similar—the pattern of repetitive transposition provides harmonic momentum and direction, and often closure as well. Ives's sequences most strongly resemble passages in later tonal music where transposition levels project not the traditional fifth relations but other intervals, usually thirds. A complete cycle is analogous with "equal subdivision of the octave" in chromatic harmony, in which an original object is transformed through various transposition levels until it reappears an octave higher.[21] In this procedure, as in Ives's work, it is the unfolding and eventual completion of the sequence or cycle that gives the progression its identity and sense of completion, in part as compensation for the absence of more conventional tonal unifying forces.[22]

Ives's short piano pieces include many examples of cyclic writing and projections of large operands. Example 7.12 shows a passage from *Rough and Ready* in which each hand is controlled by a different cycle. In the right hand the operand is ten sixteenths in duration and is projected downward through the levels of a T_{10} cycle as bracketed in the score.[23] Each operand is subdivided into two five-sixteenth-note groups, with each group beginning on an accented trichord. Indeed, such a grouping encourages a subdivision of the overall progression into two T_{10} cycles, one comprising all first groups and the other comprising all second groups. The grouping also allows a secondary line to emerge between the highest notes of the accented chords, consisting of a rising minor third within each operand (<C–D♯> in the first operand, <A♯–C♯> in the second, etc.). The progression reaches cyclic completion at m. 15:1, and then the entire sequence is repeated an octave lower in mm. 15:2–22:2, after which the texture changes and a new section begins.

In the left hand a completely different operand is projected upward through the levels of a T_2 cycle, as bracketed beneath the score in Example 7.12. Thus the hands together suggest a wedgelike mirroring between converging T_{10} and T_2 cycles, although involving only general shape, not specific mirrorings between the hands. Also distorting the mirroring effect is a discrepancy in length of operand: the left-hand operand is ten quintuplet sixteenths in duration, as opposed to the ten actual sixteenths of the right-hand operand. As a result, the left hand moves through its cycle faster than does the right hand (1.25 measures per operand in the right hand, 1 measure per operand in the left). The operands in the left hand are subdivided, as is the right hand, into two five-note groups. In this hand the lowest accented notes of the groups are related by rising half steps, thus filling in the rising whole step in the lowest voice from one operand to the next. Again, the T_1 cycle is embedded in the T_2.

Because of the difference in rate of presentation between the hands, the left hand's T_2 cycle finishes in m. 13, two measures earlier than the completion of the T_{10} cycle. Measure 14 is a transitional measure for the left hand, and lies at a T_1, rather than T_2, relationship with m. 13. But then m. 14 becomes the beginning of a new T_2 sequence of the same operand, starting a major seventh higher than the first one did (m. 8). The new cycle reaches octave completion in m. 19, before filling in the remaining measures of the section (waiting for the right hand to complete its T_{10} cycle) by changing the transposition pattern. In mm. 20–22 the transpositions are calculated so that the lowest note at the beginning

|| = end of cycle

Example 7.12. *Rough and Ready*, mm. 8–22

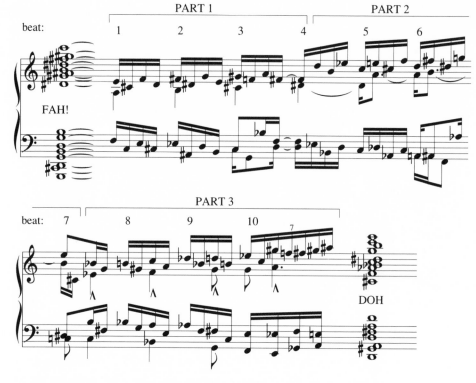

Example 7.13. *Study No. 8,* FAH-DOH connection. © Theodore Presser Co. Used by Permission.

of each group (on each beat) unfolds a segment of a T5 cycle: D and G in m. 20, C and F in m. 21, and B♭ and E♭ in m. 22.

A passage from another short piano work, *Study No. 8* (1907–?1908), also employs cyclic transpositions of large operands. The piece begins with an interplay of large verticalities Ives labels DOH, SOH, FAH, followed by passages of patterned and free linear writing occasionally interrupted by restatements of one of the verticalities.[24] Example 7.13 shows a section in the center of the *Study* that begins with a FAH chord and concludes with a restatement of DOH. Following FAH, the right hand ascends chromatically in broken minor thirds, while the left hand states the tetrachord <F–C–E–C♯> and then its T10 transposition, <E♭–A♯–D–B>. The material in both hands is then repeated, with some variation, at T10, starting at the second sixteenth of beat 4, and again at T6 starting at the third sixteenth of beat 7; this is the basis of the subdivision of the excerpt into three parts in the example.

We can subdivide the passage further by following a line notated in longer durations in a second treble voice (stems down) that begins on A and ascends by mostly whole steps. As this line rises from A on beat 1 through B on beat 2, C♯ on beat 3, and D♯ on beat 4, each right-hand beat begins to sound like an operand; we can say that from this point of view not just the inner voice but all the right-hand material ascends by whole steps from one beat to the next. (The left hand does not unfold the same kind of beat-to-beat sequence.) In part 2 the sequence is interrupted—the right hand's broken minor thirds suddenly shift to a higher register in beat 4, as does the inner voice in beat 5. Then part 3 returns to the register where part 1 left off, on the next logical third in the broken-third sequence of part 1 and on the same inner-voice note (E♭) that ended part 1. The sequence in part 3 concludes by completing the T2 cycle begun in part 1, in the inner-voice notes <E♭–F–G–A> in beats 7–10. Thus the T2 cycle shapes the entire linkage between the FAH and DOH chords, defining the basic movement of the progression, establishing a developmental context from which part 2 makes a departure, and showing the way toward closure.

We close our discussion of larger operands by mentioning two instances where cycles other than T2 or T10 control a sequential passage. The first is the piano accompaniment in the excerpt from the song "The See'r" (?1913) shown in Example 7.14. Measure 20 shows the basic operand: a D augmented triad in the left hand is answered by an E augmented triad plus F♯ in the right hand— thus completing the even whole-tone collection—and then the left hand moves down to C augmented and the right hand moves out of the even collection to F augmented. This operand (bracketed in the example) is projected via falling minor thirds, or a T9 cycle. The second occurrence (m. 21) is rhythmically varied slightly in the second half of the bar, and the third occurrence (mm. 22:1–23:1) begins a sixteenth late and is still more rhythmically varied. At the end of the sequence (mm. 23:1–24:1), what begins as a fourth projection of the operand dissolves into a transition to the song's final section, though the operand is still recognizable: the left hand falls by half steps in m. 23 as if filling in the expected whole step, and the right hand states the expected G augmented triad plus A, but then states F augmented instead of the sequentially consistent A♭ augmented. Nonetheless, the left hand does arrive at its originating pitch classes at the downbeat of m. 24, to complete the descent from m. 20. The left hand of mm. 23–24 recalls a series of augmented triads in the song's introduction (mm. 2–3) and thereby prepares the return of several previous ideas in the final section of the song.[25]

Our second and last example of a large operand projected by a non-whole-tone sequence is taken from the third movement of the Second String Quartet. Example 7.15 shows the entire operand, spanning a distance of almost six measures. Mostly, the first-violin part serves as the operand, projected upward by T3, although other parts participate occasionally. The passage is important to

Example 7.14. "The See'r," mm. 20:1–25:1

the movement and the work for several reasons. First, this material begins the second main section of the movement, coming after an Adagio section that uses quotation fragments and sustained sounds to set a kind of reverential tone that is appropriate to the title of the movement, "The Call of the Mountains." The excerpt in Example 7.15 begins a period of growing musical intensity that culminates some thirty-five bars later, in the extended statement of the hymn tune "Bethany" standing at the center of the movement (mm. 56–80, viola). As we have seen, the Finale is a trip "up the mountainside to view the firmament"(see note 10)—the growth and intensification symbolize the journey up the mountain, and the tune, with its familiar text "Nearer My God to Thee," signals the arrival. Further, in the course of the ascent the melody in the first violin restates many of the main ideas in the quartet, as if summarizing its principal musical as well as religious-philosophical themes. For example, the theme begins with a tri-chord (B–B♭–E) that is an ordered transposition of the first three notes of an

Example 7.15. String Quartet No. 2, 3rd mvt., mm. 20:4–26:2

expansive canonic line that dominates the structure of the second movement.[26] The melody also recalls cyclic ideas from both the first and second movements by briefly presenting a T4 cycle in the notes G♯, C, and E (mm. 21:3 – 22:2), and outlining a T3 cycle in the notes D♯, F♯, A, and C (mm. 22:3 – 23:4). Finally, the melody is supported by some closely interrelated chord structures similar to those seen throughout the work (see Ex. 7.3). In mm. 21 – 22 two pc sets appear in rapid alternation: X is pc [E01357] and Y is pc [24689T], as circled and labeled in Example 7.15. Since X and Y are literally complementary members of sc 6–22 (012468), they combine to form complete aggregates in rapid succession.

Example 7.16 shows the second stage in the series of T3 transpositions. While the first violin of this passage is consistently T3 of the previous first-violin line—with minor rhythmic variations—the other parts exhibit only occasional transpositional relationships with the previous accompaniment (Ex. 7.15). In m. 28, for example, the chord on beat 2 is mostly T3 of the chord at the

Example 7.16. String Quartet No. 2, 3rd mvt., mm. 26:3–31:4

parallel place in the operand, m. 22:3, but the surrounding sonorities are not so closely related. And there are other examples of connections between the accompanimental material of the two passages (all with at least one inconsistent note), but the basic sense of the writing is that of a melodic repetition with freely varied accompaniment.

Example 7.17 summarizes the first violin's entire cyclic projection: version 1 is the first-violin line of Example 7.15, version 2 is T3 of version 1 presented in the first-violin line of Example 7.16, version 3 is the next stage, T6 of version 1, and version 4 completes the cycle with T9 of version 1. The melodies of versions 1, 2, and 4 differ from each other in only minor details, while that of version 3 has more rhythmic variation and is cut short after three measures.[27]

Immediately following version 4, the tempo changes (to Andante con spirito) and the music begins its final approach to the central presentation of the hymn

Example 7.17. String Quartet No. 2, 3rd mvt., 1st violin, mm. 19:4–35:1, 39:1–44:4

tune. The texture at this point consists of rapidly moving violin parts and a walking quarter-note cello line that evolves into a whole-tone scale when the viola begins the hymn quotation (starting in m. 56). This cello line thus adumbrates the cello part of the concluding measures of the work, some of which we saw in Example 7.2, in addition to recalling many previous uses of this cycle, such as those mentioned in Chapter Five (Ex. 5.3). It is the most extensive use, up to this point in the piece, of cycles to represent the goal of a spiritual journey. As we observed earlier in this chapter, these symbols then return at the end of the work to characterize the ultimate spiritual destination. Cycles also bring to mind such manifestations of circularity in nature as life cycles or planetary orbits. Ives makes this connection, somewhat obliquely, in his frequent quotation of the "Westminster Chimes" (the familiar chiming tune of bell towers) throughout the quartet, to allude to the cyclic nature of the passage of time over the course of a minute, hour, day, or year.[28] As the upward projection of the $T3$ cycle portrays the ascent up the mountain, its four stages correlate with the four-part division of the hour created by the chimes. The transposition cycle gives unity and structure to the ascent of the mountain, just as the cyclic passage of time gives unity and structure to day-to-day existence.

8 Analysis III: "The Cage"

Cycles hold metaphorical possibilities that Ives never tired of exploring. That is part of their appeal as systematic resources: they provide not only compositional sense but also a rich vehicle for many of the extramusical ideas that find their ways into his scores. We have just seen, in the Second String Quartet, an example of cycles communicating a thoughtful and serious message, and we will see more such uses in the chapters that follow. But Ives can also employ cycles to speak in a lighter and more playful voice. That is how he uses them in "The Cage."

"The Cage" is a rare example of an Ives song that is offbeat and systematically organized yet also accessible and popular. It is frequently included in recordings and recital programs,[1] and it is familiar to countless undergraduate theory students by virtue of its immortalization in Burkhart's *Anthology for Musical Analysis*.[2] It is also a model illustration of Ives's wit and ingenuity, and a lucid musical portrayal of a profound philosophical question. In the short time "The Cage" takes to perform—it can last less than a minute—the listener receives a rudimentary introduction to some of the composer's progressive musical ideas, all tied together into a coherent and artistically satisfying whole. The song is, in other words, an ideal window into Ives's musical language.

The music of "The Cage" was first conceived as an orchestral work, to be titled *In the Cage* and included as the first movement of the Set for Theatre or Chamber Orchestra (1906). Ives describes its origins: "[*In the Cage*] is a result of taking a walk one hot summer afternoon in Central Park with Bart Yung (one-half Oriental) and George Lewis (non Oriental), when we were all living together at 65 Central Park West in 1906 (or before). Sitting on a bench near the menagerie, watching the leopard's cage and a little boy (who had apparently been a long time watching the leopard)—this aroused Bart's Oriental fatalism—hence the text in the score and in the song" (*Memos*, 55). Though the published orchestral score has no vocal part, the original manuscript does include the vocal line and text that were later used in the arrangement for voice and piano that appears in *114 Songs*.[3] Example 8.1 gives the complete score of the song version, with analytic notations.

Though Ives did not suggest a typographical organization of the text as a poem, a logical one would contain five lines:

1. A leopard went around his cage
2. From one side back to the other side;
3. He stopped only when the keeper came around with meat;
4. A boy who had been there three hours began to wonder,
5. "Is life anything like that?"

The vocal line's incessant whole steps and eighth notes help to depict the monotony and futility of the leopard's existence.[4] There are five melodic phrases—roughly coordinating with the lines of the text—articulated by subtle changes in rhythm or in melodic intervals; these are bracketed and numbered above the vocal part in Example 8.1. The clearest phrase divisions are those where the text and melody strongly correlate: between phrases 3 and 4, where the vocal line has its only rest, and between phrases 4 and 5, after the vocal line comes to rest at its longest duration, on the word *wonder*. The division between phrases 1 and 2 also correlates with a textual division, but it is musically weaker, created simply by the occurrence of the melody's first semitone (between the words *cage* and *from*). And the division between phrases 2 and 3 is not so much weak as ambiguous: the text logically breaks at the semicolon (after *side*), but the melody is more logically divided after it pauses for a longer duration two words later (at *stopped*), and then states its second semitone (between *stopped* and *only*). These overlapping structural divisions help to highlight the word *stopped* and the necessity for the leopard to pause for nourishment, while also maintaining the musical momentum needed to stress the inevitability of the continual pacing. A performer might play up these ideas by breathing not between melodic phrases but at the text division, so that the performance highlights one division, while the music itself, especially the rhythm, brings out another.[5]

Example 8.1. "The Cage." © 1955 by Peer International Corporation. International Copyright Secured. All Rights Reserved. Used by Permission.

Because the vocal line consists of whole steps within phrases and half steps between, the phrases state alternate whole-tone collections. (The exception is phrase 4, which includes one note from the opposite collection.) Phrases 1 and 5 are identical expressions of an even whole-tone pentachord [2468T], phrase 3 states the complete even whole-tone collection, phrase 2 presents an odd whole-tone pentachord [579E1], and phrase 4 states a different odd whole-tone pentachord [79E13] plus pc 4. This symmetrical arrangement of odd and even pitch classes, plus the cyclic connotations of the melodic intervals, help to portray the sense of circularity and enclosure that is the leopard's burden.

The piano part also reflects these ideas. Just as the vocal line uses a monotony of major seconds to reflect the textual theme, the piano uses a monotony of perfect fourths. In a short introduction that is repeated "2 or 3 times," six pentachords formed of stacked fourths are followed by a widely spaced hexachord formed of a variety of intervals. The series of quartal chords symbolizes the pacing leopard, while the hexachord represents the point where the leopard stops for food. Further, the chords become progressively shorter in duration up to the hexachord, which is sustained—the leopard's pace quickens as mealtime approaches. After the introduction has set this monotonous and mechanical mood, the remainder of the accompaniment continues to state these same chord types and reinforce the symbolic associations.[6]

In Example 8.1, the letter labels underneath the introductory chords refer to pitch-class content: chords A through E are followed by a repetition of C and then the "meal" chord, chord F. The subsequent chords are numbered 1–22. All other notations in the example illustrate a process of deriving the accompaniment from the opening chords.[7] First, all the introductory chords are transposed at T_5 to derive chords 1–7. Then T_3 of chords A, B, C, and E produces chords 8, 10, 13, and 18, respectively, and $T_3(D)$ derives the pitch classes of chord 15 from top to bottom, resulting in a chord in fifths. The chords that are skipped over are usually chromatically associated with the direct derivatives: chord 9 is T_1 of chord 8, chords 10–12 ascend chromatically to fill in the minor third between chords 10 and 13, chord 14 repeats chord 10, thus returning to the sonority that began the minor-third ascent, and chords 16 and 17 reiterate the quintal structure of chord 15. Chord 19, an eleven-note chord framed by the song's highest and lowest pitches, acts as the "meal chord" for the preceding T_3 derivations, though it is not a transposition of the original meal chord. Finally, chords 20–22 return to the T_5 derivation of chords A–C as first seen in chords 1–3, paralleling the equivalence between phrases 1 and 5 of the vocal line. This last, seemingly aborted statement of the chord series cooperates with the text's final open-ended question to suggest that the song (and the pacing) in fact have no foreseeable end but that we have simply looked in on an ongoing process.[8]

We can look deeper into Ives's score to find ways in which the music depicts the text more subtly. If the consistency of the harmonic language helps to represent the futility of the leopard's existence, the cyclic implications of the chords help to depict the circularity of the leopard's behavior. As the introductory chords take us through the leopard's pacings, for example, they unfold pitch-class relationships suggesting the circumnavigation of a T_5 cycle. Example 8.2 illustrates the location of each of chords A through E in a T_5 cycle notated as a circle, with pc 3, the lowest note of chord A, in the 12 o'clock position. Reminiscent of the derivations from T_5 cycles in *In Re Con Moto Et Al* and *The Fourth of July* we saw in Chapter 7, these chords suggest a gradual progression clockwise around the circle. While B is $T_7(A)$, and thus moves counterclockwise one place to hold four pc's in common with A, C is $T_3(B)$ and thus moves clockwise three places to hold two pc's in common with B (pc's 1 and 6). Chord D is $T_8(C)$, holding only one pc in common with C (pc 9) and progressing around to the circle's other side, almost back to the beginning. E completes the circle, holding two pc's in common with D (o and 5) and two in common with A (3 and 8), both T_3 relationships ($T_3(D) = E$, $T_3(E) = A$). When the sequence then repeats chord C before the meal chord, it starts back around the circle, showing that C, which is $T_1(E)$, occupies the next five places clockwise after E (no common tones).

Even though the meal chord is more variously structured than the others, it does draw meaningful connections with the same cyclic source. The chord includes one fourth, the upper dyad <C♯–F♯>, and two fifths within the central trichord <D–A–E>, in addition to the lone low F. In the context of the preceding chords, it makes sense to locate the meal chord's ic 5s within the same cycle circumnavigated by the other chords. We can easily find a cyclic connection, for example, between the just-mentioned trichord and dyad: if we continue a sequence of fifths upward beyond the <D–A–E> trichord, we skip one note, B, and then come to the F♯ and C♯ of the dyad. To arrive at the low F, we would extend the cycle downward from the trichord and skip two notes, G and C. Example 8.3 locates all these chord tones (circled) on the same T_5 cycle we used in Example 8.2: starting with the dyad <16> and progressing clockwise, we skip pc E and then come to the trichord <492>, then skip pc's 7 and 0 and arrive at the pc 5. The meal chord thus bifurcates the T_5 cycle into complementary, identically partitioned hexachords; in the illustration, both the circled and noncircled pc's are displayed in groups of 3, 2, and 1. The partitions are symmetrically displayed in the circle, with the circled trichord <294> situated directly across from noncircled trichord <T38>, the circled dyad <16> directly across from the non-circled dyad <07>, and pc 5 directly across from pc E.

After the introduction, the transposed and varied restatements of the chord

chord: A   B   C

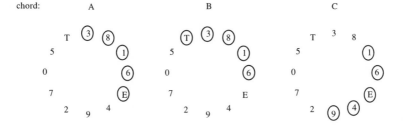

chord: D   E

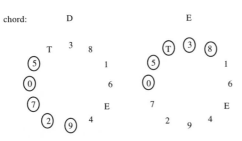

Example 8.2. "The Cage," cyclic progression of chords in sequence

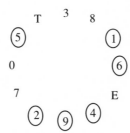

Example 8.3. "The Cage," "meal" chord within T5 cycle

series continue with circular progressions. The restatement of the entire series at T5 in chords 1–7 simply circumnavigates another circle starting a fourth higher, or one place clockwise on the circles of Example 8.2. This could be illustrated by moving each encirclement in Example 8.2 one place clockwise: in A, instead of <3816E>, circle <816E4> (= chord 1); in B, instead of <T3816>, circle <3816E> (= chord 2), and so forth. Thus the shift to illustrate chords 1–6 recalls the transpositional relationship between the first two chords in the song, save for a difference in direction: T7(A) derives chord B by moving the circling one place counterclockwise (compare with Ex. 8.2 A and B), while T5 of A–E derives chords 1–6 by moving the circlings one place clockwise.

Then when a third circumnavigation is suggested by the next set of derivatives, chords 8, 10, 13, 15, and 18, the T3 relationship recalls that same transformational relationship between the second and third chords in the song. Schematically, the T3 derivatives may be related to the chords diagrammed in Example 8.2 in the same way that chords B and C are related: by moving clockwise three places, holding two tones in common. Thus when Ives concludes the song with a restatement of the first three chords of the series (at T5), he confirms the importance of these structures in the piece, not only as the never-completed beginning of yet another progression around a circle but also as an encapsulation of the transpositional relationships that govern the song's overall design.

The sonorities that are intermixed with the derived chords further reflect aspects of the introduction and present additional metaphors of circularity. Example 8.4 organizes chords 8–13 in cycle diagrams. Pitch class 6 is in the 12 o'clock position because it is the lowest note of chord 8. The half-step relationships that predominate among these chords recall the T1 connection between chords E and C, which would be depicted as two adjacent chords on the circle with no common tones (for example, in Ex. 8.2, picture chord E followed by chord C). Example 8.4 depicts these same relationships between chords 8 and 9, and then between chords 10, 11, 12, and 13. As each chord in the latter sequence advances to the next five places in the circle, the overall progression cycles completely around and completes two thirds of a second revolution. Similar diagrams could illustrate the half-step relationship between the quintal chords 15 and 16.

Of course, the vocal line also suggests circular movement, which could be illustrated with a circle diagram containing only the six notes of a T2 or T10 cycle. But given Ives's interest in embeddings of one cycle in another, as we saw in Chapter Seven, and in the interest of a unified perspective on the song's structure, it makes sense to locate the whole-step sequences of the vocal line within a T5 cycle. We could illustrate this by taking diagrams of T5 cycles and circling alternate notes, to show the collection shifting between circled and uncircled notes in alternate phrases.

Indeed, an intercyclic connection is inherent in the interaction of individual chords with concurrent melody notes. Because alternate notes in any quartal or quintal chord are related by whole step, it is of course possible that a nearby whole-step melodic sequence will state alternate notes in the chords—a tangible illustration of the embedding of whole steps within a T5 cycle. And close inspection reveals that Ives often does use alternate chord tones as melody notes, as a kind of harmonization of the melody. The song's first two melodic pitches, for example, reflect alternate notes from the accompanying chord, chord 1. But the third melodic pitch is a "nonchord tone," an upper neighbor to the harmonized G# just before and after, and an extension of the cycle beyond its literal

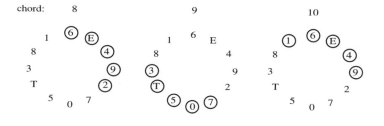

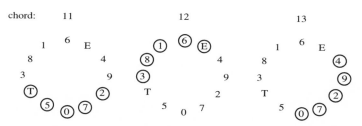

Example 8.4. "The Cage," relationships between chords 8 through 13

presence in chord 1. Other chords also imply extensions: chord 2 accompanies an F♯ chord tone and E non–chord tone, chord 4 accompanies F and G chord tones and an A non–chord tone, and so forth. In all, only chord 17 does not harmonize any of the notes it accompanies; all the other chords include at least one, and often all of the concurrent notes in the melody.

The harmonization technique also applies to the meal chords. Chord 7, which is T5(F), contains the important pc 9, on which the voice comes to a brief rest, and chord 19, which is not a transposition of chord F but which recaptures the effect of it, also contains the pc 9 where the voice makes its longest pause, on the word *wonder*. Chord 19 stands in curious contrast to the accompaniment as a whole, because it includes almost no sounds that would associate it with the predominant quartal harmonies. Rather, chord 19 is constructed of two augmented triads stating a complete odd whole-tone collection in the highest register (B–D♯–G plus A–C♯–F) and other whole-tone subsets below, thus mirroring aspects of the melodic structure. The augmented triads may be tied in with the cyclic metaphor not only as subsets of the whole-step cycles that are embedded in the T5 cycles, but also as cycles unto themselves: T4 cycles, embeddable in both T2 and T5 cycles.

Thus the cyclic pitch structures symbolize the monotony of the leopard's pacing "around its cage from one side back to the other side." But there are still other ways we can relate the music to the text, and here we move beyond the merely subtle and into the realm of the esoteric. "The Cage" is imbued with musical letter games of the type we have seen before in musical realizations of B-A-C-H and in the role of the store name in *Tone Roads No. 1* (Chapter Three). The basis of the games is the song's title and central theme—the word *cage*. Ives exploits the fact that each letter in the word is part of the musical alphabet by according musical emphasis to the notes C, A, G, and E. One aspect of this plan is inherent in the intervallic possibilities in certain arrangements of the letters. Splitting the word down the middle, for example, yields dyads that are members of ic 3: <C–A> and <G–E>. Alternate letters, <C–G> and <A–E>, are members of ic 5. Thus the word itself relates to the structure of the chords and the two main transposition levels of the chord series. Further, if we take the ic-5 dyads—<C–G> and <A–E>—and situate them within a cycle of fifths, we find only one note, D, separating them: <C–G> and <A–E> enclose or "cage in" the D. And, of course, if we include the D we have a five-note segment of the cycle of fifths, the same chord structure that dominates the accompaniment. Chord 13, the apex of the half-step ascent that begins in chord 10, states precisely these notes (C–G–D–A–E, top to bottom).

Taking the analogy a step further, the notes C-A-G-E may represent not just a specific pc set but a chord type, prime form (0358). A tetrachord of this type is, of course, a subset of all the quartal and quintal chords, but it is also present in all the meal chords, as the top four notes of chord F and chord 7, and as one of many subsets of chord 19 (though not among adjacent notes). Indeed, any expression of two ic 5 dyads that are related by T3 or T9 will be a CAGE (0358) chord type. In the introduction, for example, certain dyads from T3-related chords B and C or D and E can be combined to form CAGE chord types. To cite one of several instances, the upper dyads of chords B and C—<C♯–F♯> and <E–A>, respectively—illustrate the association of T3-related fourths to form a CAGE chord type. Analogous formations occur at the site of other direct T3 relations: chords D and E, 2 and 3, 4 and 5, 21 and 22.

But it is really the exact pitch classes of the CAGE chord that suggest the most cogent associations. The chromatic ascent from chord 10 up to chord 13, for example, not only unfolds the extended circumnavigation of the circle illustrated in Example 8.4 but also emphasizes the notes C, A, G, and E in the upper dyads: the notes A and E appear atop chord 10, starting a half-step ascent that culminates with the notes C and G atop chord 13. Chord 14 repeats chord 10 and thus the upper A and E. (Chords 15–17 then seem to echo 13 and 14, though with different intervals and with chord 16 filling in the minor-third descent.)

The four letters are also emphasized separately; they are the song's most important notes. We have already seen how the note C arrives atop chord 13 at the apex of a half-step ascent and is reiterated atop chord 15. It is the song's highest note up to that point and the highest note of any of the non–meal chords—lower only than the top of chord 19, a completely different structure. We have also remarked on the role of the note A atop the first chord in the half-step ascent (chord 10) and its repetition above chords 14 and 17. This note also plays a crucial role in the vocal line, providing points of repose at the ends of phrases 2 and 4 to emphasize crucial words in the text (*stopped* and *wonder*). And A also appears at the bottom of chord 19, as the song's lowest note. G is the song's highest note, at the top of chord 19. Finally, E appears atop chords 1 and 20, important markers in the symmetrical form, and is the last note of the vocal line. E is also the vocal line's highest pitch, first occurring in phrase 3, where it begins a whole-step descent to an E an octave lower. Perhaps this note is then reiterated as the highest note in phrase 4, even though it is foreign to the odd collection that otherwise prevails in that phrase, because a continuation of the upward whole-step sequence that phrase 4 has been presenting up to that point would progress to F, and Ives does not want to supersede E as the vocal line's highest note.

In short, the notes C, A, G, and E stand out as markers in the song's form and as registral "frames" of its pitch material. We might say they "enclose" the pitch space occupied by the song, just as the cage encloses the pacing animal. When the leopard stops a final time for a meal—at chord 19, while the text pauses to "wonder"—the chord itself is enclosed within A1 and G6. And the C and E symmetrically centered between these two pitches are nearby: C4, two octaves plus a minor third higher than A1, is also a member of chord 19, and E4, two octaves plus a minor third lower than G6, occurs prominently immediately following, as the top note of chord 20. The exact symmetrical center between A1 and G6 is not present in chord 19 or thereabouts. It is D4, the missing, or "caged" note between the dyads <C–G> and <A–E> within a cycle of fifths.

9 Combination Cycles

As we saw in Chapter Seven, Ives limits himself to the sequential use of interval cycles; he does not explore their potential as "referential collections." But his experiences with cyclic sequences surely heightened his awareness of the other issue attending composition with cycles: the limitations they impose on one's compositional resources. As we observed, few interval cycles are available, and of those, not all are equally attractive compositionally. Ives confronted this problem by developing different kinds of cyclic models that he could treat as sequences. That he did seek to enhance his language in this way is testimony to his abiding interest in systematic writing and to the importance he placed on cyclic materials to enrich his technique. If transposition cycles epitomize a "systematic" procedure, then these new ideas go one step further: they provide resources that are not only systematic but also unique.

His new approach simply introduces a second interval into a cyclic sequence— instead of repeating a single interval, the structure repeatedly alternates between one interval and another. Because the two intervals are cyclically "combined," we call this a combination cycle. Example 9.1 illustrates a combination cycle expressed in a line for the first violin from Ives's Second String Quartet. It starts with interval 6 between C and F♯, moves to interval E between F♯ and F, returns to interval 6 between F and B, returns to interval E between B and B♭, and so forth. We call this alternation between intervals 6 and E a <6E> combination cycle. Ives has various methods of determining the intervals to be alternated and thus the ultimate cyclic length, usually having something to do with aggregate completion or pc repetition or cyclic completion. In this case the intervals he uses achieve completion of the aggregate after twelve notes, at which point he breaks out of the sequence. He then restates the same pc ordering in the next twelve notes (mm. 17:4–18:2) and concludes with the first four notes of the same series (m. 18:3). The <6E> combination cycle is one of many that have meaningful compositional potential and that Ives explores throughout his systematic writing. With combination cycles Ives solves the problem of limitation, while enriching and diversifying his language and providing attractive new generators of cyclic substance.[1]

A Theory of Combination Cycles

Though the <6E> combination cycle is expressed in straight sixteenths in Example 9.1, we could impose a weighting, for illustrative purposes, that divides it into ic 6 dyads: <o6>, <5E>, <T4>, <39>, <82>, <17>. We could then pursue a unified cyclic theory by viewing these dyads as operands projected through the first six levels of a T5 cycle. Indeed, we could take a similar view of some of the transposition cycles discussed in Chapter Seven, particularly where one cycle appears embedded within another. A chromatic sequence with a whole-tone embedding, for example, could be viewed as a series of dyadic half steps projected through the levels of a T2 or T10 cycle. In the excerpt from the second *Harvest Home Chorale* shown as Example 7.11, a T10 cycle unfolds through the triad roots, and the half-step dyads are created when the third of each triad shifts from major to minor in each measure: in mm. 2–7 the dyads are <32>, <10>, <ET>, <98>, <76>, <54>. In the excerpt from *Rough and Ready* shown as Example 7.12, the accented notes in the left hand could be considered half-step operands projected through a T2 cycle: <34>, <56>, <78>, <9T>, <Eo>, <12>. Similarly, an emphasis on alternate notes in a T5 cycle could be

Example 9.1. String Quartet No. 2, 2nd mvt., 1st violin, mm. 17–18

interpreted as ic 5 operands projected through the levels of a T10 or T2 cycle. We could take this view of the brass parts in the excerpt from *Psalm 135* shown as Example 7.10, and of the excerpt from *Largo Risoluto No. 1* shown in Example 7.1, where the first violin (starting with m. 24:2) suggests ic 5 dyads projected through a T10 cycle: <7o>, <5T>, <38>, <16>, <E4>, <92>.

But in fact it will not be fruitful to encourage this kind of association between combination cycles and transposition cycles. If we did, we would simply be asserting that a combination cycle is a type of transposition cycle — that adjacent intervals in a combination cycle are important only insofar as they define the content and relationships of operands in a transposition cycle. Our method will instead treat a combination cycle as a separate kind of cycle, one with two different but equally important intervals. We thereby make combination cycles and single-interval cycles equal partners as generators of cyclic structural models. That is the way Ives seems to look at them. He uses combination cycles and single-interval cycles alongside each other and in many of the same ways. He seems to view cycles as expansions of the standard cyclic resources, not simply extensions of those already available.

We begin our investigation of combination cycles as singular phenomena by recalling the dyadic subdivisions created when a combination cycle is viewed as a projection of transposition cycle operands. We will now subdivide the sequence in a different way by extracting two cyclic "streams," one associating the first notes of the operands and the other associating all second notes. Both streams are projections of the same transposition cycle. In the <6E> combination cycle there are two streams of T5 cycles. The first starts with pc o and includes every pc in an even-numbered order position, and the second starts with pc 6 and includes all pc's in odd-numbered order positions:

op	0	1	2	3	4	5	6	7	8	9	T	E	12	13	14	15	16	17	18	19	20	21	22	23
pc	o		5		T		3		8		1		6		E		4		9		2		7	
pc		6		E		4		9		2		7		o		5		T		3		8		1

In the violin line shown in Example 9.1, Ives elects to use only the initial completion of the aggregate (op *o–E*). Thus the streams in that particular realization consist of only the first halves of the T5 cycles.

We can take the same approach to the operands implied by embeddings of one single-interval cycle within another. In the T5 sequence of *Largo Risoluto No. 1* (Ex. 9.1), for example, we extract two T10 streams:

op	0	1	2	3	4	5	6	7	8	9	T	E
pc	7		5		3		1		E		9	
pc		o		T		8		6		4		2

This shows, in effect, a T5 cycle as a <55> combination cycle. It underscores the obvious fact that both a T5 cycle and a combination cycle such as <6E> are divisible into streams but that the T5 cycle subdivides the pitch space evenly, while <6E> does not.

What we have effectively done here is subdivide streams into further streams. We started with a <6E> combination cycle, which yielded T5 streams. Now we see that those same T5 streams are further divisible into T10 streams. Thus the individual T5 streams of the <6E> combination cycle shown above can be subdivided into T10 streams as follows:

op	0	I	2	3	4	5	6	7	8	9	T	E
pc	o		T		8		6		4		2	
pc		5		3		1		E		9		7

op	0	I	2	3	4	5	6	7	8	9	T	E
pc	6		4		2		o		T		8	
pc		E		9		7		5		3		1

But we should not stop there, because a single stream of one of these cycles is itself further divisible into T8 cycles. The subdivision of the even stream <oT8642> looks like this:

op	0	I	2	3	4	5
pc	o		8		4	
pc		T		6		2

If we are truly to understand combination cycles, we must first consider how these subdivisions work. The relations between the subdivisions are revealed by the prime factors of twelve, or $2^2 \times 3$. If we take all possible combinations of these factors and divide each of them into twelve we derive all possible equal subdivisions of the aggregate—in other words, most of the standard interval cycles. First, there are five possible combinations of these factors, including the factors themselves: 2, 3, 2^2, 2×3, and $2^2 \times 3$. Thus the divisors will be 2, 3, 4 (= 2^2), 6 (= 2×3), and 12 (= $2^2 \times 3$). Our calculations will reveal both the cardinality and interval size of the resulting cycle: the divisor shows the cardinality, for it reflects the number of aggregate subdivisions, and the result shows the interval size. We start with the two single factors, 2 and 3. The calculation $12 \div 2 = 6$ reveals a T6 cycle with a cardinality of 2. In other words, a two-part equal subdivision of the aggregate is a T6 cycle. And $12 \div 3 = 4$, revealing a T4 cycle with a cardinality of 3. A three-part equal subdivision of the aggregate is a T4 cycle. We derive the other important cycles by using the other factor combinations as divisors: $12 \div 4 = 3$, revealing a T3 cycle of cardinality 4, $12 \div 6 =$

2, revealing a T2 cycle of cardinality 6, and $12 \div 12 = 1$, revealing a T1 cycle of cardinality 12. For the present purposes it will be useful to give names to these cycles: the T6 cycle will be called TRT, the T4 cycle AUG, the T3 cycle DIM, the T2 cycle WHT, and the T1 cycle CHR. Thus $12 \div 2 = $ TRT, $12 \div 3 = $ AUG, $12 \div 4 = $ DIM, $12 \div 6 = $ WHT, and $12 \div 12 = $ CHR.

From these calculations we can see how some cycles are embedded in others and thus how some cycles can potentially be divided into streams. That the integers 2 and 3 are prime confirms that the cycles revealed by these subdivisions—TRT and AUG—are not reducible to smaller cycles. But cycles derived from combinations of factors are reducible to the basic subdivisions displayed in the divisor. DIM is reducible to (2×2)—two cycles of cardinality 2. In other words, two TRTs are embedded in one DIM. We might say, 2TRT $=$ DIM. The reduction of WHT to (2×3) reveals two possible subdivisions: two cycles of cardinality 3 (2×3), or three cycles of cardinality 2 (3×2). That is, two AUGs and three TRTs are both embedded in WHT; WHT $= 2$AUG or 3TRT. Finally, the ability of CHR to host embeddings of any of the other cycles is displayed in its multiple subdivisions. One, (2×6), shows a potential subdivision into two cycles of cardinality 6 or six cycles of cardinality 2—CHR contains two WHTs or six TRTs. And of course WHT is further divisible into 2AUG or 3TRT. Mathematically, CHR $= (2 \times 6) = (2 \times (2 \times 3))$ or $(2 \times (3 \times 2))$. Another divisor is (3×4), showing a potential subdivision into three cycles of cardinality 4 or four cycles of cardinality 3—three DIMs or four AUGs. Accounting mathematically for the further divisibility of DIM into 2TRT, CHR $= (3 \times 4) = (3 \times 2^2)$. All the embeddings within CHR might be shown as follows: CHR $= 2$WHT $(= 2(2$AUG$) | 2(3$TRT$)) | 6$TRT $| 3$DIM $(= 3(2$TRT$)) | 4$AUG.

The other single-interval cycles are related to these via the operations of M, MI, or a combination. M(CHR) represents the T5 cycle, and MI(CHR) the T7 cycle; we will notate these as CHR[5] and CHR[7], respectively. Multiplicative operations also derive complementary cycles, which we will notate with an apostrophe (the complement of cycle X is X'). Thus M(AUG) $=$ the T8 cycle $=$ AUG', MI(DIM) $=$ the T9 cycle $=$ DIM', and M(WHT) $=$ the T10 cycle $=$ WHT'. That there is no TRT', because 6 is invariant under M or MI, shows that TRT has no complement. CHR' (the T11 cycle) is derived by MMI(CHR).

Now we return to combination cycles. We have seen that any cyclic structure can be reduced to the same basic roots. To see the roots of a T5 cycle, for example, we would first view it as M(CHR), and then reduce CHR to its prime factors. To find the roots of a combination cycle we simply add an additional first step of separating alternate notes into streams of transposition cycles. Then we break down the streams as we would any transposition cycle. For

<6E> we start by extracting T5 streams, and then trace the roots of T5 to M(CHR) and the various subdivisions of CHR, as usual.

When examining a combination cycle, it is always easy to know what cycle is projected in the streams, because this integer is the sum (mod 12) of the two intervals in the combination. In the case of <6E>, $6 + E = 5$. Since all combinations that sum to the same integer will have streams based on the same cycles, we may group these together as a kind of equivalence class. For example, the class of combination cycles with T5 streams includes <6E>, <7T>, <89>, <E6>, <05>, <14>, and <23> (and their retrogrades). Since all the pairs sum to the same number, this sum is in effect an index number reflecting the value of n under TnI. In other words, the contents of any given class are also TnI pairs.

But a complete listing of all members of a certain class may be more a theoretical summary than a compositional resource, because not all possible combination cycles are compositionally attractive. Some do not come close to generating the pitch-class variety that Ives usually values. To examine pitch-class variety in combination cycles, we will refer to the number of pitch classes a combination cycle generates prior to a repetition as its pitch-class length (PCL). We can make some generalizations about the PCL by focusing on the content and structure of the streams within a given combination cycle.

First let us take a look at some combination cycles with WHT streams. In an <86> combination, the WHT streams are pc equivalent. They are different rotations of the same T2 cycle:

op	0	1	2	3	4	5	6	7	8	9	T	E
pc	0		2		4		6		8		T	
pc		8		T		0		2		4		6

But in a <95> combination cycle, the WHT streams are complementary. This combination cycle completes the aggregate by alternating even and odd pitch classes:

op	0	1	2	3	4	5	6	7	8	9	T	E
pc	0		2		4		6		8		T	
pc		9		E		1		3		5		7

It is easy to tell with WHT streams whether they will be equivalent or complementary. If the two combined intervals sum to an even number, the streams are equivalent; otherwise, they are complementary.

All combination cycles containing streams with fewer than twelve elements will offer these same options—streams of WHT('), DIM('), AUG('), or TRT will be either equivalent or complementary. But of course streams with twelve elements—CHR('), CHR⁵, and CHR⁷—cannot be complementary and are always equivalent. In the exploration of cyclic PCLs, it will be useful to separate combination cycles into two groups, according to stream content: those with complementary streams and those with equivalent streams.

In cycles with complementary streams, the PCL is equal to twice the cardinality of one stream. Thus the maximum PCL for a combination cycle with WHT (or WHT') streams is 12, the maximum for DIM (or DIM') streams is 8, the maximum for AUG (or AUG') streams is 6, and the maximum for TRT streams is 4. A WHT(') complementation, such as we saw in the <95> cycle above, is a familiar juxtaposition of even and odd pitch classes. A DIM(') complementation always creates an octatonic collection. Complementations of AUG(') will produce either a whole-tone collection or sc 6–20 (014589), one of the all-combinatorial hexachords. And complementations of TRT will produce either sc 4–28 (0369), the set class of which DIM(') is a member, or sc 4–9 (0167) or 4–25 (0268), two familiar post-tonal tetrachords.

In cycles with equivalent streams, the PCL is widely variable according to the disposition of the pitch classes in the streams. To illustrate, let us return to the <86> combination and its WHT streams, which we examined earlier. The PCL of <86> is 5. Its first pc repetition occurs at op 5 (repeating op 0), which is the third note in the odd stream. We may derive other possible PCL values from these same streams by rotating one of them. For example, one rotation of the odd stream (so that it starts with pc 6) would yield a <68> combination cycle with a PCL of 6:

op	0	1	2	3	4	5	6	7	8	9	T	E
pc	0		2		4		6		8		T	
pc		6		8		T		0		2		4

But a rotation of the odd stream so that it begins on pc 0 yields a <02> cycle, with a PCL of only 1:

op	0	1	2	3	4	5	6	7	8	9	T	E
pc	0		2		4		6		8		T	
pc	0		2		4		6		8		T	

From this we can infer the range of possible PCL values for combination cycles with equivalent streams. The minimum is of course 1, as shown in <02>. In a combination with a minimal PCL, the notes of the odd stream simply echo the pitch classes that immediately precede them in the even stream. The maximum is the cardinality of one stream, as shown in the PCL of 6 for <68>. To achieve this, the streams must be rotated to maximize their differences at any given point in the cycle. In the case of <68>, any six adjacencies starting on an even op are all different pitch classes (for example, op *0–5, 2–7, 4–9,* and so on).

And there are always other rotations that will express all other PCLs lying between 1 and the maximum.

Naturally, the same is true for CHR('), CHR^5, and CHR^7 streams. Their possible PCLs range from one up to the cardinality of one stream, 12, and include all numbers in between. These combinations are particularly appealing to Ives because they provide a variety of ways to generate a large number of pitch classes. We saw one of them in Example 9.1, where CHR^5 streams are rotated so that the first halves of the streams have no common tones and thus present the aggregate. This and other cycles based on twelve-element streams are listed in Example 9.2, along with their PCLs. The columns of cycles in the table show every possible combination for each of the four streams. The rows list combination cycles with the same PCL, showing the four ways of expressing every PCL value from 1 through 12. Naturally, Ives has no use for the cycles with low PCL values, but he takes an active interest in those with higher ones, roughly those with PCLs higher than 8. When we consider these many promising new possibilities alongside some cycles with complementary streams, we can see the extent to which he has enriched his compositional language. He has overcome the limitations of the transposition cycles alone, while remaining faithful to his systematic priorities.

Some Realizations of Combination Cycles

We saw earlier how a combination cycle, such as that shown in Example 9.1, can be reinterpreted as a transposition cycle with dyadic operands. The con-

STREAMS = CHR	STREAMS = CHR'	STREAMS = CHR^5	STREAMS = CHR^7	PCL
<01>	<0E>	<05>	<07>	1
<10>	<E0>	<50>	<70>	2
<2E>	<T1>	<T7>	<25>	4
<3T>	<92>	<32>	<9T>	6
<49>	<83>	<89>	<43>	8
<58>	<74>	<14>	<E8>	10
<67>	<65>	<6E>	<61>	12
<76>	<56>	<E6>	<16>	11
<85>	<47>	<41>	<8E>	9
<94>	<38>	<98>	<34>	7
<T3>	<29>	<23>	<T9>	5
<E2>	<1T>	<7T>	<52>	3

Example 9.2. Combination cycles based on twelve-element streams

verse is also true: some of the transposition cycles we looked at in Chapter Seven have dyadic operands that can be reinterpreted as separate intervals in a combination cycle. In the right hand of the excerpt from *Study No. 8* shown in Example 7.13, for example, the broken minor thirds moving upward by half steps effectively project a <94> combination cycle. The streams are, of course, CHR, and the PCL is 7. In part 1 of the excerpt, the pitch classes are as follows:

op	0	1	2	3	4	5	6	7	8	9	T	E
pc	4		5		6		7		8		9	
pc		1		2		3		4		5		6

Example 7.12 shows an excerpt from *Rough and Ready* in which accented notes suggest an unfolding of two notes per operand. In the left hand, as we noted, the accented notes project a 2:1 chromatic:whole-tone embedding. But in the right hand the accents highlight members of a <37> combination cycle. The streams are WHT', and since the cyclic intervals are odd, we know that the pc content of the streams is complementary and thus the PCL is 12. The complete sequence (mm. 8:1–15:1, repeated down an octave in mm. 15:2–22:2) is

op	0	1	2	3	4	5	6	7	8	9	T	E
pc	0		T		8		6		4		2	
pc		3		5		7		9		E		1

And in the excerpt from "The See'r" shown in Example 7.14, the lowest voice unfolds an octatonic sequence that might be viewed as a <TE> combination cycle. Thus complementary DIM' streams express a PCL of 8:

op	0	1	2	3	4	5	6	7
pc	2		E		8		5	
pc		0		9		6		3

We have also seen alternating interval sequences in some of Ives's earlier music. The alternation of major and minor thirds in verse 4 of *Psalm 24,* for example, could be understood as an expression of a <43> combination cycle (see Chapter Four).[2] Leitmotif III in *Psalm 90* is an expression of this same combination cycle (see Ex. 4.10). And the source orderings of the chords in *Chromâtimelôdtune* alternate intervals 7 and 6 (see Ex. 5.10A). Though in our earlier discussion we treated the A and B chords as two separate sequences, we can now unite them into a single <76> combination cycle, with the A chord displayed in the first six notes (op *0–5*) and the B chord in the remainder:

op	0	1	2	3	4	5	6	7	8	9	T	E	12
pc	0		1		2		3		4		5		6
pc		7		8		9		T		E		0	

These CHR streams achieve a PCL of 11, the first repetition occurring at op *E* (pc *0*, repeating op *0*). We extend the model to op *12* to reach the twelfth pitch class and thereby explain the presence of pc o in both the A and B chords.

Rather than dwell on the many appearances of individual combination cycles in Ives's work, we will mention just two of them before moving to more extensive usages. The first is the clarinet line from *Over the Pavements* (1906–1913) shown in Example 9.3. A <47> cycle, based on CHR' streams, expresses a PCL of 9:

op	0	1	2	3	4	5	6	7	8	9	T	E	12
pc	E		T		9		8		7		6		5
pc		3		2		1		0		E		T	

In the first three measures of the excerpt the notes are stated in consistent three-sixteenth durations. The end of the PCL, the pc 7 in m. 22, is marked by a rhythmic change to sixteenths. The sixteenths continue for the remainder of the passage, as the line moves into repetitions of pc's E and T (op's *9* and *E*, first stated as op's *0* and *2*). Ives could have completed the aggregate (with repetitions in the odd stream) by extending to just one more note in the even stream (pc 4, op "*14*").

A second simple example is a particular combination cycle that recurs meaningfully throughout *In Re Con Moto Et Al*. The form of the work is organized around the number series 2-3-5-8-11-8-5-3-2 variously expressed as patterns of meter changes, phrase lengths, or rhythmic groupings.[3] To articulate the beginning of each realization of the series, Ives uses what he calls the Grit Chord (GC).[4] The GC is (bottom to top) pc <071829T4>: its first six notes arise from an alternation of intervals 7 and 6. Additionally, the GC is usually associated with a four-note sonority containing the four pc's that are absent from GC (E356). We might call this chord the Grit Chord Complement (GCC). The affiliation between GC and GCC can be explained by locating each in a <76> combination cycle starting on pc o, identical to the one used as the source

Example 9.3. *Over the Pavements,* clarinet (concert pitch), mm. 18–22

ordering for the A and B chords in *Chromâtimelôdtune* (illustrated in Ex. 5.10A). The GC is op's *0* through *5* and *7* and *8* of the <76> cycle, in order from bottom to top, and the GCC is some ordering of op's *6, 9, T*, and *12*. Pitch-class o in op *E* is excluded from GCC, presumably because it repeats op *0*. In using this chord pair to help articulate the number series, Ives introduces an element of stability and predictability into an otherwise chaotic composition.

The Ives Omnibus

As our journey through Ives's compositional language nears its conclusion, it is appropriate to examine a particular structural model that brings together many of the concepts and procedures we have visited along the way. We call this model the Ives Omnibus because it unites so many of the composer's most valued compositional principles.[5] The Ives Omnibus is a series of musical entities, often simultaneities, ordered according to a pattern of gradual, incremental structural change. It is usually realized as a series of vertical displays of transposition cycles or combination cycles placed in order according to a gradual expansion or reduction in the sizes of the formative intervals. For example, a typical Omnibus realization might begin with a chord of stacked interval 7s, followed by a chord stacking a <76> combination cycle, followed by a chord stacking a <65> combination cycle, followed by a chord stacking interval 5s, and so forth. (It could also start with smaller intervals and progress to larger ones.) Often the series reaches some kind of extreme of interval size and is then restated in reverse, to make the entire model a palindrome. Thus does the Omnibus bring together the main features of systematic composition: it is a carefully calculated structural model based on a self-generating, pitch-class-saturated transformational pattern.

The closest relatives of the Omnibus among our earlier topics of study are the structural models of Chapter Four. The pattern of gradual change in the Omnibus resembles the sequence of gradually growing or shrinking distances between voices in a wedge, although the Omnibus does not necessarily outline the shape of a wedge between its outer voices—the pattern of change in the Omnibus may occur within relatively consistent pitch-space boundaries. And when the Omnibus pattern repeats as a palindrome, the result can be a symmetrical structure of the strictest kind. Among the pieces mentioned earlier, *Psalm 24* comes closest to suggesting an Omnibus progression, as the intervallic bases of verses gradually grow larger and then smaller (see Chapter Four). Also, we saw a brief Omnibus sequence in the center of the palindromic form of "Soliloquy" (see Ex. 4.14).

Perhaps Ives first began thinking about the idea of the Omnibus during his early experiments with wedges and "chords of decreasing intervals," as notated in his father's copybook (see Ex. 1.2). A short time later he applied the idea mostly in linear structures in *Psalm 24*. Toward the end of this early period in his development, he wrote *Processional: "Let There Be Light"* (1902–1903), a work for chorus and organ or strings that is apparently his first realization of the Omnibus model as a series of vertical structures, and that shows the basic ideas that would become central to later Omnibus realizations. Example 9.4A gives the score of the first section of the work. The *Processional* continues following this excerpt with an organ interlude (mm. 19–24) that states a series of chords with a rapid contraction in interval sizes, and the work concludes (mm. 25–33) with a restatement of ideas from the initial Omnibus but with note values reduced by half.

Example 9.4B summarizes the structure of the passage. The pitch-class content of each chord, excluding the "nonessential" tones that are circled in the score, is enclosed in curly brackets. Each is arranged to start on 0—to reflect the C pedal that underlies the passage—and illustrates the ordering of the notes from low to high in the instrumental parts. The vocal parts mostly state some of the same notes but necessarily contract some chords into a narrower range.

Beneath the pitch-class notations in Example 9.4B are descriptions of the intervallic content of the chords. The Omnibus progression begins with octaves in mm. 1–2, moves to a mixture of major and minor seconds in m. 3, a mixture of thirds forming a mm7 chord in m. 4, and a stacking of interval 3 in m. 5. (The notation <x> indicates a repetition of interval x.) The process of growth continues until the arrival at octaves again at m. 18. The sense of the progression is clear; nevertheless, some of the details of that progression betray a flexibility of application that is less apparent in later Omnibus realizations. Whereas the chords in roughly the second half of the passage (starting with m. 9) are mostly consistent stackings of particular intervals or intervallic combinations, some of the chords in the first half are not so systematically structured: the diatonic cluster in m. 3, the mm7 chord in m. 4, and the major triad in m. 8. Further, in the chords that do apply systematic procedures, Ives does not seem concerned with cyclic completion, or, at least, completion of the PCL. The T_5 cycle in m. 9 stops two notes shy of completion; the <65> combination cycle in m. 10 has only eight notes, though its PCL is 12; the T_7 cycle in m. 11 states only seven notes; the <98> combination in m. 13 states six notes, though with one more note (pc 3) it could complete its PCL; the <ET> combination in m. 16 stops two notes short of its PCL of 8, which would be a complete octatonic collection; and the T_{11} cycle in m. 17 states just six notes. Of course, in many cases cyclic completion is inhibited by instrumental ranges. Nevertheless, in some later Omnibus realizations the continuation of a cycle to its conclusion, and

A. mm. 1–18

Example 9.4. Excerpt from *Processional*

m.	1-2	3	4	5	6	7
*pc:	{0}	{024579E}	{037T}	{0369}	{037T259}	{048}
**int:	8ves	"2nds"	mm7	<3>	<34>	<4>

m.	8	9	10	11	12
*pc:	{047}	{05T3816E49}	{06E5T493}	{07294E6}	{084}
**int:	M triad	<5>	<65>	<7>	<8>

m.	13	14	15	16	17	18
*pc:	{0952T7}	{0963}	{0T8642}	{0E9865}	{0ET987}	{0}
**int:	<98>	<9>	<T>	<ET>	<E>	8ves

*pc content starting on C (except circled notes)
**interval content

B. structure of chords in Example 9.4A
Example 9.4. (*continued*)

often the completion of the aggregate, become higher priorities; Ives finds ways to make them happen.

Few works by Ives are as consistently structured around the Omnibus as is the *Processional*. More common are isolated appearances of Omnibus patterns in pieces that are more stylistically or structurally diverse. In some cases there is but a hint of the model, as we saw in the palindromic center of "Soliloquy." For another such example we turn again to the work for full orchestra that is most dependent on systematic methods, *The Fourth of July*. Example 9.5 shows one measure from the string parts in which there is a rapid succession of stacked intervals E, 9, 7, 5, and <544>, followed by a half-step cluster.[6] It is a fleeting moment, perhaps a wisp of smoke from a single pyrotechnic blast, anticipating the huge explosions when the celebration becomes more boisterous later (see Exx. 5.7 and 5.8). In comparison to *Processional* (differences in scope aside), this version of the Omnibus is more attentive to the resulting registral shape. Here the voices literally converge as a wedge, mirroring the reduction in interval sizes. This result occurs naturally when the number of voices forming the chords remains constant.

intervals:	E	9	7	5	4	half-step
	E	9	7	5	4	cluster
	E	9	7	5	5	
	E	9	7	5		

Example 9.5. *The Fourth of July, m. 20, 3rd and 4th violins, viola, cello*

In *Tone Roads No. 3* (1915) a similar outlining of wedge shapes by Omnibus chords has a more explicit programmatic meaning. As Ives explains in *Memos,* an expanding and then contracting wedge in this work symbolizes the acceleration and deceleration of a subway train between stations.[7] Example 9.6 is the work's clearest depiction of this image, with four-voice chords moving through stackings of single intervals 1 through 11 and back again. Here the registral shape is so important that Ives willingly sacrifices pitch-class variety by including pitch-class repetitions where the size of the cycle is smaller than the number of voices—in the chords formed of intervals 4, 6, and 8. Elsewhere in the piece Ives depicts the wedging in less precise ways, by offering rough suggestions of the basic shape, as he does in the strings immediately following the passage shown in Example 9.6 (mm. 27–30). And the first main section of the piece concludes (in mm. 10–12) with a series of chords producing a general contraction that is at times obscured by complexities of rhythm and instrumentation.

As with cycles themselves, Ives often ascribes some kind of metaphorical significance to the Omnibus. In *Central Park in the Dark,* a repeating chord series in the strings represents "night sounds and silent darkness," providing a backdrop for a "picture-in-sounds of the sounds of nature and of happenings that men would hear . . . when sitting on a bench in Central Park on a hot summer night."[8] The first statement of the chord series is shown in Example 9.7. It is anchored on the four sustained notes in the bass line: A♭ (mm. 1–2), B♭ (mm. 3–5), F♯ (mm. 6–8), and E♭ (mm. 9–10). In the other parts, a chord formed at the beginning of each new bass note is repeated at various transposition levels

Example 9.6. *Tone Roads No. 3,* mm. 24–26

until the bass note changes, at which time a new chord is formed and then trans-posed. Thus we can look at the chord that occurs where each of the four bass notes begins to examine the harmonic structure of the entire passage. The inter-vallic structures of these chords are (bottom to top): m. 1:1, <44644>; m. 3:1, <55555>; m. 6:1, <676767>; and m. 9:1, <777777>.

It contains only a hint of the Omnibus model, but the sense of the pattern emerges in the way it is developed. Because each chord occurs several times at various transposition levels, the unfolding dwells on and features the different sounds. The transpositions of the first chord (mm. 1–2) form a palindromic arrangement of five sonorities that alternates between even and odd whole-tone collections. The remaining chords are not systematically arranged but move through the various transpositions to highlight the parallel movement under-lying the upper melodic line. Indeed, at the end of the passage we become aware of Ives's attention to the melodic line, as he writes a structurally inconsistent top note above the final chord: F♯5 (or G♭5) would be the expected top note above the stacking of fifths underneath, but instead Ives writes D♭5. The unexpected note is the only pitch class that has not occurred previously in the top line.

Example 9.7. *Central Park in the Dark,* mm. 1–10, strings

Other methods by which Ives realizes and develops the Omnibus model usually focus attention on the rhythm of the presentation in some way. In a portion of the *Robert Browning Overture,* for example, the violins present Omnibus intervals in arpeggiated four-note chords projecting intervals 1 through 7, and back to 1 (for example, mm. 124:4–127:4). Perhaps Ives's most integrated use of rhythm in an Omnibus realization is in the Cadenza of *Over the Pavements* (mm. 81–92). While the piano arpeggiates "wide-jumps" intervals, the winds present chords whose durations reflect their traditional labels: major sevenths in durations of seven sixteenths, major sixths in durations of six sixteenths (dotted quarters), perfect fifths in durations of five sixteenths, perfect fourths in durations of four sixteenths (quarter notes), major thirds in durations of three sixteenths, and major seconds in durations of two sixteenths (eighth notes).[9] In addition, the number of chords stated of each type increases by one each time the chord changes.

Rhythm also plays a role in a variant of the Omnibus model presented in the first main section of *In Re Con Moto Et Al*, just after the unfolding of T5 cycles we saw in the first measure (Example 7.4), and just prior to the first appearance of the Grit Chord and its complement. Example 9.8 shows a reduced score of the passage. The chord structures, as labeled beneath the score, start with fourths and fifths in mm. 2 and 3, move to combinations of slightly smaller intervals in mm. 4:1–5:4, and return to larger single-interval chords in mm. 5:5–6:4.[10] This suggestion of a brief contraction-expansion is supported by the durations of the chords, as indicated above the score in terms of eighth notes in mm. 2:1–5:1 and in terms of sixteenths thereafter. The resulting durational sequence 11-7-5-3-2-3-5-7-9 thus represents the first hint of the number series that is the basis for the work's overall design.

Further, these sonorities are related in a kind of wraparound process reminiscent of the unfolding of T5 cycles in the measure just preceding this passage (Ex. 7.4). The T5 cycle progresses upward in chord A (pc <1[E]6E4927>)

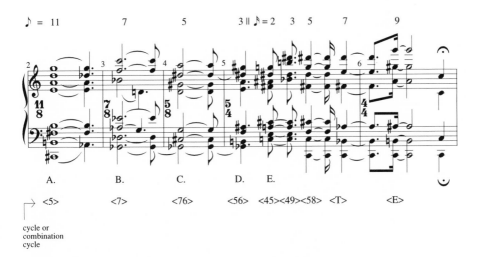

Example 9.8. *In Re Con Moto Et Al*, mm. 2–6, two-stave reduction

before wrapping around to the top of chord B and progressing downward to complete the cycle (pc <05T3816>). Subsequently, chord B's bass-note pc 6 is held over to m. 4 to serve as the anchor of chord C, making a connection between the lowest notes of chords B and C that complements the connection between the highest notes of A and B. And this weaving pattern continues subsequently, as the upper notes of the <76> combination cycle of chord C wrap around to the upper notes of the <56> combination cycle of D. This includes common tones <839> at the top of both chords: pc <6172839> going upwards in chord C, continued by pc <8394T5E6> going downwards in chord D to complete the <76> combination cycle. Finally, if the sequence of chord D were to continue downward, the next note would be pc 0, the bass note of chord E. This marks the end of the weaving and the wraparounds, as pc 0 remains in the bass for the rest of the passage.

We conclude this survey of Omnibus realizations with the song "On the Antipodes." This song has a transparent structure and has become one of the composer's most studied works.[11] Nonetheless, we owe it further attention because it so lucidly crystallizes Ives's perspective on combination cycles, the Omnibus, and systematic composition in general. The frequent appearances in the song of cycles and the Omnibus tie in closely with Ives's text, which refers to polar opposites in nature and their reflection of and relations with human existence. According to the text, nature is both relentless and kind; Eternity and today; geometry and mystery; man's master and man's slave; man's enemy and man's friend. Nature shows us both "part of life" and "all the grave." In the end Ives asks two cosmic questions: "Does Nature know the beginning of Time or the ending of Space?" and "Man! we ask you! Is nature nothing but atomic cosmic cycles around the perennial antipodes?" Thus does the composer bring together many of his most deeply contemplated metaphysical ideas. He invokes nature as a symbol of the structure and complexity of existence, as he does in "Soliloquy" (discussed in Chapter Four), and as a thing of such vast scope that it encompasses polar opposites. These themes are symbolized by cycles in the Second String Quartet, as we noted earlier, and the cyclic aspects of the Omnibus serve similar purposes in "On the Antipodes."

Example 9.9 shows the occurrence of the Omnibus in the song's opening measures, with chords labeled beneath the score according to pitch-class content.[12] Example 9.10 identifies the chords according to intervallic content. This version of the Omnibus begins with stacked fifths (chord A), moves through stackings of <76> (chord B), <65> (C), <5> (D), and so forth, stacking gradually smaller intervals until it arrives at a half-step cluster at the midpoint (chord K). These chords next appear in reverse order with three variations: the third chord in m. 3, where we expect a second occurrence of J, is instead J transposed down a whole step (labeled J'); the fourth chord in m. 3 is not chord I as expected but is a T2 cycle, labeled L; and the last chord of the passage is a stacking of interval 11s, labeled M, instead of the sequentially consistent chord A. But A does reappear at the beginning of the following measure (m. 5), accompanying the initial entrance of the voice. In sum, the sequence projects circularity both in the individual cyclic structures and in the ordering of the chords so that they "cycle back" palindromically to their starting points.

The gradual reduction of interval sizes is best understood if we view each cycle as a sum of two adjacent intervals; these sums are indicated just below the cycle labels in Example 9.10. Here we can better see the progression from chord A, sum 14, to chord K, sum 2, and back, concluding at sum 22 for chord M. The only integers from 2 through 14 that are missing from the sequence are those which generate a small number of pitch classes: sum 12 would simply be a stacking of two intervals that together form an octave, and thus would have no pitch-class variety, and sum 8 would be similarly limited, perhaps just an augmented triad. Otherwise, the cycles that Ives does select generally contain higher PCLs, as shown in the bottom line of the chart. The only one with a PCL lower than 6 is chord G, a <24> combination cycle. This chord is rhythmically de-emphasized both times it occurs.

Unlike in the earlier *Processional,* Ives often sees the cycles to their completions or to the ends of their PCLs. Chord A falls two notes short of being complete, but the <76> cycle in chord B extends beyond its PCL to state the first repeated pitch class (pc 7) at the top and bottom, chord C states the complete twelve-note PCL of a <65> cycle, chord D states a complete T5 cycle plus two repeated notes, and so forth. And the chords do effect a rough registral wedge, with the sole significant disruption being the huge cluster in the center.

By contrast, Ives seems less concerned about cyclic completion and wedge shape than he is about the pitch-class content of the upper voice. He structures the chords so that the first thirteen notes of the upper voice (atop chords A through L) present the aggregate with one repetition (pc 10, above chords E and J). This would also help explain two of the changes he makes to chords in the second half of the model. The top note in the axis chord (K), pc 3, is the tenth pitch class to be presented. As the second half begins, pc's 8 and 0 remain to be stated in the upper voice. But since these would never occur if the first half of the model were simply repeated, Ives changes the next two chords after K accordingly: he transposes J down a whole step so that its top note is pc 8, and he replaces I with a chord (L) that has the same sum (4) and PCL (6) as I but that has pc 0 as its top note.

After chord M, the voice enters and the accompaniment begins an elaborated version of the Omnibus that continues throughout the song. Rather than being

Example 9.9. "On the Antipodes," mm. 1–4. © 1935 Merion Music, Inc. Used by Permission.

chord:	A	B	C	D	E	F	G	H	I	J	K
cycle:	<7>	<76>	<65>	<5>	<54>	<43>	<24>	<32>	<31>	<12>	<1>
sums:	14	13	11	10	9	7	6	5	4	3	2
PCL:	12	11	12	12	8	8	4	6	6	8	12

chord:	J'	L	H	G	F	E	D	C	B	M
cycle:	<12>	<2>	<32>	<24>	<43>	<54>	<5>	<65>	<76>	<E>
sums:	3	4	5	6	7	9	10	11	13	22
PCL:	8	6	6	4	8	8	12	12	11	12

Example 9.10. Structure of Example 9.9

stated as a verticality, each chord is essentially arpeggiated and sometimes developed slightly.[13] The chords are presented in this way in their original order up through J' (m. 13), at which point an interruption parodies tonal conventions, setting the text "Sometimes Nature's nice and sweet, as a little pansy" (mm. 14–17). This is followed by a second chordal statement of the complete model, just like that at the beginning of the song, except in shorter durations (mm. 18–19). The arpeggiated Omnibus resumes, stating chords L, H, G, and so forth, back to B, and concludes on M (mm. 20–27). After this, the Omnibus is stated one final time as chords, as the voice asks its key question about "atomic cosmic cycles." Thus in the entire song, only the passage of tonal comic relief (mm. 14–17) is not directly derived from the Omnibus model. The Omnibus articulates the song's structure both broadly, in the unfolding and expansiveness of the arpeggiated version, and compactly, in the three chordal versions that become formal signposts and microcosms of the larger design.

The complete score of the final chordal Omnibus is shown in Example 9.11. The text is proclaimed in the pc ordering we discussed back in Chapter Five (Ex. 5.5), an aggregate partitioned into equivalent trichords.[14] As shown in the letter labels beneath the score, the intervals Ives uses to construct the Omnibus chords are essentially the same as those for the earlier versions (Exx. 9.9 and 9.10), except that chords I and L exchange places, J is the same on both sides of the center, and the realization concludes on chord A, not M. But in the way these chords are structured, this version departs significantly from the earlier ones. Each chord is anchored on pc 0, supported by an organ pedal. And Ives places much greater emphasis on cyclic completion and completion of the aggregate than he has. In the first four chords, for example: the A chord is a complete stacking of interval 7; the B chord is the eleven-note PCL of the <76> combination cycle plus the first repetition, pc 0, at the top of the chord; the C chord is the complete twelve-note PCL of the <65> cycle; and the D chord is a complete stacking of interval 5. The other chords, except K, have smaller PCLs, but they all state as many pitch classes as possible, often returning to pc 0. For example, chord E completes its eight-note PCL and then reiterates its first three notes at the top, and chord H completes its eight-note PCL and continues repeating until pc 0 returns, at which point (in m. 30) the cycle continues in a downward direction.

Other sonorities have moments of cyclic imprecision, but the overall progression is clear: the chords cycle upward from pc 0 and eventually return to that pitch class, either literally, at the top of the chord, or figuratively, in an implied connection from the top of one chord to the bass note of the next one. Rather than a wraparound or weaving process, it is a vivid portrayal of the circularity that is central both to the Omnibus itself and to the main ideas in the text.

Example 9.11. "On the Antipodes," mm. 28–34. © 1935 Merion Music, Inc. Used by Permission.

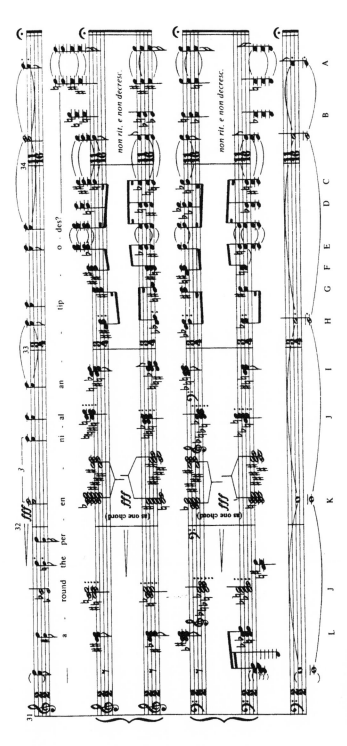

Example 9.11. (continued)

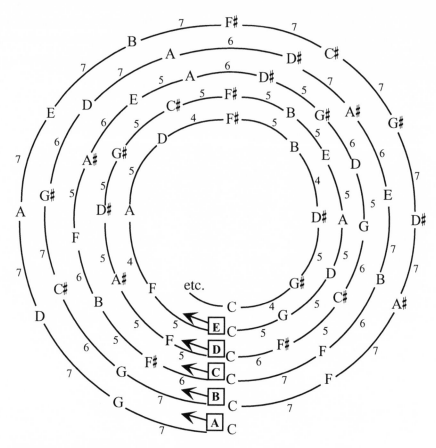

Example 9.12. Omnibus spiral

Example 9.12 notates this process as a spiral. Chord A, a T7 cycle, forms the spiral's outer layer, and its return to pc o after a complete revolution coincides with the beginning of the next chord, the <76> combination cycle of chord B, on the next inner layer. Each successive layer corresponds to each subsequent chord, following the process of gradual reduction in sums, so that each member of the chordal cycle is represented by one revolution. (It is the progression of sums, not any pattern of change in PCL or chord size, that the spiral most vividly portrays.) The chords spiral "inward" in the first half of the pattern and reverse direction to return to the outer layer at the conclusion of the realization.

It is hard to imagine a more trenchant metaphor for the "atomic cosmic cycles" of nature. The spiral is "atomic" in the structure and ordering of its individual layers, reflecting the sequence of intervallic content within the Omnibus. But it is also "cosmic" in its encapsulation of formal processes in the song as a whole. And surely the structures of this formal macrocosm symbolize the cosmic cycles in nature itself, such as life cycles and planetary orbits. Just as nature realizes an organic unity between these cosmic realities and the smallest microscopic phenomena—just as natural laws reconcile vast differences between polar opposites—so does "On the Antipodes" embrace a single structural law in its smallest details and broadest gestures. Again Ives calls upon cycles, with their implications of circularity and universality, to communicate some of his deepest philosophical and spiritual messages. There is no clearer example, in his music, of a systematic manner expressing ideas of great substance.

The song also expresses Ives's view that nature is vast and complex, but ultimately penetrable—that nature has an order and logic that is not visible on the surface. Like his systematic music, the structure of nature becomes apparent only after close scrutiny, and only if considered with a mind open to its idiosyncrasies and singular laws of organization. In "On the Antipodes" and elsewhere, the Omnibus becomes a kind of idealized musical organization of these ideas—not only a presentation of the cycles but a manner of presenting them that is as orderly and logical as nature itself. These are themes Ives would explore in a most eclectic and grandiose way in his *Universe Symphony*. We conclude our journey in the next chapter with a tour of Ives's *Universe*.

10 "A Universe in Tones"

In our ascent of this mountain of craft and ingenuity, we have followed paths leading to the technical core of Ives's substance. We have paused to take in some of the metaphorical allusions that his methods help to create. And we have been guided by the substance of the man himself, the musical values and spiritual beliefs that lie at the heart of his artistic imagination. As we approach the summit, a view emerges, encompassing all the paths we have traveled and places we have visited, a single vista that gives unity and context to the full range of his musical and philosophical ideals. It is the view of an ambitious and monumental work Ives called the *Universe Symphony*. Like the four men in the Second String Quartet who heed the call of the mountains and "view the firmament," we conclude our own ascent with a look at Ives's *Universe*.

Indeed, the symphony was also a kind of conclusion for Ives. He first began working on it sometime early in the second decade of this century, but it seems to have occupied his thoughts both during his composing years and later; in early 1932 he said of the symphony, "I haven't worked on this since [1915], but hope to finish it this summer" (*Memos,* 106). Though he never completed the work, the *Universe Symphony*—or at least the *idea* of the *Universe Symphony*—looms as a goal toward which many of his creative energies are ultimately directed. One might even suggest that he wrote compositions of narrower scope as "warm-ups" for the more substantive creation that was always in the back of his mind—that he continued working through ideas until he felt they were complete and he was ready to bring them all together. Meanwhile his philosophical ideas were also evolving and no doubt suggesting potential musical parallels. The work he conceived would be the ultimate, ideal application of systematic methods: the *Universe Symphony* would be constructed from Ives's best and most sophisticated principles of organization, and it would use these methods to communicate his deepest and most substantial spiritual beliefs.[1]

Ives explains his conception of the symphony in a marginal inscription on one of the sketch pages: "The 'Universe in Tones,' or a Universe Symphony. A striving to present and to contemplate in tones rather than in music as such— that is, not exactly within the general term or meaning as it is so understood— to paint the creation, the mysterious beginnings of all things, known through God to man, to trace with tonal imprints the vastness, the evolution of all life, in nature of humanity from the great roots of life to the spiritual eternities, from the great inknown to the great unknown."[2] On another page he explains the main ideas in a little more depth:

> As the eternities are unmeasured, as the sources of universal substances are unknown—the earth, the waters, the stars, the ether—yet these elements as man can touch them with hand and microscope, and label them as chemicals and atoms as the eternal motions, life of all things. . . . They are not single and exclusive strains, but incessant myriads for ages ever and always changing growing, but for ages ever and always a permanence in humanity of the earth for a man's lifetime of life and death and future life—the only known is the unknown, the only hope of humanity is the unseen spirit. What can't be done but what we are reaching out to do (as we feel like trying it) is to cast eternal history, the physical universe of all humanity past, present, and future, physical and spiritual—to cast them in a "universe of Tones."[3]

Ives seems to contradict himself: he says that the essence of the universe, in all its vastness and complexity, cannot be captured by any human act, but then suggests that this is precisely what he aspires to do in the *Universe Symphony*. Yet when he speaks of what cannot be captured, he is mostly talking about a spiritual essence that transcends language: the "unknown," the "unseen spirit." Surely he would agree that music is capable of capturing the spirit of such intangibles; what he must mean is that these intangibles can only be experienced, not described. The forces that can be symbolically represented and described, then, are the elements of the physical universe—to "touch them with hand and microscope, and label them as chemicals and atoms." This is what Ives's "universe in tones" aspires to do: to capture both the tangible realities and the more elusive ones. Its intricate manner serves as a metaphor for the physical universe; its substance reflects the spiritual essence of the actual universe and, by extension, of life itself.[4]

When Ives describes the symphony as a "universe in tones," and as a contemplation "in tones rather than in music as such," he emphasizes his intent to depict the creation and evolution of the universe through pure musical relationships, not (or not just) with conventional uses of themes and formal designs. He intends, in other words, to use musical ideas whose structure and development are metaphors for natural processes. And as we have seen in "Soliloquy" and "On the Antipodes," the world as Ives sees it is a strongly rational one, filled with logical patterns and overt structural regularity. In this sense he joins a long tradition of searches for natural laws in musical sounds, reaching back to the Pythagorean harmony of the spheres. Systematic methods are thus once again ideal means for Ives's artistic vision. He must only find ways to present his ideas that will both symbolize the tangible reality and at the same time communicate the unknowable spiritual essence.

Ives conceived the symphony in three main sections, which he labeled with the letters A, B, and C; he also wrote a Prelude for percussion orchestra. In *Memos* (pp. 106, 108) he says that the work is "fairly well sketched out, but not completed," and that "the themes and general plan are quite clearly indicated in the sketch." But the extant archival materials do not provide a complete picture of his intentions: the sketches for the Prelude and section A are almost complete, but only a few sketch pages survive for sections B and C.[5] In addition, Ives is said to have envisioned a performance scenario in which "several different orchestras, with huge conclaves of singing men and women, are to be placed about in valleys, on hillsides, and on mountain tops."[6] But the sketches do not clearly indicate a division into separate orchestras, nor are there any notations for chorus. Ives says, "In case I don't get to finishing this, somebody might like to try to work out the idea" (*Memos*, 108). In a sense, we will accept his offer by working through the symphony, since we must do a good deal of piecing together fragmentary sketches and speculating about missing material.[7]

Ives calls the percussion Prelude the "pulse of the universe's life beat" (*Memos*, 107). It is an extensive layering of nineteen percussion instruments ranging from various sizes of drums, to bells, xylophones, and piano. There is also a part for piccolo. The Prelude represents a kind of cosmic pulse for the universe, a fundamental source of life and energy. After it is played through once as a prelude, it is repeated during the performance of sections A, B, and C, as a pulse underlying the creation and evolution of the physical universe. Larry Austin's realization and completion of the symphony includes a faithful reconstruction of this Prelude, which was premiered alone in 1984.[8] Austin explains his realization and the structure of the Prelude in an article published shortly after the first performance.[9]

Ives determines that the Prelude will have ten sections, each based on a pattern of accumulating metric subdivisions. In the first section, for example, m. 1 contains only a low long note, which Ives calls the BU (apparently "basic unit"); m. 2 contains the BU plus two notes played on a slightly higher-pitched instrument that divide the BU in half; m. 3 repeats the contents of the first two measures and adds a third still higher instrument that divides the BU into thirds; and so forth. Gradually, ever smaller subdivisions accumulate and progress to smaller and higher-pitched instruments. At the point where all the instruments have entered, the BU is subdivided into 2, 3, 4, 5, 6, 7, 8, 9, 10, 11, 12, 13, 14, 17, 19, 22, 23, 29, and 31 equal parts, performed by the gamut of percussion instruments. This maximal accumulation then becomes the midpoint of the pattern, as the instruments then begin gradually to drop out in reverse of the order in which they entered, thereby suggesting a giant pyramid. Ives refers to this Omnibuslike palindrome as a cycle, noting the analogy with "the motion and cycles of the earth, the sun, all planets and known occurrences of the firmament or universe."[10]

After the first cycle there are nine more, all similarly structured around accumulating subdivisions, although with certain variations in the exact values. Ives usually does not notate precise details of the cycles but suggests them in verbal instructions, including general descriptions of free variations or improvisations around the prescribed metric patterns. Austin supplies many of these unnotated parts in his realization, following the basic framework that Ives originally set down.[11] But for Austin the most important model was "Ives's metaphor for humanity's role on Earth: Man, the 'life pulse' of the Universe, his birth, growth, and transcendence beyond death." Austin's realization is "born and slowly grows in intensity and complexity," and finally concludes with a return to "simpler iterations."[12] The result is a primitive, elemental effect that serves as a fitting introduction and foundation for the symphony. In Austin's words, "It does, indeed, seem like the life pulse of the Universe."[13]

With the Prelude completed, the cosmic pulse established, the symphony proper begins and the Prelude begins its repetitions.[14] In section A, according to Ives, we look back into the past and witness the "Formation of the waters and mountains." By the time section B begins, we have arrived in the present, where we view the "Earth, evolution in nature and humanity." And in the final section we look into the future and observe "Heaven, the rise of all to the spiritual."[15] Ives recalls that his first thoughts about how these ideas would be presented centered on "a parallel way of listening to music, suggested by looking at a view

(1) with the eyes toward the sky or tops of the trees, taking in the earth or foreground subjectively—that is, not focussing the eye on it—(2) then looking at the earth and land, and seeing the sky and the top of the foreground subjectively. In other words, giving a musical piece in two parts, but played at the same time—the lower parts (the basses, cellos, tubas, trombones, bassoons, etc.) working out something representing the earth, and listening to that primarily—and then the upper [parts] (strings, upper woodwind, piano, bells, etc.) reflecting the skies and the Heavens."[16]

"Heaven" and "earth" strata are apparent throughout the sketches for section A. They are especially visible in Example 10.1, which is a facsimile of the fourth sketch page for this section. This page has two score systems (staves 1–8, 9–16), and includes marginal commentary regarding instrumentation and musical metaphors. The heaven stratum comprises the top five staves of each system (1–5, 9–13), the earth stratum the lower three (staves 6–8, 14–16). In addition, each stratum is divided into instrumental groups. For example, Ives says that in the heaven stratum there are four or five groups, each with its own "chord system" (*Memos*, 107). He lists the contents of the groups for the heaven stratum across staves 3 through 5, by specifying four groups, each containing at least two flute parts. (In some groups, each part is notated divisi, so that the number of different notes can be double the number of parts.) In the musical notations we can see the moment where each group begins: the first starts at the beginning of stave 1, the second enters at the end of stave 2, the third begins in the second measure of stave 11, the fourth commences in the seventh measure of stave 12, and a fifth group—not specified in the list but written for celeste, bells, and harp—joins the stratum at the end of stave 13.

In the left margin, before stave 2, Ives indicates that these groups represent clouds. The structure of the clouds is usually fairly straightforward—most of them are typical Ivesian chord structures transposed to various pitch levels, thus projecting parallel movement between individual parts. The first group (stave 1), for example, starts with the chord <Bb−F−B−E−G#−C> in m. 1, then moves to <A−D#−G−C#−F#−D> in m. 2, then reiterates the first chord in m. 3, then moves to T9 of the first chord, <G−D−G#−C#−F−A> in m. 4. Thereafter, Ives uses the identical intervallic structures of the chords in mm. 1, 3, and 4 as the basis for much subsequent material in this group. The intervals in these chords are <76544> (bottom to top), a hint of a chord of decreasing intervals. Ives probably uses interval 4 twice at the top, instead of the sequentially consistent interval 3, in order to avoid a pc duplication. Stave 9 begins with the same <76544> chord as in mm. 1 and 3 of stave 1, and this is followed by the same structure transposed up a whole step. But thereafter Ives simply writes the top line, indicating (with the *etc.* in stave 9, m. 2) that this same chord structure is to

Example 10.1. *Universe Symphony,* facsimile of section A, p. 4 (q3029). The Charles Ives Papers, Yale University Music Library. Used by Permission.

continue in parallel movement underneath the notated line for the remainder of this stave.

The other cloud groups unfold similarly. The second group begins with <B–D–G–C–E♭> (end of stave 2) and then embarks on a series of transpositions resembling those of the first group (stave 10, indicated with only the upper line and *etc.,* as before). Its intervallic structure is symmetrical, <3553>. The third group is a series of trichords of adjacent intervals <65> (bottom to top). Last, the fourth group begins with <A–D#–F#–A#>, intervals <634>, but includes some free writing that is not transpositionally interrelated, and the fifth group is a mostly free emphasis on tritones and sevenths.

Meanwhile, the earth stratum contains two substrata—one linear, the other chordal. Ives describes the linear substratum as "lines starting at different points and at different intervals—a kind of uneven and overlapping counterpoint sometimes reaching nine or ten different lines." He describes the chordal substratum as "masses of chords built around various sets of intervals." And he says that the lines represent "ledges, rocks, woods, . . . roads, rivers, . . . and mountains," while the chord masses represent "the body of the earth, . . . whence the rocks, trees and mountains rise."[17] The earth stratum in Example 10.1 mostly contains lines, usually angular melodies to be played by the lower winds and strings. Typical of the writing in section A, these lines are unsystematic structures intended to expand polyphonic activity and create a dense, complex texture.

The chordal substratum is represented only by the two vertical sonorities at the end of staves 6–8. The first, in which whole steps predominate, includes whole-tone subsets and thereby anticipates important intervallically repetitive structures in sections B and C. The second, however, is a chord that assumes central significance throughout section A. It is a <65> combination cycle that stops one note short of completing its twelve-note PCL. Ives indicates that this chord is to be sustained throughout this and other pages of section A: just above the chord (at the far right of staves 5 and 6) he writes, "Earth created / chord for 1st Rigid Theme"; just before stave 8 he writes, "Keep Earth chord"; and below stave 16 he writes, "Keep low Earth chord through here." His comments draw attention to a <65> combination cycle notated as a verticality back on the first sketch page for section A (q3027), which he had named the "earth chord." In most of section A, Ives uses this chord to represent the "body of the earth," sustaining throughout to provide a harmonic foundation for the concurrent evolutionary processes. The earth thus displays a fundamental cyclic structure, reinforcing the metaphor of the Prelude, where cycles represent "the motion and cycles of the earth, the sun, all planets."[18] The earth chord also has the potential, if and when the cycle is seen to its completion, to encompass a kind of universe of its own—the totality of the pitch-class universe.

The sketch page of Example 10.1 illustrates the nature of the writing throughout section A. The heaven and earth strata grow and develop to symbolize natural evolution and the formation of the structure of the earth. In the initial pages of this section the mood is quieter and the texture sparser, whereas in subsequent pages the music builds in intensity and complexity. And as the structure of the earth evolves, systematic techniques begin to play ever greater roles, depicting the emergence of order in nature. For example, the upper heaven

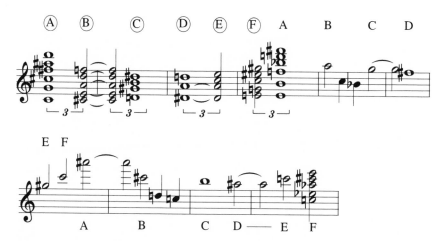

Example 10.2. *Universe Symphony,* excerpt from section A, p. 5 (q3030), literal transcription

group on the page after the one we just looked at (q3030) unfolds a chord pattern derived from the previous separate cloud groups. The first ten measures of this pattern are transcribed in Example 10.2. The plan is established in the first six chords, which Ives labels A–F. Chord A reflects the structure of the chords in the first group of the previous page (intervals <76544>, as in Ex. 10.1), chords B and F recall the previous second group (intervals <3553>), chords C and E reiterate the structure of the chords in the fourth group (intervals <634>), and chord D displays the intervals of the third group (intervals <65>). After the chords have been stated, Ives writes a melody that is to serve as the upper voice of subsequent repetitions of these same chord structures. He uses only the letter labels to indicate which chords accompany which melodic pitches. Example 10.2 shows the first two uses of chords A–F in this way, initiating a pattern of melodic-chordal affiliation that continues for some two pages. By the time section A comes to a close, this kind of patterned writing joins with other predominantly free harmonies and melodic lines to create a massive orchestral texture that represents the myriad complexity of the evolutionary process, which has now reached an important stage.

Example 10.3 shows Ives's notations for the final measures of section A.[19] They are organized around four three-instrument groups, each making a brief flourish of three-voice counterpoint and then coming to rest on a trichord. The first group is the basses (bottom stave), the second is the trombones (next stave up), the third is the cellos (next stave up), and the fourth is the horns (next stave up). The concluding trichords of each group combine to complete the aggregate: pc <1Eo> in the basses, <93T> in the trombones, <256> in the cellos, and <784> in the horns. And since all the trichords are sustained once they

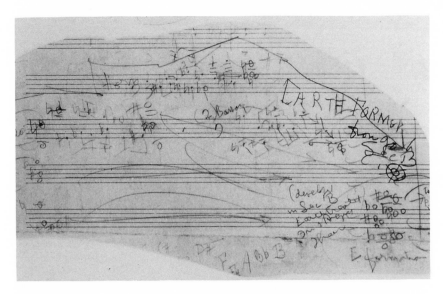

Example 10.3. *Universe Symphony,* facsimile of patch for end of section A (q3035). The Charles Ives Papers, Yale University Music Library. Used by Permission.

arrive, at the end they converge as a single sonority to mark the conclusion of the symphony's first section. Hence this important point in the formation of the universe is marked by a formation of the pitch-class universe. Above the final sound, Ives writes, "EARTH FORMED / from [here] go to Sec[tion] B."[20]

The materials that survive for section B are much less clearly formulated than those for section A. Only two pages resemble score sketches (3050, q3045), and the other pages contain at best preliminary sketches and diagrams.[21] Nonetheless, the ideas that do survive are rich and provocative, and they provide enough information to give a reasonably clear account of what Ives must have had in mind for section B. Two pages are of particular interest. One is a full page of various short sketches of chords and themes (q3038), and the other is a preliminary sketch for the beginning of section B (q3036) that begins to give musical realization to some of the ideas on the other page. In the top margin of the preliminary sketch Ives writes, "and now the Earth and the Firmament and the Heavens are now formed and situated and the waters, the land 'have taken their shape.'"

Let us first look at 3038, the page of short sketches. Example 10.4 is a literal transcription of the entire page, with only the boldface boxes labeled A through J added. The page contains a few melodic lines that are either identical or similar to lines on other pages, but what is most interesting is the notes enclosed in the added boxes, which are abstract notations of various cyclic structures. Example 10.5 lists the intervallic content, pc content, and PCL of each boxed collection.

Example 10.4. *Universe Symphony*, sketch toward section B (q3038), literal transcription

The notations illustrate a variety of ways of cyclically generating a large number of pitch classes. There are two single-interval cycles, T10 (C) and T11 (D), but there are also a variety of combination cycles, exhibiting every PCL value from 7 through 12. Three are based on CHR streams: <94> (A), <58> (E), and <67> (I). And two are based on CHR' streams: <47> (F) and <56> (G). These illustrate several contents of the streams with respect to each other, and thus various PCLs, including 7 in <94>, 9 in <47>, 10 in <58>, 11 in <56>, and 12 in <67>. Ives always notates only the notes of the PCL, so that none of the structures have pitch-class duplications. The <59> cycle (B) has complementary WHT streams and thus a PCL of 12, while the <45> and <21> cycles (H and J) are based on complementary DIM' and DIM streams, respectively, and thus are octatonic collections with PCLs of 8.

Then on page 3036, the preliminary sketch, we can begin to see how these

	cycle	pc	PCL
A.	<94>	<091T2E3>	7
B.	<59>	<0527496E81T3>	12
C.	<T>	<0T8642>	6
D.	<E>	<0ET987654321>	12
E.	<58>	<0516273849>	10
F.	<47>	<04E3T2918>	9
G.	<56>	<6E5T4938271>	11
H.	<45>	<04916T37>	8
I.	<67>	<061728394T5E>	12
J.	<21>	<0235689E>	8

Example 10.5. *Universe Symphony,* boxed notes in Example 10.4

cycles would be used in the symphony. This page is literally transcribed in Example 10.6. As in section A, a textural stratification represents heaven and earth; here heaven is depicted in staves 1–5, before which Ives writes "Heaven and Planetary Skies and Clouds," and earth is depicted in staves 7–16, before which Ives writes "EARTH formed." Before stave 6, Ives reminds us that the "Pulse of 12 [sic] Percussion" continues as well. The heaven stratum contains some chord types from section A; the chord in stave 1, for example, is intervals <76544>, the same as in the previous first group, and the chord in stave 2 is intervals <3553>, the same as in the previous second group. Thus the chord structures that evolved in section A remain firmly in place as part of the substance of the universe. But there are also some new ideas for the heaven stratum: Ives's sketchings and verbal instructions scattered within the first five staves specify, among other structures, a large chord of decreasing intervals, chords of fifths or fourths with some notes inflected by quarter tones, and a chord made up of notes in an overtone series.

Many new ideas also make their appearance in the earth stratum, some of which seem to have been inspired by the notations on page 3038 (see Exx. 10.4 and 10.5). The chords notated in the left margin of staves 7–16 are apparently to be sustained for long periods of time, perhaps throughout section B. Ives gives a key to the structure of these chords in the bottom margin, where he calls them groups and specifies their instrumentation and intervals. Groups 1–4 reiterate combination cycles from page 3038: the double-bass parts of group 1, on staves 15–16, project <67> (Exx. 10.4 and 10.5, formation I);[22] the trombone parts of group 2, on staves 13–14, form <65> (sketched as <56>, Exx. 10.4

and 10.5, G); the horn parts of group 3, on staves 10–11, construct <58> (Exx. 10.4 and 10.5, E); and the trumpet and oboe parts of group 4, on staves 7–8, display <94> (Exx. 10.4 and 10.5, A).[23] Group 5 is the odd assortment of intervals surrounding the first barline in stave 7. In the right-hand and lower left-hand margins of the page, Ives names the sonorities of all of these groups Earth formation chords.

The remainder of the earth stratum on page 3036 consists of melodic lines in the four marked-off measures of staves 10–14. Two of these are linearizations, one with slight variations, of the preceding chords: the melody in stave 14 linearizes the group 2 chord (<65> cycle) with one note out of place (pc E), and the melody in stave 12 linearizes a <67> cycle, recalling the structure of the group 1 chord. Ives calls these the rigid lines; they apparently reflect regular and predictable aspects of nature. He does not comment on the lines in staves 10 and 11, but he does explain that the line in stave 13 represents "free evolution and humanity." This line does not evolve from a chord; it apparently symbolizes those aspects of nature which are not easily defined and described. And yet its structure is hardly haphazard: its first twelve notes (excluding the four grace notes in the first measure) complete the aggregate, and then the next twelve (again, excluding the four grace notes) are a melodic inversion of the first twelve. Even nature's less tangible features reflect some kind of order.

The relationships between melodies and chords on this page express a basic metaphor that Ives might have intended to explore throughout section B. The earth, symbolized by cyclic chords, provides the structural foundation for the forms of life that grow out of it, symbolized by the melodies. The structural relationships between the chords and melodies reflect a basic natural organicism. It is easy to imagine a continuation of these ideas throughout section B in which many more chords would be sustained, presumably including more of the cyclic collections from page 3038 as well as other cyclic structures, and many additional melodies would evolve out of the sustained sounds. Meanwhile, perhaps the sustained chords in the heaven stratum would also become more numerous and clearly formed.

Another page of disorganized sketches (q3045) is apparently the final page of section B. But from this it is hard to tell exactly how Ives planned to conclude the section. What is clear is that by the end of section B a vast amount of material has come together to form some kind of broadly defined unity. At one point, for example, he indicates that some of the structures on this page should "join as one Cloud chord."[24] And at the very end of the page—*after* a double bar—he makes a vertical list of twelve notes that are probably supposed to form an aggregate. (All pitch classes are represented except pc 2, and pc 3 occurs as both D♯ and E♭—perhaps Ives erroneously placed a sharp sign after the D.)

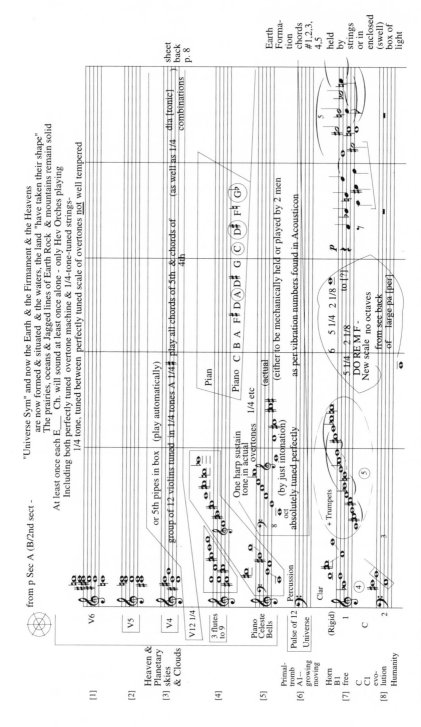

Example 10.6. *Universe Symphony,* preliminary sketch for beginning of section B (q3036), literal transcription

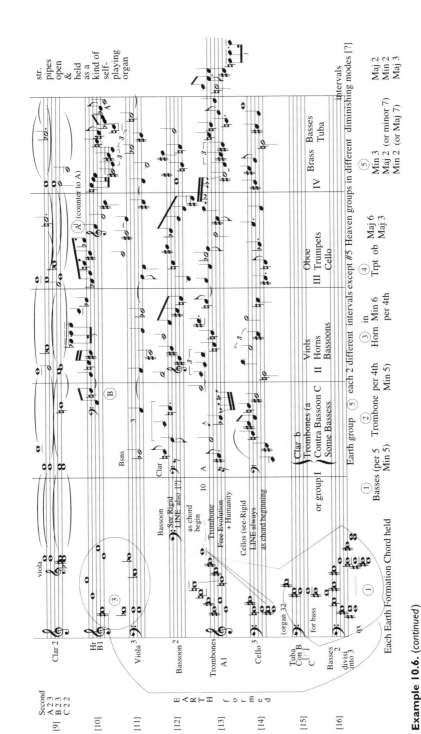

Example 10.6. (continued)

This seems to indicate a conclusion for section B not unlike that of section A—a use of the pitch-class universe to symbolize the actual one.

A reconstruction of section C, "the rise of all to the spiritual," calls for even more speculation. As is the case for section B, very little of the surviving section C material exists in something approaching a "score" form; mostly there are sketches and diagrams.[25] Example 10.7 is a transcription of the most interesting page (q3039), which is headed "Universe Sym[phony] 3rd Section Foreground Harmonic Basis." It is hard to say exactly how this page would be used in the symphony—and we will take up this matter in a moment—but the "harmonic basis" itself is instantly recognizable: it is a kind of Omnibus based on both cycles and combination cycles within a quarter-tone (twenty-four-pitch-class) system. It has twenty-four chords marked off in separate measures of two score systems. The chords are numbered 1 through 24 near the top of both systems (the first four numbers are Ives's, the others [bracketed] continue his numbering).

The bottom notes of the chords, specified in the fourth stave of both systems, unfold a rising quarter-tone scale that reaches completion at the conclusion of the pattern. The first bass note is C3, and the next is notated as C3 but accompanied by the indication *quart,* obviously meaning to raise the note by a quarter tone. The bass note for chord 3 is C♯3, and the chord 4 bass note is this pitch raised a quarter step. The quarter-tone ascent continues up through B3 in chord 23, and although the measure where chord 24 should appear is empty, we can assume that the bass note for this chord would be a quarter-tone inflection of B3.

The chords themselves, which are either notated or described on the upper two or three staves of the systems, follow a related pattern of quarter-tone inflection every other measure—chords in the odd-numbered measures contain notes from the twelve-pitch-class system, chords in the even-numbered measures from a twenty-four-pitch-class system. Most of the odd-numbered chords are cycles or combination cycles, and the even-numbered ones are formed by inflecting alternate intervals in the chord just preceding. For example, chord 1 is a stacking of perfect fifths, and chord 2 is an alternation of perfect fifths and inflected perfect fifths—a combination cycle that alternates regular and inflected intervals.[26] Similarly, chord 4 is formed by inflecting alternate intervals in the <76> combination cycle of chord 3. Ives's instructions say to form every even-numbered chord through chord 22 in this way. He gives no instructions for chord 24.

Most of the chords contain a variety of pitch classes, but Ives does not always notate them to reach their cyclic completions or PCLs. Nevertheless, it seems likely that in some subsequent sketch Ives would have paid more attention to this matter, as he did in "On the Antipodes." In the first measure he twice writes "6 or more," apparently referring to chord tones, and to the right of staves 1–4 he writes "and return on this basis until a same note in the scale then stop." This latter inscription seems to be a directive to continue a cycle until it arrives at its PCL.

Example 10.8 summarizes what is inscribed on this page by notating the intervals of each chord in quarter tones (quarter tone = 1, m2 = 2, etc.). The pattern begins as an Omnibus with strict quarter-tone gradations: a <14> (*fourteen*, not *one-four*) cycle in chord 1, a <14,13> combination cycle in chord 2, a <14,12> combination cycle in chord 3, and a <13,12> combination cycle in chord 4. But chords 5 and 6 are symmetrical rather than cyclic. And chords 7 and 8 are symmetrical except for the top interval, chords 9 through 12 are strictly cyclic, and chords 13 and 14 display another symmetrical structure disrupted by the top interval.[27] Chord 15 is a sequence of three intervals <846846>, but this pattern is not preserved when alternate notes are inflected to derive chord 16. (Instead, chord 16 has one of each interval from 3 to 8.) Chords 17–22 are chords of decreasing intervals (top to bottom). Up to this point we have a general sense of an Omnibus progression, most clearly articulated in roughly the first half and thereafter suggested in the lower portions of the chords. Indeed, a survey of just the lowest intervals of the chords—left to right in the bottom row of the chart—reveals a meandering but steady progression from interval 14 down to interval 1, skipping only 6 and 5. Finally, chord 23 is an aggregate, which Ives marks as "a 12-note chromatic." Perhaps chord 24, instead of inflecting alternate notes in chord 23, would have been a quarter-tone inflection of the entirety of chord 23, so that the final two chords in the model would comprise the twenty-four-pitch-class aggregate.

There are only hints about how this chord sequence would be used in section C. In the lower right-hand margin of the same page Ives writes, "Each chord system, on each of the 24 notes, will be used for the themes, and in each section of the 3rd section of the U[niverse] Sym[phony] thus each Theme of the 24 will be its own and not the same as any other—i.e., literally all differ[en]t. A kind of 24 scales, varying intervals and overtone vibrations, each its own tonal plan." When he says, "Each chord system . . . will be used for the themes," he seems to be saying that each chord will be linearized, as we saw at the beginning of section B. But his next statement—"in each section of the 3rd section . . . thus each Theme of the 24 will be its own and not the same as any other"—is more ambiguous. It could mean that section C will have twenty-four subsections, each based on a different chord from the series—a vast unfolding of the chords resembling the large-scale presentation of the Omnibus in "On the Antipodes." Or it could mean that each of the twenty-four themes will be present at all times,

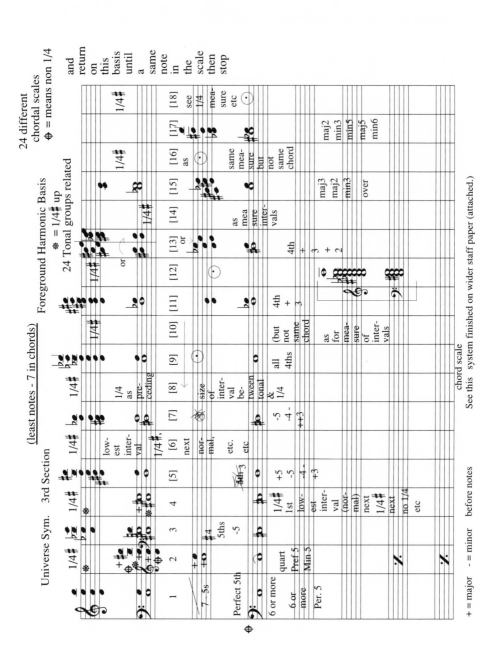

Example 10.7. *Universe Symphony,* sketch toward section C (q3039), literal transcription

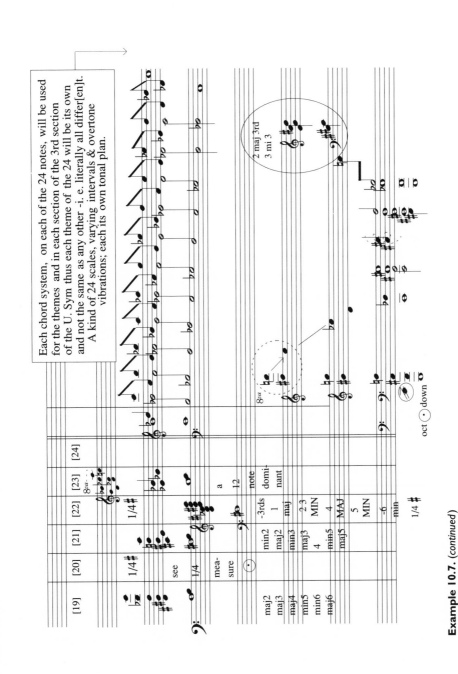

Example 10.7. (continued)

chord #	1	2	3	4	5	6	7	8	9	10	11	12
intervals:									10	10	8	8
					14	13			10	9	10	9
	14	14	12	12	12	12	10	10	10	10	8	8
	14	13	14	13	10	9	12	11	10	9	10	9
	14	14	12	12	8	8	10	10	10	10	8	8
	14	13	14	13	10	9	8	7	10	9	10	9
	14	14	12	12	12	12	10	10	10	10	8	8
	14	13	14	13	14	13	12	11	10	9	10	9

chord #	13	14	15	16	17	18	19	20	21	22	23	24
intervals:											10	
											2	
											4	
											10	
											2	
											4	
	8	8	6	6	16	16	18	18	14	14	6	
	10	9	4	3	14	13	16	15	12	11	8	
	8	8	8	8	12	12	12	12	8	8	8	
	4	3	6	5	8	7	10	9	6	5	6	
	8	8	4	4	6	6	8	8	4	4	6	
	10	9	8	7	4	3	4	3	2	1	2	

Intervals measured in number of quarter tones.

Example 10.8. Interval content of chord sequence in Example 10.7

in each of twenty-four subsections. Indeed, it would seem consistent with Ives's apparent conception of the symphony to establish twenty-four orchestral groups, each elaborating a different chord from the Omnibus, that are all playing simultaneously. One page (q3042) appears to be a rough score sketch from the end of section C—it is headed "end of Sec C / Universe Sym"—but it does not offer any clues to how the chord series would be used.

Regardless of how the sketches would be realized, however, the significance of section C in the symphony's overall conception is clear. We can see this by glancing back to the previous sections. Section A begins with the earth chord, a <65> combination cycle with a PCL of 12 that represents an underpinning of all things, a complete statement of the twelve-pitch-class universe whose structure mirrors cyclic forces in the actual universe. But most of the other material at the beginning of the symphony is not so systematically formed. The universe is here represented only by its structural essence; otherwise it is formless. Then as section A progresses, some chords and themes begin to exhibit greater clarity and rigidity of structure, reflecting the universe's evolving form. By the time section A concludes and we arrive at the notations at the beginning of section B, a quite precise clarity of structure in the various earth chords and their melodic derivatives has developed. Meanwhile, chords in the heaven stratum also present organized patterns. It seems safe to assume that the melodic-chordal relationships would continue to develop throughout section B, perhaps growing in number and intensity. Finally, in the chord series of section C we see musical ideas of the utmost clarity and organization. This is Ives's vision of heaven: a pervasive organization and logic that brings order to all the previous diverse ideas, as if resolving all the ambiguities and conflicts of life on earth. Presumably, section C would also have discontinued the previous stratification symbolizing heaven and earth. Ives would thereby have concluded on a unified final resting place for the symphony, as for humanity—the spirit that will survive when evolution has run its course, and a transcendentalist's vision of ultimate unity between earth and heaven.

For those who know Ives only as a composer of impulsive, free inspiration—the composer of sweeping romantic gestures in the *Concord* Sonata or brilliantly evocative images in *Three Places in New England*—the rigidity and seeming sterility of his experiments in systematic composition have been an enigma. His interest in patterns and calculations and cerebral musical machinations have seemed odd, trivial, tangential, even a little crazy. But the *Universe Symphony* helps to put it all in perspective. Ives spent so much of his composing life exploring musical order and logic because he saw the universe ultimately as inherently orderly and logical. If he could capture the spirit of a historical event or a metaphysical idea in music that sprang freely from his soul, he could also capture the essence of nature and natural laws with music that issued primarily from his intellect. And after all, the natural laws that systematic composition emulates are fundamental forces underlying any earthly event, whether it is valued chiefly for its spiritual essence or for its organic logic.

But at the same time a complementary truth holds: the spiritual essence of earthly events stands at the center of Ives's compositional objectives, whether they arose from the soul or the intellect. Ives did not conceive the *Universe Symphony* just as a technical representation of the structural evolution of the world. He also envisioned a grand musical expression of those aspects of life and nature which are beyond literal representation—a use of music to express what words cannot, the unknowable, the "unseen spirit." It is exactly what Ives has in mind when he speaks of the "substance" of an artwork (see Chapter One), and a strong presence in many of his major efforts, notably the *Concord* Sonata, the Second String Quartet, and the Fourth Symphony. But only in the *Universe Symphony* did he seek to achieve such a harmonious combination of spiritual depth and structural strength.

The *Universe Symphony* provides a sharper lens for viewing the complete history of Ives's quest for substance in music. Early on, his father instilled in him the value of compositional sense as a component of good music. Some of his subsequent music may seem overburdened by this sense, as if overwhelmed by the strength of the methods and the depth of his artistic vision. But this is precisely the point: substance is a powerful and elusive goal that may inspire a lifelong pursuit. In the *Universe Symphony* we can see the status of Ives's quest in its final stages and imagine where he might have gone had he remained compositionally active during the last thirty-odd years of his life. And yet the symphony also reveals more sobering realities—the difficulty of the goal and the idealism of the one who conceived it. Ultimately, the union Ives envisioned—the perfect marriage of artistry and technique—remained an elusive dream.

Burkholder blames such high artistic standards in part for the cessation of Ives's compositional activity by the early 1920s. He cites the *Essays Before a Sonata* as the source of "exalted ideals and purposes for music that . . . became impossible for [Ives] to live up to." More succinctly, "His artistic aims had exceeded his grasp."[28] We can see a parallel process of realization in the pages of Ives's systematic music, as his search for new technical means for expressing substance lags behind his broadening artistic ideals. And if the *Universe Symphony* represents his most ardent quest to realize these goals, it is hardly surprising that he left it incomplete. Ives is said to have expressed regret at not finishing the symphony, saying, "If only I could have done it."[29] But Henry Cowell says that Ives never intended to complete the work, that it is "so gigantic, so inclusive and so exalted that he feels its complete realization is beyond any single man."[30] In Feder's view, "This was music that was meant to be imagined, not performed."[31] Indeed, if there is any work of art that could justifiably remain incomplete, surely it is the *Universe Symphony*. As the symphony shows, the many ambiguities and uncertainties of earthly existence find their resolution only on a higher spiritual plane. Ives would not resolve his own difficulties with art, society, politics—with the contents of his personal universe—until he had completed his own spiritual journey.

Appendix A: Alphabetical List of Works Discussed

This list includes all works of Ives mentioned in the text, regardless of the extent of the citation. Dates of composition are based on: 1) the Kirkpatrick *Catalogue;* 2) the list of works that follows Kirkpatrick's article on Ives in the *New Grove;* and 3) information from Gayle Sherwood via her dissertation, her article in the *Musical Quarterly* (1994), and personal communications. Any conjectural datings (indicated with question marks) are Kirkpatrick's. The information from these sources, plus the weight of overwhelming musical and biographical evidence, have produced a basic chronology that cannot be substantively challenged by Maynard Solomon's speculations about a "systematic pattern of falsification" in Ives's own attempts at dating his work. (See Maynard Solomon, "Charles Ives: Some Questions of Veracity," *Journal of the American Musicological Society* 40/3 (1987): 443–470.) Given the vast amount of information Solomon must ignore in order to validate his revisionist agenda, one is not compelled to accept his interpretation of the dating problems he does describe or to give serious consideration to a radically rewritten chronology of Ives's work.

Also included are data on publications, if any, although the published version may not be the one used as a source (see Preface). Unpublished works are identified by their number in the Kirkpatrick *Catalogue.*

"Aeschylus and Sophocles" (1922). Voice, piano, string quartet. *19 Songs,* pp. 12–15 (Merion Music, 1935).

All the Way Around and Back (1906). Chamber ensemble (Peer, 1971).

"The Cage" (1906). Voice and piano. *114 Songs,* p. 144 (Peer, 1955).

Calcium Light Night (1911). Chamber orchestra (Merion Music, 1964).

The Celestial Country (1898–1902). Chorus and chamber ensemble [vocal score] (Peer, 1973).

Central Park in the Dark (1906). Chamber orchestra. Ed. John Kirkpatrick and Jacques-Louis Monod (Boelke-Bomart, 1973).

Chromâtimelôdtune (?1919). Chamber orchestra. Arr. Gunther Schuller (MJQ Music, 1963).

"A Farewell to Land" (1909). Voice and piano. *19 Songs,* p. 10 (Merion Music, 1935).

The Fourth of July (1911–1913). Orchestra. Ed. Wayne Shirley (Associated Music Publishers, 1988).

From the Steeples and the Mountains (1901–?1902). Trumpet, trombone, bells (Peer, 1965).

"From *The Swimmers*" (1915). Voice and piano. *114 Songs,* pp. 62–67 (Merion Music, 1933).

Fugue in Four Keys on "The Shining Shore" (1896). Trumpet, flute, and strings. Ed. John Kirkpatrick (Merion Music, 1975).

The General Slocum (1904). Orchestra. Cat. no. 1B4.

George Ives's Copybook. Cat. no. 7A2.

The Gong on the Hook and Ladder (?1911). Chamber orchestra. Ed. James B. Sinclair (Peer, 1979).

Hallowe'en (1906). Piano quintet (Boelke-Bomart, 1949).

Harvest Home Chorales (c. 1902, reconstructed 1914–1919). Chorus and chamber ensemble [Chorus/organ score] (Mercury, 1949).

Hymn (1904). String quintet (Peer, 1966).

In Re Con Moto Et Al (1913). Piano quintet (Peer, 1968).

Largo Risoluto No. 1 (1906). Piano quintet (Peer, 1961).

Largo Risoluto No. 2 (1906). Piano quintet (Peer, 1961).

"Like a Sick Eagle" (?1906). Voice and piano. *114 Songs,* p. 61 (Merion Music, 1933).

"Luck and Work" (?1913). Voice and piano. *114 Songs,* p. 49 (Merion Music, 1933).

"Majority" (1914–1915). Unison voices, orchestra. Cat. no. 5B10. Voice and piano version, *114 Songs,* pp. 1–5 (Merion Music, 1935).

"On the Antipodes" (1915–1923). Voice and piano (four hands). *19 Songs,* pp. 44–47 (Merion Music, 1935).

Over the Pavements (1906–1913). Chamber orchestra (Peer, 1954).

Overture and March "1776" (1903). Chamber orchestra. Ed. James B. Sinclair (Merion Music, 1976).

Piano Sonata No. 2: *(Concord, Mass., 1840–60)* (1910–1915) (Associated Music Publishers, 1947).

Processional: "Let There Be Light" (1902–1903). Chorus and instruments (Peer, 1967).

Psalm 24 (1898–1902, reconstructed c. 1914). Chorus (Mercury, 1955).

Psalm 25 (1898–1902, reconstructed c. 1914). Chorus and organ. Ed. John Kirkpatrick and Gregg Smith (Merion Music, 1979).

Psalm 54 (c. 1902). Chorus. Ed. John Kirkpatrick and Gregg Smith (Merion Music, 1973).

Psalm 67 (1898–1902). Chorus (Associated Music Publishers, 1939).

Psalm 90 (c. 1923). Chorus, organ, bells. Ed. John Kirkpatrick and Gregg Smith (Merion Music, 1970).

Psalm 135 (c. 1902, rev. 1914). Chorus and instruments. Ed. John Kirkpatrick (Merion Music, 1981).

Robert Browning Overture (1908–1912). Orchestra. Ed. Henry Cowell and Lou Harrison (Peer, 1959).

Rough and Ready et al and/or The Jumping Frog (1906–1907). Piano. Cat no. 3B16ii.

Scherzo ("Holding Your Own") (1903/1914). String quartet (Peer, 1958).

"The See'r" (?1913). Voice and piano. *114 Songs,* pp. 69–70 (Associated Music Publishers, 1957).

"Soliloquy" (1907). Voice and piano. *34 Songs,* p. 50, *New Music* vol. 7, no. 1, Oct. 1933.

Sonata No. 3 for Violin and Piano (1913–?1914). Ed. Sol Babitz and Ingolf Dahl (Merion Music, 1951).

"Song for Harvest Season" (1893). Voice and instruments or organ. *34 Songs,* p. 68, *New Music* vol. 7, no. 1, Oct. 1933.

"Song in 5's" (?1913). Piano(?). Cat. no. 7E38.

"Songs My Mother Taught Me" (1895). Voice and piano. *114 Songs,* pp. 250–251 (Peer, 1955).

String Quartet No. 2 (1907–1913) (Peer, 1954).

Study No. 2 (1907–?1908). Piano. Cat. no. 3B17 (#2).

Study No. 5 (1907–?1908). Piano. Ed. Alan Mandel (Merion Music, 1988).

Study No. 6 (1907–?1908). Piano. Cat. no. 3B17 (#6).

Study No. 8 (1907–?1908). Piano. Cat. no. 3B17 (#8).

Study No. 20 (?1908). Piano. Ed. John Kirkpatrick (Merion Music, 1981).

Study No. 21: Some Southpaw Pitching! (?1909). Piano. Ed. John Kirkpatrick (Mercury, 1975).

Study No. 22 (?1909). Piano. Ed. John Kirkpatrick (Merion Music, 1973).

Symphony No. 4 (1909–1916). Orchestra. Ed. Theodore A. Seder, Romulus Franceschini, and Nicholas Falcone (Associated Music Publishers, 1965).

Three-Page Sonata (1905). Piano. Ed. John Kirkpatrick (Mercury, 1975).

Three Places in New England (from the First Orchestral Set) (1908–?1914). Ed. James B. Sinclair (Mercury, 1976).

Three Quarter-Tone Pieces (1923–1924). Two pianos. Ed. George Pappastavrou (C. F. Peters, 1968).

Tone Roads No. 1 (1911). Chamber orchestra (Peer, 1949).

Tone Roads No. 3 (1915). Chamber orchestra (Peer, 1952).

Trio (1904–1911). Violin, cello, piano. Ed. John Kirkpatrick (Peer, 1987).

Universe Symphony (1911–1928). Orchestra. Cat. no. 1A9.

Variations on "America" (?1891). Organ (Mercury, 1949).

Varied Air and Variations (?1923). Piano. Ed. John Kirkpatrick and Garry Clarke (Merion, 1971).

A Yale-Princeton Football Game (?1898). Orchestra. Cat. no. 1B3.

Appendix B: Chronological List of Works Discussed

Variations on "America" (?1891)
"Song for Harvest Season" (1893)
"Songs My Mother Taught Me" (1895)
Fugue in Four Keys on "The Shining Shore" (1896)
A Yale-Princeton Football Game (?1898)
The Celestial Country (1898–1902)
Psalm 67 (1898–1902)
Psalm 24 (1898–1902, reconstructed c. 1914)
Psalm 25 (1898–1902, reconstructed c. 1914)
From the Steeples and the Mountains (1901–?1902)
Psalm 54 (c. 1902)
Processional: "Let There Be Light" (1902–1903)
Psalm 135 (c. 1902, rev. 1914)
Harvest Home Chorales (c. 1902, reconstructed 1914–1919)
Overture and March "1776" (1903)
Scherzo ("Holding Your Own") (1903/1914)
The General Slocum (1904)
Hymn (1904)
Trio (1904–1911)
Three-Page Sonata (1905)
All the Way Around and Back (1906)
"The Cage" (1906)
Central Park in the Dark (1906)
Hallowe'en (1906)
Largo Risoluto No. 1 (1906)
Largo Risoluto No. 2 (1906)
"Like a Sick Eagle" (?1906)
Rough and Ready et al and/or The Jumping Frog (1906–1907)
Over the Pavements (1906–1913)
"Soliloquy" (1907)
Study No. 2 (1907–?1908)
Study No. 5 (1907–?1908)
Study No. 6 (1907–?1908)
Study No. 8 (1907–?1908)
String Quartet No. 2 (1907–1913)
Study No. 20 (?1908)
Robert Browning Overture (1908–1912)
Three Places in New England (1908–?1914)
"A Farewell to Land" (1909)
Study No. 21: Some Southpaw Pitching! (?1909)

Study No. 22 (?1909)
Symphony No. 4 (1909–1916)
Piano Sonata No. 2: *(Concord, Mass., 1840–60)* (1910–1915)
Calcium Light Night (1911)
Tone Roads No. 1 (1911)
The Gong on the Hook and Ladder (?1911)
The Fourth of July (1911–1913)
In Re Con Moto Et Al (1913)
"Luck and Work" (?1913)
"The See'r" (?1913)
"Song in 5's" (?1913)
Sonata No. 3 for Violin and Piano (1913–?1914)
"Majority" (1914–1915)
"From *The Swimmers*" (1915)
Tone Roads No. 3 (1915)
"On the Antipodes" (1915–1923)
Chromâtimelôdtune (?1919)
"Aeschylus and Sophocles" (1922)
Psalm 90 (c. 1923)
Varied Air and Variations (?1923)
Three Quarter-Tone Pieces (1923–1924)
Universe Symphony (1911–1928)

Notes

Chapter 1: The Composer and His Language

1 Burkholder, *Ives*, 48.

2 Ives's early education and musical activities are chronicled and discussed by Wallach, "New England Education," 110–153; Rossiter, *Ives and His America*, 44–53; and Burkholder, *Ives*, 43–57.

3 Burkholder, *Ives*, 48. Other studies with similar perspectives include Winters, "Additive and Repetitive Techniques"; Lambert, "Compositional Procedures"; and Nicholls, *American Experimental Music*.

4 Burkholder explains both the experimental and artistic orientations in the context of Western traditions in "Evolution," 640–644.

5 See, for example, Burkholder, "Evolution," and *Ives*.

6 Burkholder offers a similar explanation of Ives's artistic objectives in highlighting the "rhetorical" and "organic" aspects of Ives's work, supporting his depiction of the composer as an inheritor of Western art-music traditions. Burkholder's views differ from those presented here, however, in their linkage of these two concepts to the notions of concert and experimental music, respectively. See "Evolution," 630–666.

7 Burkholder speaks of an analogous interdependence to explain the dual creative streams within Ives's compositional evolution: a desire to "represent experience" inspires experimentation with new techniques, which in turn inspires "more daring aims" and then further experimentation. See *Ives*, 18–19.

8 *Ives*, 49. This notion is supported by, among others, Winters, "Additive and Repetitive Techniques" (chapter 5, 287–318), and Lambert, "Compositional Procedures" (397–402).

9 Ward, "Ives," 132–133. Burkholder disputes Ward's explanation, saying "it would be a serious mistake to assume that the process was as linear as this paradigm suggests" (*Ives*, 18).

10 A similar perspective is embodied in Larry Starr's explanation of the evolution of Ives's use of style. Starr observes a general tendency in Ives's early music to be stylistically consistent within single works but wildly inconsistent from work to work. Then in later pieces he explores the same stylistic diversity within the same work. See Starr, "Early Styles."

11 Burkholder, *All Made of Tunes*. Earlier studies of Ives's borrowings include Marshall, "Ives' Quotations"; Cyr, "Intervallic Structural Elements"; and Ballantine, "Ives and the Meaning of Quotation." See also Henderson, *Charles Ives Tunebook*.

12 See, for example, Starr, *Union of Diversities*; Gingerich, "Processes of Motivic Transformation"; and Gingerich, "Technique of Melodic Motivic Analysis."

13 The *Essays*, which were first published privately in 1920, are reprinted in Ives, *Essays*.

14 See Burkholder, *Ives*, 4–7; and Burkholder, "Ives and His Fathers."

15 Burkholder, *Ives*, 6.

16 Ibid., 5–6.

17 Kavanaugh, "Music and American Transcendentalism," 193.

18 *Essays*, 73–77.

19 Burkholder, *Ives*, 11.

20 In his essay "Some Remarks on Value and Greatness in Music," Leonard Meyer develops a similar explanation for the artistic process (*Music, the Arts, and Ideas,* 22–41). Meyer's *content* is akin to *values,* and his *greatness* is virtually indistinguishable from Ives's *substance.* (For a different interpretation see Isham, "Musical Thinking.") Meyer says, for example, that greatness is "a quality of experience which transcends the syntactical" (p. 38). As for the next step, Meyer is more accepting than Ives; he speaks of the potential of this phase, which he terms *values,* for simplicity, complexity, elegance, and economy (p. 37). Ultimately, Meyer offers a dualistic reasoning similar to that in Ives's *Essays:* "The greatest works would be those which embody value of the highest order with the most profound . . . content" (p. 39).

21 Emerson, *Selected Essays,* 23–24.

22 For more on this aspect of Emerson and its connections with the *Essays,* see Robinson, "Children of the Fire"; and Hertz, *Angels of Reality,* 31–33.

23 The inscription is fully transcribed in Kirkpatrick, *Catalogue,* 126–127.

24 Hertz, *Angels of Reality,* 31.

25 Kirkpatrick points this out by using italicized parentheses (*Memos,* 91).

26 Ives's comment is directed at performers who fail to recognize substance in unconventional technical requirements. Charles Ward discusses this and other aspects of the quotation in "Ives's Concept of Music." The comment itself is reminiscent of a passage from Thoreau: "The expressions of the poet cannot be analyzed; his sentence is one word, whose syllables are words. There are, indeed, no *words* quite worthy to be set to his music. But what the matter if we do not hear the words always, if we hear the music?" See "Thursday" in *A Week on the Concord and Merrimack Rivers* (Boston: Ticknor and Fields, 1868), 347, cited and discussed by Kavanaugh, "Music and American Transcendentalism," 47.

27 Emerson, *Selected Essays,* 25.

28 "The Amount to Carry," excerpted in *Essays,* 235–240.

29 Ibid., 239–240. Italics in original, Howard Boatwright's interpolation.

30 Marshall, "Ives' Quotations," 46.

31 Ibid., 56. Italics in original.

32 Starr, *Union of Diversities,* 18. Italics in original.

33 Starr analyzes the song both in *Union of Diversities* (20–30) and in "Style and Substance." The quotation is from the latter, p. 33.

34 There are other aspects of Starr's views that do not harmonize so neatly with those expressed here. For example, about a systematically organized cadenza in *Over the Pavements* Starr writes, "Such passages represent, to my way of thinking, the *least* significant aspect of Ives the creator. They attest to his conceptual inven-

tiveness, but they lack that profound quality of true *musical* invention found so often elsewhere in his output, in those passages and pieces where the drive for expression and meaning is paramount over any interest in arbitrarily engendered sound phenomena, and where technique is subservient to content" (48, italics in original). But the main point of his study is that Ives embraced a multitude of styles to fill his expressive needs: Why could not a systematically generated passage be one of them? It would seem that a passage of this sort would simply represent yet one more aspect of Ives's stylistic heterogeneity, serve as yet another indicator of the range of his expressive resources. And it would provide further support for statements Starr makes elsewhere in the book: to accept Ives's stylistic diversity, he says, "is not only to accept the validity of a new and broader usage of style and form in musical expression, but also to accept, by implication, a world (a universe?) of change, inconsistency, diversity, and non-recurrence (at least, non-*literal* recurrence)" (28).

35 Burkholder, *All Made of Tunes,* 6. Later Burkholder concludes, "Whether working out a technical experiment, creating a musical analogue to a text or a program, or reworking borrowed material, [Ives] followed a similar pattern of elaborating a central, usually simple idea that served as the starting point" (417).

36 Cohn, "Transpositional Combination"; Cohn, "Inversional Symmetry and Transpositional Combination"; Cohn, "Bartók's Octatonic Strategies"; Cohn, "Properties and Generability"; Lewin, "Transformational Techniques"; Lewin, *Generalized Musical Intervals and Transformations;* Lewin, *Musical Form and Transformation.*

37 Anton Webern, *The Path to New Music,* ed. Willi Reich, trans. Leo Black (Bryn Mawr: Theodore Presser Co., 1963), 51. Originally published as *Wege zur Neue Musik,* ed. Willi Reich (Vienna: Universal Edition, 1960).

38 Henry Cowell, *New Musical Resources* (New York: Knopf, 1930), 41–42.

39 Kirkpatrick, *Catalogue,* 219, 7C5. Two of the versions are in Ives's hand in his father's copybook (Kirkpatrick, *Catalogue,* 214–215, 7A2), and the third is on a separate page. For a fuller discussion of the three versions, and another perspective on Ives's reasons for writing them, see Burkholder, "Critique of Tonality."

40 Ives sometimes manipulates the rhythm also. See *Memos,* 46–47 and the "London Bridge" arrangement discussed by Burkholder, "Critique of Tonality," 205–207.

41 *Memos,* 44. Ives does not cite his father's inspiration for this technique, but Kirkpatrick does: "Ives told George Roberts that his father had him do chromatic scales with each interval a minor 9th—'If you must play a chromatic scale, play it like a man'" (in Kirkpatrick's footnote 5, *Memos,* 44).

42 See category 7A2 in Kirkpatrick, *Catalogue,* 214–215.

43 An indication of direction in a transformational label indicates pitch transformation, in this case a transposition up five pitch-space half steps. Nondirectional labels indicate transformations in pitch-class space.

44 Kirkpatrick, *Catalogue,* 230, 7E77.

45 Kirkpatrick, *Catalogue,* 220, 7A13.

46 Kirkpatrick, *Catalogue,* 220, 7C10. For a summary of the various instances when Ives uses wedges, including both converging and diverging wedge shapes, see Burkholder, "Critique of Tonality," 215. Triad wedges are also discussed by Winters, "Additive and Repetitive Techniques," 26–27.

47 Kirkpatrick, *Catalogue,* 219, 7C1.

Chapter 2: Contrapuntal Foundations

1 Reti, *Tonality in Modern Music,* 170–174. Reti cites this concept as an innovation of Ives's, noting that the polyphony of Schoenberg and Stravinsky remains "rooted in the classical example."

2 *Memos,* 47. Italics in original. Kirkpatrick's interpolation.

3 Ives's early contrapuntal training is discussed in more detail by Wallach, "New England Education," 110–290; and Lambert, "Ives and Counterpoint."

4 Burkholder, "Evolution," 644–666, and Burkholder, "Critique of Tonality."

5 Kirkpatrick, *Catalogue,* 220, 7C16, 7C17. The exposition may be a portion of a longer fugue that continued onto pages that are now missing.

6 The fugal "Song for Harvest Season" begins with subject entries related by perfect fourths (?); it originated as a sketch in George Ives's copybook (Kirkpatrick, *Catalogue,* 163–164, 6B18). The subject entries in the "Shining Shore" fugue are related by fifths (?), the same as in the sketches mentioned in the previous note.

7 In *Memos* (115), Ives mentions that his father "even let me try out 'two keys to once,' as an Interlude in an organ piece, *Variations on America*." However, such an interlude was not notated on the original manuscript of the piece (Kirkpatrick, *Catalogue,* 105–106). The familiar published version of the *Variations* (Mercury, 1949) includes this interlude plus another polytonal one that were apparently interpolated into the manuscript at a later time.

  The canon in Example 2.2 is number 7C14 in Kirkpatrick, *Catalogue,* 220.

8 For a discussion of the tonal aspects of the "Song for Harvest Season," see Wallach, "New England Education," 223–231.

9 The works are commonly known by a title such as this, although Ives actually called them "fugues with the theme in four different keys" (*Memos,* 49), which seems somewhat more accurate.

10 Burkholder, "Evolution," 498–538.

11 Cf. George Perle: "In the absence of the restrictive criteria of simultaneity and progression that are characteristic of tonal music, a rigorous contrapuntal scheme [in a post-tonal work] . . . is not the formidable achievement that it is often taken to be." George Perle, *Wozzeck,* vol. 2 of *The Operas of Alban Berg* (Berkeley: University of California Press, 1980), 15.

12 For a discussion of Ives's contrapuntal studies under Parker, see Wallach, "New England Education," 233–290, and Lambert, "Ives and Counterpoint," 125–129.

13 One possible source of inspiration for inversional transformations appears in the pedagogical materials Ives might have used. In *Memos* (49), Ives recalls that he used texts by Jadassohn with his father and at Yale. Inversional canon, called "canon

in contrary motion," is treated in chapter 2 of Salomon Jadassohn, *A Course of Instruction on Canon and Fugue,* 2nd ed., trans. Gustav (Tyson-) Wolff (Leipzig: Breitkopf und Härtel, 1904; first English edition 1888), 22–30.

14 For a more comprehensive discussion of this work, see Rinehart, "Ives' Compositional Idioms," 9–10, 43, 70–71, 97–99, 119–120, 126–131, 159–161; and Nicholls, *American Experimental Music,* 21–25.

15 The change occurs in the trombone, at the B♮ at the end of m. 22. Prior to this, the trombone is T9 of the trumpet; starting with the B, it is T8.

16 At the end of the score Ives writes, "From the Steeples—the Bells!—then the Rocks on the Mountains begin to shout!"

17 Cf. Percival Price, *The Bells of Man* (Oxford: Oxford University Press, 1983), 235–239. Change ringing dates back to the sixteenth century and is still practiced in England. In the usual bell-tower sequence, sometimes known as plain bob, these two scale-degree patterns would not actually occur in direct succession.

18 Ives's comments on this work are appended to the published score (ed. John Kirkpatrick and Jacques-Louis Monod, 1973), [31].

19 For example, see mm. 5–8 in the trombone and clarinet.

20 Ives's marginal comment is transcribed in Kirkpatrick, *Catalogue,* 65. The canon begins in m. 10.

21 This work is discussed briefly in Rinehart, "Ives' Compositional Idioms," 131–133, and Nicholls, *American Experimental Music,* 52–53.

22 This work is discussed briefly by Rinehart, "Ives' Compositional Idioms," 133–136, and Nicholls, *American Experimental Music,* 53–54 (citing the erroneous title *Largo Risoluto No. 3*).

23 The latter quote refers, of course, to composing fugues the wrong way. Certainly the same advice would apply to unorthodox conceptions of canon.

24 The Trio is also discussed by Rinehart, "Ives' Compositional Idioms," 137–139, and Nicholls, *American Experimental Music,* 31.

25 The *comes* voices echo the scale content of the *dux* voices but may introduce minor variations in the exact pitch-class succession. This is apparently what leads Nicholls to conclude that "the music is not truly canonic" (ibid., 31).

26 For further information on the latter work, see Schoffman, "Songs," 185–208. The song is based on an earlier exercise entitled *Greek Fugue* (cf. Kirkpatrick, *Catalogue,* 63).

27 For a history of Ives's early studies in fugal composition, see Wallach, "New England Education," 261–272, and Lambert, "Ives and Counterpoint."

28 Neither of Ives's best-known fugues is fully a product of his mature writing. The fugue he revised as the third movement of the Fourth Symphony was mostly composed when he was in college. The fugal first movement of the Fourth Violin Sonata draws extensively from one of his father's student fugues (cf. Kirkpatrick, *Catalogue,* 216, 7A3 ("4th fugue in B flat")).

Chapter 3: *Tone Roads No. 1*

1 Transcribed in Kirkpatrick, *Catalogue,* 50. Kirkpatrick notes that "Hartwell's . . . was a large store in Danbury, now Hartwell & Brady" (*Memos,* 63).

2 As transcribed in Kirkpatrick, *Catalogue,* 50.

3 The exact quote is from Voltaire (letter to Mme. de Fontaine, Sept. 23, 1750), but the original source is apparently Chaucer (from the Prologue to *The Astrolabe*): "Diverse pathes leden diverse folk the righte way to Rome." *Dictionary of Quotations,* collected and arranged and with comments by Bergen Evans (New York: Delacorte, 1968), 598.

4 Eliade, *Myth,* 18.

5 Some aspects of the structure of this piece are discussed by Nicholls, *American Experimental Music,* 64–67.

6 Information about transpositional distances is included here not to suggest particular transformational patterns or relationships, but simply to point out precise derivational connections.

7 There are striking similarities between this type of model-based thematic variation and development and Ives's treatment of borrowed material as explained in Burkholder, *All Made of Tunes.*

8 Subsequent presentations of this material confirm that the trichord at m. 12:3 in Example 3.5A should be C♯3–F♯3–B3, as indicated in parentheses, not the F♯2–B2–E3 that appears in the original. Ives apparently miscalculated this in his sketches.

9 Other appearances of B-A-C-H in Ives's music are mentioned in Chapter Five.

10 See, for example, the excerpt from *Study No. 5* shown in Example 6.6. Another instance is the canonic line in the second movement of the Second String Quartet, mm. 66–73.

11 Some aspects of this passage are discussed in Rinehart, "Ives' Compositional Idioms," 67–69, and Nicholls, *American Experimental Music,* 66–67.

12 To be precise, the measures following the arrival point (33–41) are a first ending that begins at the common destination but then regresses into a retransition and return of road A, leading to a repetition of mm. 5–32. The second ending is essentially the first measure of the first ending. This analysis ignores the retransition and repetition and treats both the beginning of the first ending and the entirety of the second ending as the arrival points of the roads.

13 This passage has been renotated in $\frac{3}{2}$ (from $\frac{4}{4}$ with triplets) for convenience of reading.

14 See *Memos,* 42. Such "piano-drum" chords are discussed in detail in Lambert, "Ives's 'Piano-Drum' Chords."

Chapter 4: Structural Models

1 Perle, *Serial Composition and Atonality,* 24.

2 This is the approach taken by Winters, "Additive and Repetitive Techniques."

3 Ives's wedges are also discussed by Schoffman, "Serialism"; Burkholder, "Evolution," 573–582; Winters, "Additive and Repetitive Techniques," 24–126; and Lambert, "Aggregate Structures." Each author approaches the topic from a different perspective, without necessarily using the term *wedge* or invoking the concept of structural model.

4 Ives, *Memos,* 120. See also p. 33 and the question in 47: "If two major or minor 3rds can make up a chord, why not more?"

5 The Interlude appears on p. 169 in the copybook; see Kirkpatrick, *Catalogue,* 107, 3D6ii. It is transcribed in Cowell, *Ives,* 35.

6 In particular, this Interlude comes across as a variation on the Prelude before No. 2.

7 In addition, this same Interlude is performed immediately following the Intermezzo but with a B♭-major triad added at the end.

8 See *Memos,* 61. The converging wedges represent the formation of blockers running ahead of a ball carrier. Some of the voices include whole steps mixed in with the half steps. The passage is transcribed and discussed in Winters, "Additive and Repetitive Techniques," 24–25.

9 Hitchcock makes this same point in *Ives,* 31–32.

10 The alto line in m. 10 appears here as in the original sketch (Kirkpatrick, *Catalogue,* 138, no. 2338). In later versions the note at m. 10:1 is G♮.

11 The complete song is given in Example 4.14.

12 Actually, Bach's fugue subject is two pitch classes short of being a complete chromatic wedge. See also the main theme of Bartók's Bagatelle for piano, op. 6, no. 2, one of the principal melodies in the first of Berg's op. 4 orchestral songs (first presented in the viola, mm. 10:1–15:1), and the tone row of R. Murray Schafer's *Patria.*

13 Kirkpatrick discusses the problems of dating this work in *Memos,* 159, 169. 1906 is a reasonable assumption, based on a comment of Ives in *Memos* (59), but the manuscript is dated 1909, which could be the date not of the original orchestral work but of the song arrangement (see Kirkpatrick, *Catalogue,* 192). To complicate matters, the version in *114 Songs* is dated 1920.

14 The model calls to mind some pitch structures from *Wozzeck* (e.g., II/3, mm. 380–381) and Berg's "master array" of interval cycles, as discussed in Perle, "Berg's Master Array."

15 For further discussion of this model and this song, see Schoffman, "Songs," 36–45.

16 Four complete transpositions (including the first one) plus a final incomplete one create an expansion from an initial tritone (F♯3–C4, m. 1:2) to a distance of four octaves plus a tritone (F♯0–C6, m. 4:2), beyond the normal range of the modern piano.

17 *Memos,* 91. Although the canonic and tonally stratified string parts of *Hallowe'en* have received ample analytical scrutiny (cf. Rinehart, "Ives' Compositional Idioms," 41–42, 62–66, 118–119, 142–144, and Hitchcock, *Ives,* 69–71), the piano part has not.

18 Winters, "Additive and Repetitive Techniques," 24–126.

19 It is Winters's broad definition of *wedge* that enables him to link it to palindrome. His wedges include not just pitch-space unfoldings but also any process of graduated change. This definition encompasses many such processes that are organized palindromically.

20 This song is analyzed in full in Chapter Eight.

21 The labels are printed in the published score (Merion Music, 1981).

22 Grantham, "Harmonic 'Leitmotif' System."

23 Grantham (ibid., 13) gives a similar chart of the structure, but does not point out any palindromic associations.

24 Grantham recognizes the latter type of recurrence, as is evident when he states, "Occasionally, a leitmotif will not return literally, and in these cases some intervallic characteristic of the leitmotif usually serves as a source for the harmonic material of the verse setting" (ibid., 4). For the most part, however, he focuses on recurrences of LMs in something like their original forms.

25 For further discussion of this work, see Rinehart, "Ives' Compositional Idioms," 43–44, 70–71, 97–99, 119–120, 126–131, 159–161; and Winters, "Additive and Repetitive Techniques," 105–112.

26 Winters describes this work in "Additive and Repetitive Techniques," 112–118.

27 See *Memos* Appendix 17, 266. Ives says, "*Calcium Light Night* was started as, or at least had something like, the 'piano stunts' of and around college days" (*Memos,* 61).

28 In the score arranged by Henry Cowell (in the Ives Archive at Yale), the units are identified by upper-case letters. These letters do not appear in the score available from the Presser Rental Library.

29 Ives identifies this tune, as well as two others used in the piece, in a memo described in Kirkpatrick, *Catalogue,* 49. The tune notated in Example 4.12A was used by members of the Psi Upsilon fraternity, and the other two are "DKE Song" and "DKE Marching Song," associated with the Delta Kappa Epsilon fraternity. For more information see Henderson, *Charles Ives Tunebook,* 146–147, 194.

30 As described in *Memos,* 61–62.

31 This work is discussed in depth in Maske, *Kammermusik,* 14–15, 62, 105, 112–114, 134; and Winters, "Additive and Repetitive Techniques," 100–104.

32 Schoffman ("Songs," 46) notes that this text is similar to a passage in the *Essays Before a Sonata* (31) in which Ives paraphrases Emerson.

33 Kirkpatrick, *Catalogue,* 191.

34 Ives uses a similar technique in *Over the Pavements* (1906–1913), mm. 81–92.

35 The next arpeggio in the pattern would consist of nine notes separated by interval 13s, which would require a total of 105 keys (spanning $8 \times 13 = 104$ half steps).

36 Kirkpatrick, "Ives."

Chapter 5: Transformational Techniques

1 The theoretical discussion here borrows most extensively from Lewin, *Generalized Musical Intervals and Transformations.* It is also influenced by Morris, *Composition with*

Pitch-Classes. A canonical transformation should not be confused with the contrapuntal technique of canon.

2 This is a group in the mathematical sense, as explained by Lewin, ibid., 3–4.

3 See Lewin, ibid., 104.

4 Morris summarizes the canonical groups defined in the various studies (though using different terminology) in "Set Groups, Complementation, and Mappings Among Pitch-Class Sets," *Journal of Music Theory* 26 (1982): 101–104. See also Morris, *Composition with Pitch-Classes,* 78–81. The advocates of transposition are Hubert Howe, "Some Combinational Properties of Pitch Structures," *Perspectives of New Music* 4/1 (1965): 45–61; and Eric Regener, "On Allen Forte's Theory of Chords," *Perspectives of New Music* 13/1 (1974): 191–212. See also the discussion of "Tn-types" in Rahn, *Basic Atonal Theory,* 74–77.

5 As best known from Forte, *Structure of Atonal Music.* See also Rahn, *Basic Atonal Theory.*

6 Daniel Starr, "Sets, Invariance, and Partitions," *Journal of Music Theory* 22 (1978): 136–183; Morris, "Set Groups, Complementation, and Mappings," 102; and Morris, *Composition with Pitch-Classes,* 66.

7 Morris, *Composition with Pitch-Classes,* 78–81. He emphasizes, however, that an orientation around Tn and TnI "should not be taken as prescriptive or normative." His discussion establishes why Tn and TnI make up a strong group, not why other groups are less desirable.

8 This occurs in mm. 40:1–43:1, which are transposed and contrapuntally inverted as 43:4–46:4. In a later passage of the same piece the hands switch parts without transposing (mm. 57–62 = 63–68).

9 T0 occurs in mm. 25:1–28:1, T4I in mm. 28:3–31:2.

10 The top voice of mm. 1:1–4:1 recurs at T4 in an inner voice in mm. 5:1–7:2, and then at T4I in the top voice starting in m. 10 and discontinued in m. 11. Measures 1–11 are repeated as mm. 12–22.

11 Other occurrences of B-A-C-H in the *Three-Page Sonata,* of which there are many, are identified in Kirkpatrick's "Editor's Notes" for the published version of the work (Mercury, 1975) and in Gingerich, "Processes of Motivic Transformation," 126–155. The extensive use of B-A-C-H calls to mind J. S. Bach's final fugue ("Contrapunctus XIX," left incomplete) from *The Art of the Fugue,* in which the motive is used in a third subject (m. 193 ff.).

12 Example 5.1 also illustrates some of the problems with the publication of the overture. The bracketed notes accompanying Examples 5.1A, 5.1B, and 5.1D show errant notations that appear in the published score; the examples themselves include corrections of those bracketed notes. Since the complete original sketch of the work is not extant, some of the corrections are speculative, based on a comparison of the questionable material with appearances of the same ideas elsewhere in the piece. For example, the corrected version of the theme in Example 5.1A, or some transformation thereof, appears numerous times in the piece. Unfortunately, the portion of the sketch that would contain this particular occur-

rence of the theme is missing, and Ives's first full score, which is the earliest available evidence in his hand, contains the errant version. (See Kirkpatrick, *Catalogue*, 32–33.) On the basis of what happens elsewhere in the piece, it does not seem likely that Ives intended to give this melody the form in which it ultimately appears. For a fuller discussion of problems such as these in the overture, see Hilliard, "Ives' *Robert Browning Overture.*"

13 John Kirkpatrick and Garry Clarke, in their Editors' Notes to the 1971 Merion Music edition, point out some discrepancies between the pc ordering of the theme and that of the variation.

14 In general, studies of unordered (Tn/TnI) pitch-class sets in the music of Ives have not been uniformly illuminating. An introductory study by Allen Forte provocatively suggested numerous avenues to pursue, but those who have attempted to follow up his efforts, such as Gregory Danner and J. Timothy Kolosick, have not achieved nearly the same degree of success. See Forte, "Ives and Atonality"; Danner, "Ives' Harmonic Language"; and Kolosick, "Computer-Assisted, Set-Theoretic Investigation."

15 For additional information on this subject, including discussion of aggregates formed by using both systematic and other methods, see Lambert, "Aggregate Structures."

16 The first chord of *Central Park in the Dark* (m. 1, upper strings) is transposed up three half steps to the second chord. See Example 9.7. In "A Farewell to Land," the first chord in the piano (m. 1:2) is transposed by T1.

17 In the orchestral piano (both parts), mm. 46–50.

18 Ives's article on quarter-tone composition, entitled "Some 'Quarter-Tone' Impressions," was originally published in the *Franco-American Music Society Bulletin,* March 26, 1925. It is reprinted in *Essays,* 107–119.

19 Cf. Perle, *Serial Composition and Atonality,* 95. Perle cites m. 212 of the *Ode.* Ives forms an aggregate from nonoverlapping triads that are not equivalent in *Study No. 20,* m. 94. This chord comprises, from bottom to top, CM, B♭+, F+, and G♯m triads.

20 This is page 1219 (Kirkpatrick, *Catalogue,* 27). The formation has no obvious connection to the violin sonata but would not be out of place among the pitch structures of the symphony.

21 The full title of this piece is *Rough and Ready et al and/or The Jumping Frog.* It is the second in Kirkpatrick's grouping of *Five Take-Offs.*

22 Webern's row is <ET2376845019>, forming adjacent intervals <E414E281718>. The trichords are additionally equivalent via the four twelve-tone operations. If the initial trichord is X, the other three are, in order, RI(X), R(X), and I(X).

23 They could also be considered rotated retrograde inversions, since B-A-C-H is RI-invariant.

24 Kolosick alludes to these relationships in "Computer-Assisted, Set-Theoretic Investigation," 69–70. Gingerich identifies versions a and b of the motive, as well as other motives, in the theme ("Processes of Motivic Transformation," 145–147).

25 Morris, *Composition with Pitch-Classes,* 107. Morris's INT identifies ordered pitch-class intervals between all pairs of consecutive pc's in a segment, not just the adjacent ones.

26 See Morris, *Composition with Pitch-Classes,* 108–109. For example, if segment X = <1427>, INT(X) = <3T5>, INT(T3(X)) (pc <475T>) = <3T5>, INT(T1I(X)) (pc <09E6>) = <927>, INT(RT3I(X)) (pc <T574>) = <729>, and INT(RT1I(X)) (pc <6E90>) = <5T3>. Thus INT(Tn(X)) = R(INT(RTnI(X))) and INT (TnI(X)) = R(INT(R(X))).

27 Morris, *Composition with Pitch-Classes,* 114.

28 To be precise, one new interval is added—i.e., the "wraparound" interval between the pc originally in the last position and the pc originally in the first position—and one is removed—i.e., the new wraparound. Morris (in *Composition with Pitch-Classes*) handles this situation by defining a *cyclic INT* (CINT), which includes all the adjacent intervals plus the wraparound.

29 Morris, *Composition with Pitch-Classes,* 115. The order mappings (OM) of a segment are the order positions, starting with 0. This is symbolized for a segment X by OM$_x$X, where the subscript indicates the segment that defines the ordering—called the reference segment—and the final symbol (X) indicates the segment with which the reference segment is being compared. Thus OM$_x$X gives the order of the reference segment; it compares X with itself. OM$_x$Y compares the order mappings of X with a different ordering of the same pitch classes in segment Y—the order mappings of X as they appear in Y.

30 The oboe's final D♯5 recalls the initial pitch of the series before the twelfth pc (0) arrives in the first oboe at the beginning of the next measure. Example 5.8C skips over the D♯ and shows the systematically consistent pc 0 in brackets.

31 We are using Morris's notation for rotation, from *Composition with Pitch-Classes,* 108. If r$_r$A = B, A$_n$ = B$_{(n+r)}$ where (n+r) is taken mod #A. That is, "r$_r$A means that we take the last r pcs of . . . A and place them at A's beginning."

32 These are by Gunther Schuller (Columbia MS-7318), Gerard Schwarz (Nonesuch H-71222), and Kenneth Singleton (Columbia M-32969). The editors discuss their versions and performance-related matters in "Three Realizations of *Chromâtimelôdtune,*" in Hitchcock and Perlis, *An Ives Celebration,* 87–109. Singleton's is the most faithful to Ives's apparent intentions. The versions are discussed further in Lambert, "Another View of *Chromâtimelôdtune.*"

33 For an analysis and discussion of the other pages, see Lambert, "Another View of *Chromâtimelôdtune.*"

34 This is page q2794 (Kirkpatrick, *Catalogue,* 69). Some marginal inscriptions, mostly relating to instrumentation, have been omitted. All four pages are reproduced in facsimile—and all marginalia are transcribed—in "Three Realizations of *Chromâtimelôdtune,*" 89–93.

35 This happens at the beginning of the second page (Kirkpatrick, *Catalogue,* 69, 2796).

36 The derivation of the source ordering from the chromatic scale could be repre-

sented formally as a mapping of each note in a chromatic scale to every other note in the sequence of half-step-related fifths as follows: $C_n = S_{(n+n) \bmod 13}$, where C = the chromatic scale, S = the sequence of half-step-related fifths, and n = 0–12. (C should wrap around to pc 0 (C_{12} = pc 0) for us to be able to map twelve pc's onto thirteen.)

37 Cf. Milton Babbitt's discussion of combinational and permutational systems in "Twelve-Tone Invariants as Compositional Determinants," *The Musical Quarterly* 46 (1960): 247–248.

38 Sherwood ("Questions and Veracities," 441) lists the dates for *Psalm 25* as "1898–1902 (original)" and "ca. 1914 (reconstruction and ink copy)." As observed by John Kirkpatrick and Gregg Smith in the critical notes accompanying the published edition (Merion, 1979, p. 25), most of the passage under discussion here was clearly part of the original sketches.

39 This process may be quantified using Morris's CC measurement of order similarity (*Composition with Pitch-Classes*, 120–121). The CC varies from −1 to 1, where 1 is identity and −1 is identity under R. Most of the CC values between adjacent segments in the *Psalm 25* passage are between .8 and .97, while CCs between non-adjacencies are smaller, and the CC between the first and last segment is .427.

40 The example omits an additional reordering that is cut short after four notes, mm. 36:1–39:2.

41 See mm. 1–12. The scramblings occur in the quintuplets, within a single measure. Usually, segments presented in the first half of the measure reappear permuted in the second half.

42 For example, chromatic wedges move through patterns of half-step transpositions in the low strings of mm. 55–136.

43 See, for example, the violins of mm. 107–112.

44 Ives employs similar procedures to reorder a chromatic scale in the orchestral version of "Majority" (1914–1915). This happens in verse 6, in music that is excluded from the published voice-piano version. See Kirkpatrick, *Catalogue*, 126, q2975.

45 Multiplication by seven maps the chromatic scale onto the cycle of fifths. See Morris, *Composition with Pitch-Classes*, 65–67.

Chapter 6: *Study No. 5*

1 This is the G4 sustained in the right hand starting at the bottom of p. 12 of the Merion edition and ending in the second system of p. 13 (see voice 2 of Example 6.13). Mandel calls this "one of those Ivesian ideas that are impossible to realize in performance, except by judicious repetition" ("Editorial Notes" to the Merion edition, p. 5). He quotes Kirkpatrick as commenting that "the long G reminds one that Bach, in his keyboard-string music, seems to have used an organ notation of the long notes, because some instruments need more repetition" (ibid.).

2 Inscribed on the bottom margin of p. 2 of manuscript; Kirkpatrick, *Catalogue*, 97, q1787. Alan Mandel, who premiered and edited the work (Merion Music, 1988), plays the entire piece without assistance, but says that it is "quite appropriate to

call on an assisting pianist" ("Performance Notes" introducing the Merion edition, p. 4).

3 "Three Realizations of *Chromâtimelôdtune*," 100.

4 Because there are few barlines, I use beat numbers, following the numbering of quarter-note beats in the Merion edition to refer to specific points in the score.

5 In his sketch Ives places an *X* under each note of the first aggregate (beats 55–62) plus three repeated notes (63–64). Perhaps he was crossing off pitch classes to ensure that he had stated all of them.

6 He uses barlines in a few other places, such as beats 33, 41, and 49 in section I. They do not always mark an obvious division in the formal or pitch structure.

Chapter 7: Transposition Cycles

1 See, for example, Gary Karpinski, "The Interval Cycles in the Music of Claude Debussy," paper delivered at the annual meeting of the Society for Music Theory, Oakland, California, November 10, 1990; Antokoletz, *Bartók;* Antokoletz, "Interval Cycles"; and Perle, "Berg's Master Array."

2 Perle, *The Listening Composer,* 92.

3 This is Perle's characterization of musical cycles; he borrows the phrase from James Gleick's study of chaos (*The Listening Composer,* 55–92).

4 A preliminary investigation of this subject was undertaken in Lambert, "Interval Cycles." Portions of Chapters Seven through Ten are revisions and extensions of ideas first presented in that article.

5 See Lewin, "Transformational Techniques," *Generalized Musical Intervals and Transformations,* and *Musical Form and Transformation.*

6 See Cohn, "Transpositional Combination," and "Inversional Symmetry and Transpositional Combination."

7 See especially Perle, "Berg's Master Array," and Antokoletz, "Interval Cycles."

8 Ives used virtually the same ideas in the *Overture and March "1776"* (1903), mm. 42–56, strings. This material was added sometime after the piece was composed, possibly after the composition of *Largo Risoluto No. 1.*

9 See Morgan, "Spatial Form."

10 This inscription appears on the first page of a sketch of the first movement. See Kirkpatrick, *Catalogue,* 60, q1386.

11 Ives characterizes the end of the Fourth Symphony this way by quoting Henry Bellamann's program notes for the work in *Memos,* 66. Kirkpatrick finds no source for the quote in Bellamann's writings about the symphony (ibid., note 9).

12 For a discussion of the sacred mountain in a mythological context see Mircea Eliade, *Myth,* 12–14. Also see Rathert, "Paysage imaginaire," 133, for a valuable investigation of this kind of imagery as it relates to Ives, and specifically to the *Universe Symphony.*

13 See Joseph Campbell, *The Power of Myth* (New York: Doubleday, 1988), 214–217. See also the chapter on "The Universal Round" in Joseph Campbell, *The Hero with a Thousand Faces,* 2nd ed. (Princeton: Princeton University Press, 1968), 261–269.

14 For example, the opening trombone motive, pc <92>, is answered by the trumpet's, <70>, forming the interval 5 sequence <9270> (mm. 6–7).

15 Kirkpatrick does not suggest a date for this sketch (*Catalogue*, 226, 7E38). The "Thoreau" movement was composed around 1910–1915. The ideas in the sketch do not appear to have been used in the movement or elsewhere, although there are vague resemblances between the sketch and some of the movement's harmonies. See Babcock, "Ives' 'Thoreau'" for a discussion of passages from "Thoreau" that have some connection to T5 cycles.

16 The chords in this passage assume considerable significance in the analysis of this work by Arthur Maisel, "*The Fourth of July* by Charles Ives: Mixed Harmonic Criteria in a Twentieth-Century Classic," *Theory and Practice* 6/1 (1981): 3–32.

17 Marshall, "Ives' Quotations," demonstrates the pervasive importance of this tune in *The Fourth of July*.

18 When the song was published in *New Music* in 1933, Ives added some accidentals to this passage that would alter the cyclic unfoldings described here. The most substantial changes affect the stems-up bass-clef voice, which was revised to read G♯–A♮–A♯–C♮–C♯–D♭–D♮–E♭–E♯–F♯, very nearly a T1 cycle. Ives also replaced the sharp before the A2 in the T2 cycle with a natural, thereby introducing a chromatic moment into the otherwise whole-step ascent.

19 Burkholder, "Critique of Tonality," 216–217, cites this passage within a discussion of Ives's methods of supplanting tonal forces.

20 The triad sequence in the first two measures, for example, is C major, B♭ minor, A♭ minor, G♭ major, A♭ minor, B♭ minor.

21 See Edward Aldwell and Carl Schachter, *Harmony and Voice Leading*, 2nd ed. (New York: Harcourt Brace Jovanovich, 1989), 542–551.

22 Ives's "Songs My Mother Taught Me" (1895) is noteworthy in this connection. It is a very traditional song, written during his Yale years in a quite conventional language, but its key structure suggests an equal division of the octave into major thirds: E♭ major (mm. 1–14), G major (mm. 17–19), B major (mm. 20–26), and back to E♭ major (mm. 27 to the end). The pattern is articulated only by the key areas; the material that expresses each tonality is not transpositionally related.

23 It becomes immediately apparent that the sequence is slightly inconsistent as a result of changes in the right hand's accented chords if we compare the ones in m. 8 (sc's 3–3 and 3–4) with the ones in m. 9 (sc's 3–6 and 3–4). Then the next four accented chords (in mm. 10–12) follow sequentially from m. 9, alternating 3–6 and 3–4. Starting in m. 10, however, all accented chords are members of sc 3–6. These inconsistencies do not affect the sequential regularity of the top voice.

24 The "DOH" chord is an aggregate formed of overlapping and nonoverlapping triads, very similar to the final sonority of *Rough and Ready* shown in Example 5.4. "SOH" and "FAH" also include prominent triads, although not exclusively, and not within complete aggregates. These factors help to suggest a hierarchization of the three chords, by analogy to the eponymous chord functions in tonality.

Ives explores the idea of using vertical aggregates as formal signposts in several of his short piano works. For example, he uses a nontriadic 12-pc chord as the opening sound of *Study No. 2* (1907–?1908).

25 For example, mm. 25:1–34:1 in the piano are T1 of mm. 4–9, with some variation.

26 The canonic line in the second movement begins in the viola in m. 42 and is answered by the first violin starting in m. 43, by the cello in m. 44, and by the second violin in m. 46.

27 One pitch in version 4, both in the original manuscript and in the printed score, does not fit the transposition pattern. In an exact transposition, the A4 in m. 43 would be A♯4.

28 Davidson, "Transcendental Unity," cites the time structure of a day as an important symbol of unity in Ives's writings.

Chapter 8: "The Cage"

1 Richard Warren's discography lists six recordings of the song in the Ives Collection as of 1972; perhaps the best-known recording released since then is by Jan DeGaetani and Gilbert Kalish (Nonesuch H-71325). See Warren, *Ives Discography*, 7–8. See also Block, *Ives*, 67–69.

2 Charles Burkhart, *Anthology for Musical Analysis*, 4th ed. (New York: Holt, Rinehart, and Winston, 1986), 470–471.

3 The manuscript is q2849 in Kirkpatrick, *Catalogue*, 45. In *114 Songs* Ives dates the arrangement for voice and piano 1906, but this may refer to the date of composition, not to the date of the arrangement.

4 In the original sketch and in the published orchestral version, the melody is doubled a perfect fourth higher. And in the sketch only—not in any published version—Ives writes additional lines in mirror inversion with the main melody. In *Memos* (56) Ives recalls, "The main line in 4ths had two lines of inverted counterpoint going with it (see old manuscript). Whether this was meant to increase the fatalism or reduce it, I don't know. It was left out of the printed score and the song copy (I can't remember exactly why, except [that] it's hard to play, and for some lady-boys to listen to)."

5 Jan DeGaetani does this in her recording mentioned earlier (note 1).

6 Larry Starr finds an aural and visual parallel between the chords in the sequence and the bars on a cage (*Union of Diversities*, 128).

7 Some of these relationships are pointed out by Schoffman, "Songs," 28–35; Euteneuer-Rohrer, "Ives: 'The Cage'"; and Nicholls, *American Experimental Music*, 40–42.

8 In Starr's words, "The verbal and musical unanswered question hangs in the shocked silence, lingering beyond the point where the piece stops—as Ives's fermata clearly indicates" (*Union of Diversities*, 128). Starr mentions "The Cage" as one of several examples in Ives's work where a song is complete in one sense but incomplete in another.

Schoffman notes in his description of the open-ended ending that the last three chords plus chord 19 begin a rhythmic diminution series that recalls, but never completes, the rhythmic series of the introduction ("Songs," 31).

Chapter 9: Combination Cycles

1 Combination cycles are also discussed, somewhat differently, in Lambert, "Interval Cycles."

2 Sequences of alternating major and minor thirds recall the opening of the fourth movement of the *Hammerklavier* Sonata. In m. 10, immediately preceding the Allegro risoluto, Beethoven constructs chords above a bass sequence of intervals <98> that concludes at the first pitch-class repetition: A–F♯–D–B–G–E–C–A–F–D. This is followed by a return to A. The passage is discussed by Charles Rosen, *The Classical Style* (New York: Norton, 1972), 429. A similar sequence occurs in the second movement of the Ninth Symphony (mm. 159–171).

3 This process is described by Nicholls, *American Experimental Music,* 73–81.

4 *Memos,* 101.

5 My choice of terminology is inspired from a use of the word *omnibus* in Victor Fell Yellin's study (unpublished) of a cyclic chromatic chord progression found in music of Mozart and Schubert, among others, cited by Robert W. Wason, *Viennese Harmonic Theory from Albrechtsberger to Schenker and Schoenberg* (Ann Arbor: UMI Research Press, 1985), 16–19. Though there are similarities between registral patterns in Yellin's omnibus and in Ives's, the choice here reflects simply the quality of pervasiveness conveyed by the word *omnibus.*

6 This fifth sonority is notated as shown here in later sketches and scores, but in the earliest sketch (q3111) the natural sign preceding the D4 appears to be marked over a sharp sign (Kirkpatrick, *Catalogue,* 11). With a D♯ the chord would be formed of intervals <444>, consistent with the Omnibus pattern. Perhaps Ives changed the D♯ to D♮ to avoid a pc repetition between the bottom and top notes.

7 "The Subway was started, and 'blocks' were regular things—getting out of the block and back into it again" (*Memos,* 64).

8 As explained by the composer in notes accompanying the score.

9 For a more detailed explanation of this passage, see Rinehart, "Ives' Compositional Idioms," 44–46, 91–93, and Schoffman, "Serialism," 25.

10 The <49> combination in m. 5 excludes the bottom two notes, which are held over from the previous chord.

11 See Rinehart, "Ives' Compositional Idioms," 71–86; Argento, "Digest Analysis"; Hitchcock, *Ives,* 18–20; Schoffman, "Songs," 209–234; and Schoffman, "Serialism," 28–29.

12 Ives uses a very similar labeling in a sketch (Kirkpatrick, *Catalogue,* 210, q2908, q3048), except that he makes a distinction (with superscripts) between separate statements of the same chords.

13 In the sketch Ives points out the derivations by labeling the arpeggiations with the same letters he uses for the chordal version (Kirkpatrick, *Catalogue,* 210). Argento ("Digest Analysis") describes the arpeggiation process completely.

14 Ives adds a lower voice in smaller noteheads just below the primary ones for "lower voice, or voices, if there be a chorus" (footnote to the Merion edition, p. 44). In the original sketch (q2908) this voice formed an aggregate, if the G♯ in m. 28 can be considered shared between both voices. But in later versions, and as shown in Example 9.11, he destroyed the aggregate completion by changing the first new lower-voice note of m. 31 from A to G♯. The trichords of the original lower-voice aggregate (including the G♯ in m. 28) were 3–5, 3–5, 3–10, and 3–3.

Chapter 10: "A Universe in Tones"

1 Feder has a different view of the *Universe Symphony* (*Ives*, 292–297). He regards the symphony's conception and materials as evidence of mental dysfunction, viewing the systematic methods as "formulae" that Ives fell back on because of an "ebbing creative impulse" (p. 296). This view is consistent with much of the rest of Feder's study, in which systematic pieces tend to play minor and marginal roles in Ives's oeuvre. It is an unfortunate view, not only because such a wealth of musical ideas deserves greater attention but also because Ives's interest in systematic methods would seem to provide further supporting evidence for Feder's theories about the influence of George Ives on his son.

2 Sketch page q3011 (Kirkpatrick, *Catalogue*, 27). The quote has been edited slightly to resolve ambiguities of syntax.

3 Sketch page q3040 (Kirkpatrick, *Catalogue*, 28). The quote has been edited to reduce syntactical confusion, although much remains.

4 For further commentary on the symphony and its metaphors, see Kavanaugh, "Music and American Transcendentalism."

5 See Kirkpatrick, *Catalogue*, 26–28. As is often the case with Ives's manuscripts, it is unclear whether a large number of pages for the symphony have simply been lost or destroyed or whether the work was never fully sketched out to begin with.

6 This is Cowell's description in *Ives and His Music*, 201. Ives is also said to have described the symphony this way to Christine Loring, who did secretarial work for him in his later years, and to George F. Roberts, his favorite copyist. See Perlis, *Ives Remembered*, 117, 188. There is, however, no extant description of the hilltop scenario by Ives himself.

7 Larry Austin has taken Ives's offer quite seriously. Culminating some twenty years of reconstruction and study, Austin's "realization and completion" of Ives's *Universe Symphony* was premiered on January 29, 1994, in Cincinnati, by the Cincinnati Philharmonia Orchestra conducted by Gerhard Samuel. A recording was released on Centaur (CRC 2205). Austin explains, "My intent in transcribing and interpreting Ives's sketches has been to realize and complete both Ives's explicit and implicit compositional, formal, and aesthetic intent for the work. Hence, to the extent intended and possible, I have meant this realization and completion of Ives's *Universe Symphony* to be experienced and appreciated in performance as a 100% Ives composition" (liner notes to Centaur CRC 2205, 3). There can be no doubt that Austin is as much a collaborator as a reconstructor, and that some

other "realization and completion" could sound quite different from this one. But there can also be no doubt that Austin has created a moving and powerful work that is readily "experienced and appreciated as a 100% Ives composition." One can easily imagine Ives's being delighted with the results.

Johnny Reinhard, by contrast, feels that Ives essentially completed the symphony. Reinhard produced a realization based exclusively on sketch materials that was premiered on June 6, 1996, in New York. Certainly it is true that Reinhard found enough sketch material to make a performable whole; whether the result can be considered "complete" and faithful to Ives's artistic vision is an issue that deserves extensive consideration.

8 At the North American Festival of New Music, State University of New York at Buffalo.

9 Austin, "Ives's 'Life Pulse Prelude.'"

10 Page 3025 (Kirkpatrick, *Catalogue,* 26). The quote has been edited slightly for clarity.

11 As explained in Austin, "Ives's 'Life Pulse Prelude,'" 75–76.

12 Ibid., 75.

13 Ibid., 81. One is reminded of Kenneth Singleton's comments about *Chromâtimelôdtune,* cited in Chapter Six with regard to a similar effect in *Study No. 5.*

14 It is not clear whether the percussion cycle and the rest of the orchestra are to be metrically coordinated or whether they should remain autonomous entities. Austin ("Ives's 'Life Pulse Prelude,'" 69) suggests that one page of the Prelude sketches (3020) might be an attempt to coordinate them, but this seems doubtful. In his version of the whole work Austin treats the percussion as an autonomous group—indeed, it is one of several autonomous orchestral groups.

15 Descriptions taken from *Memos,* 106–108.

16 Ives, *Memos,* 106. Kirkpatrick's interpolation.

17 All quotes in this paragraph taken from *Memos,* 106–107.

18 See note 10 and the corresponding text.

19 This "patch" for section A originally appeared on two sketch pages for section C (q3041, q3046).

20 Ives's idea of a complete pitch-class universe forms a striking parallel with some of Scriabin's ideas. In preliminary sketches for a never-completed work entitled *Mysterium* (remarkably similar in conception to Ives's *Universe Symphony*), Scriabin forms aggregates by combining two tetrachordal subsets of an octatonic collection with the four pitch classes that are not part of that collection. See Perle, "Scriabin's Self-Analyses," 119–120. This structure would apparently play a symbolic role in a depiction of the history of the universe, including musical representations of evolution and humanity. Indeed, Faubion Bowers's description of the basic outline of *Mysterium* could virtually apply to the *Universe Symphony:* "from Oneness to Duality, into Multiplicity and finally to return to the initial Oneness." See Faubion Bowers, *The New Scriabin: Enigma and Answers* (New York: St. Martin's Press, 1973), 124. Ultimately, Scriabin's conception was more exotic and bizarre

than Ives's: his ideas for *Mysterium* included some kind of cosmic act of sexual intimacy that would culminate in the actual destruction of the world.

21 Actually, the two score-sketch pages (3050, q3045) are not clearly marked by Ives and cannot definitively be linked to section B. The musical ideas in them are typical of what one would expect to find in this section, and Kirkpatrick lists them that way (*Catalogue,* 27), but we cannot be sure.

22 This chord reveals one apparent calculation error. The <67> sequence starts with the C2 and progresses upward to F#2, C#3, G3, and D4, and then down to G#3. The next note should be D#3, not D3, as Ives writes. Subsequent notes follow in correct sequence from the D3.

23 Ives inscribes alternative instrumentations of groups 1 and 4 in and between staves 15 and 16.

24 Inscribed within the fifth and sixth staves from the bottom of the page.

25 Some of the pages that Kirkpatrick considers part of section C may have been intended for other sections. The material on q4449, for example, bears a strong resemblance to parts of sections A and B—the same heaven chords, a similar use of cycles in both chords and melodies, and so forth. Kirkpatrick places this page in section C because of a large *III* at the top, but this could refer to a chord or an instrumental group. Also, inscriptions at the top read "The Earth and the Heavens" and "and lo now it is night / and lo the Earth is of the Heavens / (on the Plateau, Keene Valley Oct. 1915)." Perhaps this is one of the first pages Ives wrote, as he recalls in *Memos* (106): "When we were in Keene Valley, on the plateau, staying in the fall of 1915 . . . I started something I'd had in mind for some time . . . trying out a parallel way of listening to music." And the title "The Earth and the Heavens" resembles a reference on the first page of the score sketch of section A (q3027) to "Symphony The Earth and the Firmament."

26 That this is Ives's intent is clear from his verbal instructions, even though some of the musical notations show something slightly different. In the second chord, for example, rather than inflecting every other *interval* in chord 1, he appears to begin inflecting every other *note*. Doing this does not result in the intervallic structure he wants; perhaps he discontinued writing out the inflected chords, choosing just to describe them, after he realized as much.

27 Actually, chord 13 has three options. Example 10.8 chooses the second (top two staves, second half of the measure).

28 Burkholder, *Ives,* 114.

29 He said this to Christine Loring, his occasional secretary. Quoted in Perlis, *Ives Remembered,* 117.

30 Cowell, *Ives,* 203. Ives's copyist George Roberts also said that Ives did not intend to finish the symphony; see Perlis, *Ives Remembered,* 188.

31 Feder, *Ives,* 296.

Bibliography

Antokoletz, Elliott. *The Music of Béla Bartók: A Study of Tonality and Progression in Twentieth-Century Music.* Berkeley: University of California Press, 1984.

————. "Interval Cycles in Stravinsky's Early Ballets." *Journal of the American Musicological Society* 34/3 (1986): 578–614.

Argento, Domenick. "A Digest Analysis of Ives' 'On the Antipodes.'" *Student Musicologists at Minnesota* 6 (1975–1976): 192–200.

Austin, Larry. "Charles Ives's 'Life Pulse Prelude' for Percussion Orchestra: A Realization for Modern Performance from Sketches for his *Universe Symphony.*" *Percussive Notes* 23/6 (1985): 58–84.

Babcock, Michael J. "Ives' 'Thoreau': A Point of Order." *Proceedings of the American Society of University Composers* 9 and 10 (1976): 89–102.

Ballantine, Christopher. "Charles Ives and the Meaning of Quotation in Music." *The Musical Quarterly* 65/2 (1979): 167–184.

Block, Geoffrey. *Charles Ives: A Bio-Bibliography.* New York: Greenwood Press, 1988.

Burkholder, J. Peter. "Charles Ives and His Fathers: A Response to Maynard Solomon." Newsletter of the Institute for Studies in American Music 8/1 (1988): 8–11.

————. *Charles Ives: The Ideas Behind the Music.* New Haven: Yale University Press, 1985.

————. "The Critique of Tonality in the Early Experimental Music of Charles Ives." *Music Theory Spectrum* 12/2 (1990): 205–207.

————. "The Evolution of Charles Ives's Music: Aesthetics, Quotation, Technique." Ph.D. diss., University of Chicago, 1983.

————. "'Quotation' and Emulation: Charles Ives's Uses of His Models." *The Musical Quarterly* 71/1 (1985): 1–26.

————. *All Made of Tunes: Charles Ives and the Uses of Musical Borrowing.* New Haven: Yale University Press, 1995.

Cohn, Richard. "Bartók's Octatonic Strategies: A Motivic Approach." *Journal of the American Musicological Society* 44/2 (1991): 262–300.

————. "Inversional Symmetry and Transpositional Combination in Bartók." *Music Theory Spectrum* 10 (1988): 19–42.

————. "Properties and Generability of Transpositionally Invariant Sets." *Journal of Music Theory* 35/1–2 (1991): 1–32.

————. "Transpositional Combination in Twentieth-Century Music." Ph.D. diss., Eastman School of Music of the University of Rochester, 1986.

Cowell, Henry. *New Musical Resources.* New York: Knopf, 1930.

Cowell, Henry, and Cowell, Sidney. *Charles Ives and His Music.* 2nd ed. New York: Oxford University Press, 1969. Reprint, 1975.

Cyr, Gordon. "Intervallic Structural Elements in Ives's Fourth Symphony." *Perspectives of New Music* 9/2 and 10/1 (1971): 291–303.

Danner, Gregory. "Ives' Harmonic Language." *Journal of Musicological Research* 5 (1984): 237–249.

Davidson, Audrey. "Transcendental Unity in the Works of Charles Ives." *American Quarterly* 22/1 (1970): 35–44.

Eliade, Mircea. *The Myth of the Eternal Return; or, Cosmos and History.* Trans. Willard R. Trask. Princeton, N.J.: Princeton University Press, 1971.

Emerson, Ralph Waldo. *Selected Essays, Lectures, and Poems.* Edited and with a foreword by Robert D. Richardson, Jr. New York: Bantam Books, 1990.

Euteneuer-Rohrer, Ursula Henrietta. "Charles Ives: 'The Cage.'" *Neuland* 1 (1980): 47–52.

Feder, Stuart. *Charles Ives, "My Father's Song": A Psychoanalytic Biography.* New Haven: Yale University Press, 1992.

Forte, Allen. "Ives and Atonality." In *An Ives Celebration: Papers and Panels of the Charles Ives Centennial Festival-Conference,* edited by H. Wiley Hitchcock and Vivian Perlis, 159–186. Urbana: University of Illinois Press, 1977.

———. *The Structure of Atonal Music.* New Haven: Yale University Press, 1973.

Gingerich, Lora Louise. "Processes of Motivic Transformation in the Keyboard and Chamber Music of Charles E. Ives." Ph.D. diss., Yale University, 1983.

———. "A Technique of Melodic Motivic Analysis in the Music of Charles Ives." *Music Theory Spectrum* 8 (1986): 75–93.

Grantham, Donald. "A Harmonic 'Leitmotif' System in Ives's *Psalm 90.*" *In Theory Only* 5/2 (1979): 3–14.

Henderson, Clayton W. *The Charles Ives Tunebook.* Warren, Mich.: Harmonie Park Press, 1990.

Hertz, David Michael. *Angels of Reality: Emersonian Unfoldings in Wright, Stevens, and Ives.* Carbondale: Southern Illinois University Press, 1993.

Hilliard, John Stanley. "Charles Ives' Robert Browning Overture: Style and Structure." D.M.A. diss., Cornell University, 1983.

Hitchcock, H. Wiley. *Ives: A Survey of the Music.* London: Oxford University Press, 1977. Reprint, with corrections, New York: Institute for Studies in American Music, 1983.

Hitchcock, H. Wiley, and Perlis, Vivian, eds. *An Ives Celebration: Papers and Panels of the Charles Ives Centennial Festival-Conference.* Urbana: University of Illinois Press, 1977.

Isham, Howard. "The Musical Thinking of Charles Ives." *The Journal of Aesthetics and Art Criticism* 31/3 (1973): 395–404.

Ives, Charles E. *Memos.* Edited and with appendixes by John Kirkpatrick. New York: Norton, 1972.

———. *Essays Before a Sonata, The Majority, and Other Writings.* Edited by Howard Boatwright. New York: Norton, 1970.

Karpinski, Gary. "The Interval Cycles in the Music of Claude Debussy." Paper delivered at the annual meeting of the Society for Music Theory, Oakland, California, November 10, 1990.

Kavanaugh, James Vincent. "Music and American Transcendentalism: A Study of

Transcendental Pythagoreanism in the Works of Henry David Thoreau, Nathaniel Hawthorne, and Charles Ives." Ph.D. diss., Yale University, 1978.

Kirkpatrick, John. "Ives, Charles E." In *The New Grove Dictionary of Music and Musicians*, 6th ed.

―――. *A Temporary Mimeographed Catalogue of the Music Manuscripts and Related Materials of Charles Edward Ives, 1874–1954*. New Haven: Library of the Yale University School of Music, 1960. Reprint, 1973.

Kolosick, J. Timothy. "A Computer-Assisted, Set-Theoretic Investigation of Vertical Simultaneities in Selected Piano Compositions by Charles E. Ives." Ph.D. diss., University of Wisconsin-Madison, 1981.

Lambert, Philip. "Aggregate Structures in Music of Charles Ives." *Journal of Music Theory* 34/1 (1990): 29–55.

―――. "Another View of *Chromâtimelôdtune*." *Journal of Musicological Research* 11 (1991): 237–262.

―――. "Compositional Procedures in Experimental Works of Charles E. Ives." Ph.D. diss., Eastman School of Music of the University of Rochester, 1987.

―――. "Interval Cycles as Compositional Resources in the Music of Charles Ives." *Music Theory Spectrum* 12/1 (1990): 43–82.

―――. "Ives and Counterpoint." *American Music* 9/2 (1991): 119–148.

―――. "Ives's 'Piano-Drum' Chords." *Intégral* 3 (1989): 1–36.

Lewin, David. *Generalized Musical Intervals and Transformations*. New Haven: Yale University Press, 1987.

―――. *Musical Form and Transformation: 4 Analytic Essays*. New Haven: Yale University Press, 1993.

―――. "Transformational Techniques in Atonal and Other Music Theories." *Perspectives of New Music* 21/1–2 (1982–1983): 312–371.

Marshall, Dennis. "Charles Ives' Quotations: Manner or Substance?" *Perspectives of New Music* 6/2 (1968): 45–56.

Maske, Ulrich. *Charles Ives in seiner Kammermusik für drei bis sechs Instrumente*. Kölner Beiträge zur Musikforschung, vol. 64. Regensberg: G. Bosse, 1971.

Meyer, Leonard B. *Music, the Arts, and Ideas*. Chicago: University of Chicago Press, 1967.

Morgan, Robert P. "Spatial Form in Ives." In *An Ives Celebration: Papers and Panels of the Charles Ives Centennial Festival-Conference*, edited by H. Wiley Hitchcock and Vivian Perlis, 145–158. Urbana: University of Illinois Press, 1977.

Morris, Robert. *Composition with Pitch-Classes: A Theory of Compositional Design*. New Haven: Yale University Press, 1987.

Nicholls, David. *American Experimental Music 1890–1940*. Cambridge: Cambridge University Press, 1990.

Perle, George. "Berg's Master Array of the Interval Cycles." *The Musical Quarterly* 63/1 (1977): 1–30.

―――. *The Listening Composer*. Berkeley: University of California Press, 1990.

―――. *Serial Composition and Atonality*. 5th ed. Berkeley: University of California Press, 1981.

————. "Scriabin's Self-Analyses." *Music Analysis* 3/2 (1984): 101–122.

Perlis, Vivian. *Charles Ives Remembered: An Oral History*. New Haven: Yale University Press, 1974. Reprint, New York: Norton, 1976.

Rahn, John. *Basic Atonal Theory*. New York: Longman, 1980.

Rathert, Wolfgang. "Paysage imaginaire et perception totale: L'idée et la forme de la symphonie *Universe*." *Contrechamps* 7 (1986): 129–154.

Reti, Rudoph. *Tonality in Modern Music*. New York: Collier Books, 1958.

Rinehart, John McLain. "Ives' Compositional Idioms: An Investigation of Selected Short Compositions as Microcosms of His Musical Language." Ph.D. diss., Ohio State University, 1970.

Robinson, David B. "Children of the Fire: Charles Ives on Emerson and Art." *American Literature* 48/4 (1977): 564–576.

Rossiter, Frank R. *Charles Ives and His America*. New York: Liveright, 1975.

Schoffman, Nachum. "Serialism in the Works of Charles Ives." *Tempo* 138 (1981): 21–32.

————. "The Songs of Charles Ives." Ph.D. diss., Hebrew University of Jerusalem, 1977.

Sherwood, Gayle. "Questions and Veracities: Reassessing the Chronology of Ives's Choral Works." *The Musical Quarterly* 78/3 (1994): 429–447.

————. "The Choral Works of Charles Ives: Chronology, Style, and Reception." Ph.D. diss., Yale University, 1995.

Starr, Larry. "The Early Styles of Charles Ives." *19th-Century Music* 7/1 (1983): 71–80.

————. "Style and Substance: 'Ann Street' by Charles Ives." *Perspectives of New Music* 15/2 (1977): 23–33.

————. *A Union of Diversities: Style in the Music of Charles Ives*. New York: Schirmer, 1992.

Wallach, Laurence D. "The New England Education of Charles Ives." Ph.D. diss., Columbia University, 1973.

Ward, Charles Wilson. "Charles Ives: The Relationship Between Aesthetic Theories and Compositional Processes." Ph.D. diss., University of Texas at Austin, 1974.

————. "Charles Ives's Concept of Music." *Current Musicology* 18 (1974): 114–119.

Warren, Richard, Jr. *Charles E. Ives: Discography*. New Haven: Yale University Library, 1972.

Winters, Thomas Dyer. "Additive and Repetitive Techniques in the Experimental Works of Charles Ives." Ph.D. diss., University of Pennsylvania, 1986.

Additional Credits

Index

Hallowe'en, 64; canon in, 34; as example of workmanship, 10; piano in, 219n. 17; wedge in, 62–65, 137

Harmony: chords in, 156–157; chromatic, 21; framework in, 140, 153–154, 156–157; leitmotifs, 66

Harvest Home Chorale, 141

Harvest Home Chorales, 30–31, *31,* 38, 140, 161

Hymn, for string quintet, 38

In Re Con Moto Et Al, 133, 154; rhythm in, 177–178; as systematic work, 11; use of combination cycles in, 169; use of fragmentation in, 132

Intellect, in music, 11–12, 13. *See also* Substance; Systematic composition

Intermezzo for String Quartet. See *Celestial Country, The*

Interval cycles. *See* Transposition cycles

Intervals: consonant, 29; cyclical, 160–161; dissonant, 29; early experiments with, 18–19; in order transformation, 88, 90; sizes of, 179; in *Tone Roads No. 1,* 50–51; in wedges, 56–59, 62, 73; wide-, 17. *See also* Transposition cycles

INT function, Morris's, 85, 94

Inversion, canonic. *See* Canon

Ives, Charles Edward: borrowing by, 3–4, 13, 27, 35, 77, 218n. 7; canonic writing of, 27–30; compositional evolution of, 1, 3–4, 31, 213n. 10; concern with organization, 3, 4; cooperation in, 30–31; courtship of wife by, 75; on cyclical modeling, 129–130, 167; essay on insurance, 12; experimentation by, 2–4, 15–22, 26–27; on fugues, 26–27, 38; imagery in music of, 131, 149, 151, 174, 178, 184–206; mature work of, 3, 34, 54, 61, 77, 99, 141; model of beliefs, 7–8; on modern music, 9; musical goals of, 2–3, 30, 141; on music critics, 10–11; on origins of "The Cage," 151; on other composers, 6, 7; philosophy of, 40, 149, 178, 185, 189, 205; on pitch-class universe, 230n. 20; on quarter-tone composition, 222n. 18; response to

father's admonitions, 29–30, 86; on symphony, 187; on technique, 2–13; time structure and, 227n. 28; on tonality, 88; on tradition, 10, 65, 71; on *Universe Symphony,* 29, 30, 213n. 26; use of cycles for order derivations, 135; use of modeling, 14; on workmanship in music, 10

Ives, George Edward: copybooks of, 17, 18–19, 27, *28,* 171, 215n. 39; on fugues, 26, 217n. 28; influence on son, 1, 27, 36, 54–55, 86, 206, 215n. 41, 216n. 7; musical experiments of, 15–16

Ives Omnibus, 170–185; examples of, 170–178; palindrome in, 175; progression, 201; rhythm in, 176–178; spiral model of, *184;* wedge in, 173–174

Kirkpatrick, John, 68, 74–75, 219n. 13, 224n. 38, 226n. 15, 231n. 25

Largo Risoluto No. 1, 39, 77, *130,* 134, 140, 225n. 8; combination cycles in, 162–167; mensuration canon in, 35; use of single-note operands in, 130

Largo Risoluto No. 2, 35, *36,* 39, 77

Lewin, David, 128

"Like a Sick Eagle," 62, *63,* 134

"London Bridge," 16

Loring, Christine, 229n. 6, 231n. 29

"Luck and Work," 62, 137

"Majority," 9

Mandel, Alan, 2, 224n. 1

Manner, 6–13. *See also* Substance

Marshall, Dennis, 13

Memos (Ives, Charles Edward), 5; on *Robert Browning Overture,* 78; on systematic composition, 9–13; on "The Cage," 227n. 4; on *Tone Roads No. 1,* 40, 174

Metaphorical illusions, 197, 205. *See also* Nature

Meyer, Leonard, 214n. 20

Mirror inversion, 30, 37, 46, 57, 78–80; triplet, 102, 123; wedge, 60–61, 70, 142, 173. *See also* Palindrome